Social Security Programs Throughout the World: The Americas, 2005

Social Security Administration
Office of Policy
Office of Research, Evaluation, and Statistics

ISSA · AISS · IVSS

Preface

This fourth issue in the current four-volume series of *Social Security Programs Throughout the World* reports on the countries of the Americas. The combined findings of this series, which also includes volumes on Europe, Asia and the Pacific, and Africa, are published at 6-month intervals over a 2-year period. Each volume highlights features of social security programs in the particular region.

The information contained in these volumes is crucial to our efforts, and those of researchers in other countries, to review different ways of approaching social security challenges that will enable us to adapt our social security systems to the evolving needs of individuals, households, and families. These efforts are particularly important as each nation faces major demographic changes, especially the increasing number of aged persons, as well as economic and fiscal issues.

Social Security Programs Throughout the World is the product of a cooperative effort between the Social Security Administration (SSA) and the International Social Security Association (ISSA). Founded in 1927, the ISSA is a nonprofit organization bringing together institutions and administrative bodies from countries throughout the world. The ISSA deals with all forms of compulsory social protection that by legislation or national practice are an integral part of a country's social security system.

Previous editions of this report, which date back to 1937, were issued as one volume and were prepared by SSA staff. With the introduction of the four-volume format in 2002, however, the research and writing has been contracted out to the ISSA. The ISSA has conducted the research largely through its numerous country-based correspondents, as well as its Social Security Worldwide Database and a myriad of other types of data that must be drawn together to update this report. Members of the ISSA's Information System and Databases Unit analyzed the information and revised the publication to reflect detailed changes to each social security program. *Social Security Programs Throughout the World* is based on information available to the ISSA and SSA with regard to legislation in effect in July 2005, or the last date for which information has been received.

Questions about the report should be sent to Barbara Kritzer at ssptw@ssa.gov. Corrections, updated information, and copies of relevant documentation and legislation are also welcome and may be sent to:

> International Social Security Association
> Information System and Databases Unit
> Case postale 1
> 4 route des Morillons
> CH-1211 Geneva 22
> Switzerland

This report is available at http://www.socialsecurity.gov/policy. For additional copies, please e-mail op.publications@ssa.gov or telephone 202-358-6274.

SSA staff members were responsible for technical and editorial assistance and production. Barbara Kritzer served as technical consultant and provided overall project management. Staff of the Division of Information Resources edited and produced the report and prepared the electronic versions for the Web.

Linda Drazga Maxfield
Associate Commissioner
for Research, Evaluation, and Statistics

March 2006

Contents

Guide to Reading the Country Summaries

This fourth issue in the current four-volume series of *Social Security Programs Throughout the World* reports on the countries of the Americas. The combined findings of this series, which also includes volumes on Europe, Asia and the Pacific, and Africa, are published at 6-month intervals over a 2-year period. Each volume highlights features of social security programs in the particular region.

This guide serves as an overview of programs in all regions. A few political jurisdictions have been excluded because they have no social security system or have issued no information regarding their social security legislation. In the absence of recent information, national programs reported in previous volumes may also be excluded.

In this volume on the Americas, the data reported are based on laws and regulations in force in July 2005 or on the last date for which information has been received.[1] Information for each country on types of social security programs, types of mandatory systems for retirement income, contribution rates, and demographic and other statistics related to social security is shown in Tables 1–4 beginning on page 16.

The country summaries show each system's major features. Separate programs in the public sector and specialized funds for such groups as agricultural workers, collective farmers, or the self-employed have not been described in any detail. Benefit arrangements of private employers or individuals are not described in any detail, even though such arrangements may be mandatory in some countries or available as alternatives to statutory programs.

The country summaries also do not refer to international social security agreements that may be in force between two or more countries. Those agreements may modify coverage, contributions, and benefit provisions of national laws summarized in the country write-ups. Since the summary format requires brevity, technical terms have been developed that are concise as well as comparable and are applied to all programs. The terminology may therefore differ from national concepts or usage.

---

[1] The names of the countries in this report are those used by the U.S. Department of State. The term *country* has been used throughout the volume even though in some instances the term *jurisdiction* may be more appropriate.

Sources of Information

Most of the information in this report was collated from the Social Security Programs Throughout the World survey conducted by the International Social Security Association (ISSA) under the sponsorship of the U.S. Social Security Administration (SSA). This information was supplemented by data collected from the ISSA's Developments and Trends Annual Survey. Empirical data were also provided by numerous social security officials throughout the world. (For a listing of countries and jurisdictions that responded to the survey, see page 2.) Important sources of published information include the ISSA Documentation Center; the legislative database of the International Labour Office; and official publications, periodicals, and selected documents received from social security institutions. Information was also received from the Organization for Economic Cooperation and Development, the World Bank, the International Monetary Fund, and the United Nations Development Programme. During the compilation process, international analysts at both SSA and the ISSA examined the material for factual errors, ambiguous statements, and contradictions in material from different sources.

Types of Programs

The term social security in this report refers to programs established by statute that insure individuals against interruption or loss of earning power and for certain special expenditures arising from marriage, birth, or death. This definition also includes allowances to families for the support of children.

Protection of the insured person and dependents usually is extended through cash payments to replace at least a portion of the income lost as the result of old age, disability, or death; sickness and maternity; work injury; unemployment; or through services, primarily hospitalization, medical care, and rehabilitation. Measures providing cash benefits to replace lost income are usually referred to as income maintenance programs; measures that finance or provide direct services are referred to as benefits in kind.

Three broad approaches to coverage provide cash benefits under income-maintenance programs; namely, employment-related, universal, and means-tested systems. Under both the employment-related and the universal approaches, the insured, dependents, and survivors can claim benefits as a matter of right. Under means-tested approaches, benefits are based on a comparison of a person's income or resources against a standard measure. Some countries also provide other types of coverage.

Employment-Related

Employment-related systems, commonly referred to as social insurance systems, generally base eligibility for pensions and other periodic payments on length of employment or self-employment or, in the case of family allowances and work injuries, on the existence of the employment relationship itself. The amount of pensions (long-term payments, primarily) and of other periodic (short-term) payments in the event of unemployment, sickness, maternity, or work injury is usually related to the level of earnings before any of these contingencies caused earnings to cease. Such programs are financed entirely or largely from contributions (usually a percentage of earnings) made by employers, workers, or both and are in most instances compulsory for defined categories of workers and their employers.

The creation of notional defined contributions (NDC) is a relatively new method of calculating benefits. NDC schemes are a variant of contributory social insurance that seek to tie benefit entitlements more closely to contributions. A hypothetical account is created for each insured person that is made up of all contributions during his or her working life and, in some cases, credit for unpaid activity such as caregiving. A pension is calculated by dividing that amount by the average life expectancy at the time of retirement and indexing it to various economic factors. When benefits are due, the individual's notional account balance is converted into a periodic pension payment.

Some social insurance systems permit voluntary affiliation of workers, especially the self-employed. In some instances, the government subsidizes such programs to encourage voluntary participation.

The government is, pro forma, the ultimate guarantor of many benefits. In many countries, the national government participates in the financing of employment-related as well as other social security programs. The government may contribute through an appropriation from general revenues based on a percentage of total wages paid to insured workers, finance part or all of the cost of a program, or pay a subsidy to make up any deficit of an insurance fund. In some cases, the government pays the contributions for low-paid workers. These arrangements are separate from obligations the government may have as an employer under systems that cover government employees. Social security contributions and other earmarked

Countries in the Americas that Responded to the Social Security Programs Throughout the World Survey

Antigua and Barbuda	Guatemala
Argentina	Guyana
Barbados	Haiti
Belize	Jamaica
Bermuda	Mexico
Bolivia	Nicaragua
Brazil	Panama
British Virgin Islands	Paraguay
Canada	Peru
Chile	Saint Kitts and Nevis
Costa Rica	Saint Lucia
Cuba	Saint Vincent and the Grenadines
Dominica	Trinidad and Tobago
Dominican Republic	United States
Grenada	Uruguay

income are kept in a dedicated fund and are shown as a separate item in government accounts. (For further details on the government's role in financing social security, see Source of Funds under Old Age, Disability, and Survivors.)

Universal

Universal programs provide flat-rate cash benefits to residents or citizens, without consideration of income, employment, or means. Typically financed from general revenues, these benefits may apply to all persons with sufficient residency. Universal programs may include old-age pensions for persons over a certain age; pensions for disabled workers, widow(er)s, and orphans; and family allowances. Most social security systems incorporating a universal program also have a second-tier earnings-related program. Some universal programs, although receiving substantial support from income taxes, are also financed in part by contributions from workers and employers.

Means-Tested

Means-tested programs establish eligibility for benefits by measuring individual or family resources against a calculated standard usually based on subsistence needs. Benefits are limited to applicants who satisfy a means test. The size and type of benefits awarded are determined in each case by administrative decision within the framework of the law.

The specific character of means, needs, or income tests, as well as the weight given to family resources, differ considerably from country to country. Such programs, commonly referred to as social pensions or equalization payments, traditionally are financed primarily from general revenues.

Means-tested systems constitute the sole or principal form of social security in only a few jurisdictions. In other jurisdictions, contributory programs operate in tandem with income-related benefits. In such instances, means- or income-tested programs may be administered by social insurance agencies. Means-tested programs apply to persons who are not in covered employment or whose benefits under employment-related programs, together with other individual or family resources, are inadequate to meet subsistence or special needs. Although means-tested programs can be administered at the national level, they are usually administered locally.

In this report, when national means-tested programs supplement an employment-related benefit, the existence of a means-tested program is generally noted, but

no details concerning it are given. When a means-tested program represents the only or principal form of social security, however, further details are provided.

Other Types of Programs

Three other types of programs are those delivered, in the main, through financial services providers (mandatory individual accounts, mandatory occupational pensions, and mandatory private insurance), publicly operated provident funds, and employer-liability systems.

Programs Delivered by Financial Services Providers

Mandatory individual account. Applies to a program where covered persons and/or employers must contribute a certain percentage of earnings to the covered person's individual account managed by a contracted public or private fund manager. The mandate to establish membership in a scheme and the option to choose a fund manager lie with the individual. The accumulated capital in the individual account is normally intended as a source of income replacement for the contingencies of retirement, disability, ill health, or unemployment. It may also be possible for eligible survivors to access the accumulated capital in the case of the insured's death.

Contributions are assigned to an employee's individual account. The employee must pay administrative fees for the management of the individual account and usually purchase a separate policy for disability and survivors insurance.

Mandatory occupational pension. Applies to a program where employers are mandated by law to provide occupational pension schemes financed by employer, and in some cases, employee contributions. Benefits may be paid as a lump sum, annuity, or pension.

Mandatory private insurance. Applies to a program where individuals are mandated by law to purchase insurance directly from a private insurance company.

Provident Funds. These funds, which exist primarily in developing countries, are essentially compulsory savings programs in which regular contributions withheld from employees' wages are enhanced, and often matched, by employers' contributions. The contributions are set aside and invested for each employee in a single, publicly managed fund for later repayment to the worker when defined contingencies occur. Typically, benefits are paid out in the form of a lump sum with accrued interest, although in certain circumstances drawdown provisions enable partial access to savings prior to retirement or other defined contingencies. On retirement, some provident funds also permit beneficiaries to purchase an annuity or opt for a pension. Some provident funds provide pensions for survivors.

Employer-Liability Systems. Under these systems, workers are usually protected through labor codes that require employers, when liable, to provide specified payments or services directly to their employees. Specified payments or services can include the payment of lump-sum gratuities to the aged or disabled; the provision of medical care, paid sick leave, or both; the payment of maternity benefits or family allowances; the provision of temporary or long-term cash benefits and medical care in the case of a work injury; or the payment of severance indemnities in the case of dismissal. Employer-liability systems do not involve any direct pooling of risk, since the liability for payment is placed directly on each employer. Employers may insure themselves against liability, and in some jurisdictions such insurance is compulsory.

Format of Country Summaries

Each country summary discusses five types of programs:
- Old age, disability, and survivors;
- Sickness and maternity;
- Work injury;
- Unemployment; and
- Family allowances.

Old Age, Disability, and Survivors

Benefits under old age, disability, and survivor programs usually cover long-term risks, as distinct from short-term risks such as temporary incapacity resulting from sickness and maternity, work injury, or unemployment. The benefits are normally pensions payable for life or for a considerable number of years. Such benefits are usually provided as part of a single system with common financing and administration as well as interrelated qualifying conditions and benefit formulas.

The laws summarized under Old Age, Disability, and Survivors focus first on benefits providing pensions or lump-sum payments to compensate for loss of income resulting from old age or permanent retirement. Such benefits are usually payable after attaining a specified statutory age. Some countries require complete or substantial retirement in order to become eligible for a pension; other countries pay a retirement pension at a certain age regardless of whether workers retire or not.

The second type of long-term risk for which pensions are provided is disability (referred to in some countries as invalidity). Disability may be generally defined as long-term and more or less total work impairment resulting from a nonoccupational injury or disease. (Disability caused by a work injury or occupational disease is usually compensated under a separate program; see Work Injury, below.)

The third type of pension is payable to dependents of insured workers or pensioners who die. (Pensions for survivors of workers injured while working are usually provided under a separate Work Injury program.)

Coverage. The extent of social security coverage in any given country is determined by a number of diverse factors, including the kind of system, sometimes the age of the system, and the degree of economic development. A program may provide coverage for the entire country or some portion of the workforce.

In principle, universal systems cover the entire population for the contingencies of old age, disability, and survivorship. A person may have to meet certain conditions, such as long-term residence or citizenship. Many countries exclude aliens from benefits unless there is a reciprocal agreement with the country of which they are nationals.

The extent of employment-related benefits is usually determined by the age of the system. Historically, social security coverage was provided first to government employees and members of the armed forces, then to workers in industry and commerce, and eventually extended to the vast majority of wage earners and salaried employees through a general system. As a result, public employees (including military personnel and civil servants), teachers, and employees of public utilities, corporations, or monopolies are still covered by occupation-specific separate systems in many countries.

In many countries, special occupational systems have been set up for certain private-sector employees, such as miners, railway workers, and seamen. Qualifying conditions and benefits are often more liberal than under the general system. The risk involved in an occupation, its strategic importance for economic growth, and the economic and political strength of trade unions may have had a role in shaping the type and size of benefits offered by the particular program.

Groups that might be considered difficult to administer—family workers, domestics, day workers, agricultural workers, and the self-employed—were often initially excluded from coverage. The trend has been to extend coverage to these groups under separate funds or to bring them gradually under the general system. In some countries, noncovered workers become eligible for the right to an eventual pension if they make voluntary contributions at a specified level. Some systems also provide voluntary coverage for women who leave the labor force temporarily to have children or to raise a family, or for self-employed persons not covered by a mandatory program. Some developed countries with younger programs have constructed a unified national program, thus largely bypassing the need for developing separate industrial or agricultural funds.

Most developing countries have extended coverage gradually. Their first steps toward creating a social security system have commonly been to cover wage and salary workers against loss of income due to work injury, and then old age and, less commonly, disability.

In a number of developing countries, particularly in those that were once British colonies, this initial step has come via the institutional form of provident funds. Most provident funds provide coverage for wage and salary workers in the government and private sector. A few funds have exclusions based on the worker's earnings or the size of the firm. Funds that exclude employees with earnings above a certain level from compulsory coverage may in some cases give them the option to affiliate or continue to participate voluntarily.

Source of Funds. The financing of benefits for old-age, disability, and survivor programs can come from three possible sources:

- A percentage of covered wages or salaries paid by the worker,

- A percentage of covered payroll paid by the employer, and

- A government contribution.

Almost all pension programs under social insurance (as distinct from provident funds or universal systems) are financed at least in part by employer and employee contributions. Many derive their funds from all three sources. Contributions are determined by applying a percentage to salaries or wages up to a certain maximum. In many cases the employer pays a larger share.

The government's contribution may be derived from general revenues or, less commonly, from special earmarked or excise taxes (for example, a tax on tobacco, gasoline, or alcoholic beverages). Government contributions may be used in different ways to defray a portion of all expenditures (such as the cost of administration), to make up deficits, or even to finance the total cost of a program. Subsidies may be provided as a lump sum or an amount to make up the difference between employer/employee contributions and the total cost of the system. A number of countries reduce or, in some cases, eliminate contributions for the lowest-paid wage earners, financing their benefits entirely from general revenues or by the employer's contribution.

The contribution rate apportioned between the sources of financing may be identical or progressive, increasing with the size of the wage or changing according to wage class. Where universal and earnings-related systems exist side by side, and the universal benefit is not financed entirely by the government, separate rates may exist for each program. In other instances, flat-rate weekly contributions may finance basic pension programs. These amounts are uniform for all workers of the same age and sex, regardless of earnings level. However, the self-employed may have to contribute at a higher rate than wage and salary workers, thereby making up for the employer's share.

For administrative purposes, a number of countries assess a single overall social security contribution covering several contingencies. Benefits for sickness, work injury, unemployment, and family allowances as well as pensions may be financed from this single contribution. General revenue financing is the sole source of income in some universal systems. The contribution of the resident or citizen may be a percentage of taxable income under a national tax program. General revenues finance all or part of the means-tested supplementary benefits in many countries.

Contribution rates, as a rule, are applied to wages or salaries only up to a statutory ceiling. A portion of the wage of highly paid workers will escape taxation but will also not count in determining the benefit. In a few cases, an earnings ceiling applies for the determination of benefits but not for contribution purposes. In some countries, contribution rates are applied not to actual earnings but to a fixed amount that is set for all earnings falling within a specified range or wage class.

Qualifying Conditions. Qualifying to receive an old-age benefit is usually conditional on two requirements: attainment of a specified age and completion of a specified period of contributions or covered employment. Another common requirement is total or substantial withdrawal from the labor force. In some instances, eligibility is determined by resident status or citizenship.

Old-age benefits generally become payable between ages 60 and 65. In some countries, length-of-service benefits are payable at any age after a certain period of employment, most commonly between 30 and 40 years. In recent years, several countries have increased the age limit for entitlement, in part because of budgetary constraints arising as a consequence of demographic aging.

Many programs require the same pensionable age for women as for men. Others permit women to draw a full pension at an earlier age, even though women generally have a longer life expectancy. Although the norm has been for the differential to be about 5 years, there is now an emerging international trend toward equalizing the statutory retirement age.

Many programs offer optional retirement before the statutory retirement age is reached. A reduced pension, in some instances, may be claimed up to 5 years before the statutory retirement age. Some countries pay a full pension before the regular retirement age if the applicant meets one or more of the following conditions: work in an especially arduous, unhealthy, or hazardous occupation (for example, underground mining); involuntary unemployment for a period near retirement age; physical or mental exhaustion (as distinct from disability) near retirement age; or, occasionally, an especially long period of coverage. Some programs award old-age pensions to workers who are older than the statutory retirement age but who cannot satisfy the regular length-of-coverage requirement. Other programs provide increments to workers who have continued in employment beyond the normal retirement age.

Universal old-age pension systems usually do not require a minimum period of covered employment or contributions. However, most prescribe a minimum period of prior residence.

Some old-age pension systems credit periods during which persons, for reasons beyond their control, were not in covered employment. Credits can be awarded for reasons such as disability, involuntary unemployment, military service, education, child rearing, or training. Other systems disregard these periods and may proportionately reduce benefits for each year below the required minimum. Persons with only a few years of coverage may receive a refund of contributions or a settlement in which a proportion of the full benefit or earnings is paid for each year of contribution.

The majority of old-age pensions financed through social insurance systems require total or substantial withdrawal from covered employment. Under a retirement test, the benefit may be withheld or reduced for those who continue working, depending on the amount of earnings or, less often, the number of hours worked. Universal systems usually do not require retirement from work for receipt of a pension. Provident funds pay the benefit only when the worker leaves covered employment or emigrates.

Some countries provide a number of exemptions that act to eliminate the retirement condition for specified categories of pensioners. For instance, the retirement test may be eliminated for workers who reached a specified age above the minimum pensionable age or for pensioners with long working careers in covered employment. Occupations with manpower shortages may also be exempted from the retirement test.

The principal requirements for receiving a disability benefit are loss of productive capacity after completing a minimum period of work or having met the minimum contribution requirements. Many programs grant the full disability benefit for a two-thirds loss of working capacity in the worker's customary occupation, but this requirement may vary from one-third to 100 percent.

The qualifying period for a disability benefit is usually shorter than for an old-age benefit. Periods of 3 to 5 years of contributions or covered employment are most common. A few countries provide disability benefits in the form of an unlimited extension of ordinary cash sickness benefits.

Entitlement to disability benefits may have age limitations. The lower limit in most systems is in the teens, but it may be related to the lowest age for social insurance or employment or to the maximum age for a family allowance benefit. The upper age limit is frequently the statutory retirement age, when disability benefits may be converted to old-age benefits.

For survivors to be eligible for benefits, most programs require that the deceased worker was a pensioner, completed a minimum period of covered employment, or satisfied the minimum contribution conditions. The qualifying contribution period is often the same as that for the disability benefit. The surviving spouse and orphans may also have to meet certain conditions, such as age requirements.

Old-Age Benefits. The old-age benefit in most countries is a wage-related, periodic payment. However, some countries pay a universal fixed amount that bears no relationship to any prior earnings; others supplement their universal pension with an earnings-related pension.

Provident fund systems make a lump-sum payment, usually a refund of employer and employee contributions plus accrued interest. In programs that have mandatory individual accounts, options for retirement include purchasing an annuity, making withdrawals from an account regulated to guarantee income for an expected lifespan (programmed withdrawals), or a combination of the two (deferred annuity).

Benefits that are related to income are almost always based on average earnings. Some countries compute the average from gross earnings, including various fringe benefits; other countries compute the average from net earnings. Alternatively, some countries have opted to use wage classes rather than actual earnings. The wage classes may be based on occupations or, for administrative convenience, on earnings arranged by size using the midpoint in each step to compute the benefit.

Several methods are used to compensate for averages that may be reduced by low earnings early in a worker's career or by periods without any credited earnings due, for example, to unemployment or military service, and for the effects of price and wage increases due to inflation. One method is to exclude from consideration a number of periods with the lowest (including zero) earnings. In many systems the period over which earnings are averaged may be shortened to the last few years of coverage, or the average may be based on years when the worker had his or her highest earnings. Other systems revalue past earnings by applying an index that usually reflects changes in national average wages or the cost of living. Some assign hypothetical wages before a certain date. Alternatively, others have developed mechanisms for automatic adjustment of workers' wage records based on wage or price changes.

A variety of formulas are used in determining the benefit amount. Instead of a statutory minimum, some systems pay a percentage of average earnings—for instance, 35 percent or 50 percent—that is unchanged by length of coverage once the qualifying period is met. A more common practice is to provide a basic rate—for example, 30 percent of average earnings—plus an increment of 1 percent or 2 percent of earnings either for each year of coverage or for each year in excess of a minimum number of years. Several countries have a weighted benefit formula that returns a larger percentage of earnings to lower-paid workers than to higher-paid workers.

Most systems limit the size of the benefit. Many do so by establishing a ceiling on the earnings taken into account in the computation. Others establish a maximum cash amount or a maximum percentage of average earnings set, for example, at 80 percent. Some systems combine these and other, similar methods.

Most systems supplement the benefit for a wife or child. The wife's supplement may be 50 percent or more of the basic benefit, although in some countries the supplement is payable only for a wife who has reached a specified age, has children in her care, or is disabled. It may also be payable for a dependent husband.

Minimum benefits are intended to maintain a minimum standard of living in many countries, although that objective is not always achieved. A maximum that reduces the effect large families have on benefits is commonly used to limit total benefits, including those of survivors, in the interest of the financial stability of the program.

In some countries, benefits are automatically adjusted to reflect price or wage changes. In other countries, the process is semiautomatic—the adequacy of pensions is reviewed periodically by an advisory board or other administrative body that recommends a benefit adjustment to the government, usually requiring legislative approval.

Disability Benefits. Under most programs, provisions for disability benefits for persons who are permanently disabled as the result of nonoccupational causes are very similar to those for the aged. The same basic formula usually applies for total disability as for old age—a cash amount usually expressed as a percentage of average earnings. Increments and dependents' supplements are generally identical under the total disability and old-age programs. For the totally disabled, a constant-attendance supplement, usually 50 percent of the benefit, may be paid to those who need help on a daily basis. Partial disability benefits, if payable, are usually reduced, according to a fixed scale. The system may also provide rehabilitation and training. Some countries provide higher benefits for workers in arduous or dangerous employment.

Survivor Benefits. Most systems provide periodic benefits for survivors of covered persons or pensioners, although some pay only lump-sum benefits. Survivor benefits are generally a percentage of either the benefit paid to the deceased at death or the benefit to which the insured would have been entitled if he or she had attained pensionable age or become disabled at that time.

Survivor benefits are paid to some categories of widows under nearly all programs. The amount of a widow's benefit usually ranges from 50 percent to 75 percent of the deceased worker's benefit or, in some cases, 100 percent. In some countries, lifetime benefits are payable to every widow whose husband fulfills the necessary qualifying period. More commonly, the provision of widows' benefits is confined to widows who are caring for young children, are above a specified age, or are disabled.

Lifetime benefits are ordinarily payable to aged and disabled widows. Those awarded to younger mothers, however, are usually terminated when all children have passed a certain age, unless the widow has reached a specified age or is disabled. Most widows' benefits also terminate on remarriage, although a final lump-sum grant may be payable under this circumstance. Special provisions govern the rights of the divorced. Age limits for orphan's benefits are in many cases the same as for children's allowances. Many countries fix a somewhat higher age limit for orphans attending school or undergoing an apprenticeship or for those who are incapacitated. The age limit is usually removed for disabled orphans as long as their incapacity continues. Most survivor programs distinguish between half orphans (who have lost one parent) and full orphans (who have lost both parents), with the latter receiving benefits that are 50 percent to 100 percent larger than those for half orphans. Special payments are also made to orphans under the family allowance programs of some countries.

Benefits are payable under a number of programs to widowers of insured workers or pensioners. A widower usually must have been financially dependent on his wife and either disabled or old enough to receive an old-age benefit at her death. A widower's benefit is usually computed in the same way as a widow's benefit.

Many systems also pay benefits to other surviving close relatives, such as parents and grandparents, but only in the absence of qualifying widows, widowers, or children. The maximum total benefit to be split among survivors is usually between 80 percent and 100 percent of the benefit of the deceased.

Administrative Organization. Responsibility for administration generally rests with semiautonomous institutions or funds. These agencies are usually subject to general supervision by a ministry or government department but otherwise are largely self-governing, headed by a tripartite board that includes representatives of workers, employers, and the government. Some boards are bipartite with representatives of workers and employers only or of workers and the government. Where coverage is organized separately for different occupations, or for wage earners and salaried employees or self-employed workers, each program usually has a separate institution or fund. In a few cases, the administration of benefits is placed directly in the hands of a government ministry or department.

Sickness and Maternity

Sickness benefit programs are generally of two types: cash sickness benefits, which are paid when short-term illnesses prevent work, and health care benefits, which are provided in the form of medical, hospital, and pharmaceutical benefits. Some countries maintain a separate program for cash maternity benefits, which are paid to working mothers before and after childbirth. In most countries, however, maternity benefits are administered as part of the cash sickness program. (Benefits provided as a result of work injury or occupational disease are provided either under work injury or sickness programs. Details of the benefits are discussed under Work Injury.)

Cash sickness and maternity benefits as well as health care are usually administered under the same branch of social security. For this reason, these programs are grouped together in the country summaries.

An important reason for grouping these numerous benefits together is that each deals with the risk of temporary incapacity. Moreover, in most instances, such benefits are furnished as part of a single system with common financing and administration. Most countries provide medical care services for sickness and maternity as an integral part of the health insurance system and link those services directly with the provision of cash benefits. In some instances, however, maternity cash grants are covered under family allowance programs. Occasionally, medical care services are provided under a public health program, independent of the social insurance system. Where this dual approach is followed, it has been indicated in the summaries.

Where health care is dispensed directly by the government or its agencies and the principal source of funds is general revenue, the cash benefit program usually continues to be administered on an insurance basis, funded by payroll contributions, and merged in some instances with other aspects of the social insurance system such as old age and disability. However, countries that deliver health care primarily through private facilities and private funding are also likely to have developed separate programs. Where the social security program operates its own medical facilities, both types of benefits are usually administered jointly.

Benefits designed to assist in the provision of long-term care, often at home, are generally supported by a special tax. Benefit levels are normally set to the level of care required. These benefits may be payable in cash, as care services, or as a combination of the two.

Coverage. The proportion of the population covered by sickness programs varies considerably from country to country, in part because of the degree of economic development. Coverage for medical care and cash benefits is generally identical in countries where both types of benefits are provided through the same branch of social insurance. In a number of systems, particularly in developing countries, health care insurance extends only to employees in certain geographic areas. A common procedure is to start the program in major urban centers, then extend coverage gradually to other areas. Both cash sickness and health care programs may exclude agricultural workers, who, in some countries, account for a major proportion of the working population. Where a health insurance system (as distinguished from a national health service program) exists, most workers earning below a certain ceiling participate on a compulsory basis. Others, such as the self-employed, may be permitted to affiliate on a voluntary basis. In several countries, higher-paid employees are specifically excluded from one or both forms of sickness insurance, although some voluntary participation is usually permitted.

Many countries include pensioners as well as other social security beneficiaries under the medical care programs, in some cases without cost to the pensioner. Elsewhere, pensioners pay a percentage of their pension or a fixed premium for all or part of the medical care coverage. Special sickness insurance systems may be maintained for certain workers, such as railway employees, seamen, and public employees.

Where medical care coverage is provided through a national health service rather than social insurance, the program is usually open in principle to virtually all residents. However, restrictions on services to aliens may apply.

Source of Funds. Many countries have merged the financing of sickness programs with that of other social insurance benefits and collect only a single contribution from employees and employers. More commonly, however, a fixed percentage of wages, up to a ceiling, is contributed by employees and employers directly to a separate program that administers both health care and cash benefits for sickness and maternity. Some countries also provide a government contribution. Where medical care is available to residents, generally through some type of national health service, the government usually bears at least the major part of the cost from general revenues.

Qualifying Conditions. Generally, a person becoming ill must be gainfully employed, incapacitated for work, and not receiving regular wages or sick-leave payments from the employer to be eligible for cash sickness benefits. Most programs require claimants to meet a minimum period of contribution or to have some history of work attachment prior to the onset of illness to qualify. Some countries, however, have eliminated the qualifying period.

The length of the qualifying period for cash sickness benefits may range from less than 1 month to 6 months

or more and is ordinarily somewhat longer for cash maternity benefits. Usually the period must be fairly recent, such as during the last 6 or 12 months. In the case of medical benefits, a qualifying period is usually not required. In instances where such a requirement does exist, it is generally of a short duration. Most programs providing medical services to dependents of workers, as well as to the workers themselves, do not distinguish in their qualifying conditions between the two types of beneficiaries. A few programs require a longer period of covered employment before medical services are provided to dependents.

Cash Benefits. The cash sickness benefit is usually 50 percent to 75 percent of current average earnings, frequently with supplements for dependents. Most programs, however, fix a maximum benefit amount or do so implicitly through a general earnings ceiling for contributions and benefits. Benefits may be reduced when beneficiaries are hospitalized at the expense of the social insurance system.

A waiting period of 2 to 7 days is imposed under most cash sickness programs. As a result, benefits may not be payable if an illness or injury lasts for only a few days. Similarly, in the case of a prolonged inability to work, benefits may not be payable for the first few days. Under some programs, however, benefits are retroactively paid for the waiting period when the disability continues beyond a specified time, commonly 2 to 3 weeks. A waiting period reduces administrative and benefit costs by excluding many claims for short illnesses or injuries during which relatively little income is lost and can also help reduce the potential for the inappropriate use of the system by workers.

The period during which a worker may receive benefits for a single illness or injury, or in a given 12-month period, is ordinarily limited to 26 weeks. In some instances, however, benefits may be drawn for considerably longer and even for an unlimited duration. A number of countries permit the agency to extend the maximum entitlement period to 39 or 52 weeks in specific cases. In most countries, when cash sickness benefits are exhausted, the recipient is paid a disability benefit if the incapacity continues.

Cash maternity benefits are usually payable for a specified period, both before and after childbirth. A woman is almost always required to stop working while receiving maternity benefits, and usually she must use the prenatal and postnatal medical services provided by the system. In some countries, cash maternity benefits are also payable to working men who stay home to care for a newborn child while the mother returns to work. Cash payments may also be available for a parent, usually the mother, who is absent from work to care for a sick child under a specified age.

The proportion of earnings payable as a cash maternity benefit differs considerably from country to country but, like cash sickness benefits, is usually between 50 percent and 75 percent of current earnings. However, in a number of countries, maternity benefits are set at 100 percent of wages. Benefit payments usually start approximately 6 weeks before the expected date of childbirth and end 6 to 8 weeks afterward.

A nursing allowance—usually 20 percent or 25 percent of the regular maternity benefit and payable for up to 6 months or longer—may be provided in addition to the basic cash maternity benefit. A grant for the purchase of a layette—clothes and other essentials for the new-born baby—or the provision of a layette itself is furnished under some programs. Finally, a lump-sum maternity grant may be paid on the birth of each child. The wives of insured men may be eligible for this grant. Similar benefits may be provided under the family allowance program.

Medical Benefits. Medical services usually include at least general practitioner care, some hospitalization, and essential drugs. Services of specialists, surgery, maternity care, some dental care, a wider range of medicines, and certain appliances are commonly added. Transportation of patients and home-nursing services may be included.

There are three principal methods of meeting the cost of health care: direct payment to providers by the public system or its agents, reimbursement of patients, and direct provision of medical care. These methods may be used in different combinations and may be varied for different kinds of services.

Under direct payment, the social security or public medical care system pays providers directly for services. Patients usually have little or no direct financial dealings with the care provider. Payments for care are commonly made on the basis of contracts with service providers or the professional groups representing them, such as practitioner or hospital associations. Remuneration may take the form of a specified fee for each service, a capitation payment in return for providing all necessary services to a given group of persons, or a salary.

Under the reimbursement method, the patient makes the initial payment and is reimbursed by social security for at least part of the cost. A maximum is sometimes placed on the refund, expressed as a percentage of the bill or a flat amount that can vary with the nature of the service as stipulated in a schedule of fees. The ceiling on medical bills can be placed on the provider when presenting the bill or on the patient when applying for reimbursement. In the latter case, the patient may be reimbursed for only a small portion of the bill.

Under the direct-provision method, the social security system or the government owns and operates its own medical facilities, largely manned by salaried staff. Countries using this method may contract for services of public or private providers. The patient normally pays no fee for most of these services, except insofar as part of the social security contribution may be allotted toward health care funding.

Regardless of the funding method used, all national health care programs provide for at least a small degree of cost-sharing by patients, usually on the assumption that such charges discourage overuse. Thus, the patient either pays part of the cost to the provider or social security agency or receives less than full reimbursement. Even under the direct-provision method, with its emphasis on basically free medical services to the whole population, patients are generally required to pay a small fixed fee per medical treatment or prescription or per day of hospitalization.

Some health care systems have no limit on how long medical care may be provided. Other systems fix a maximum, such as 26 weeks, for services provided for any given illness. Some set limits only on the duration of hospitalization paid for by social security. Where time limits are imposed, they may be extended.

Maternity Care. Prenatal, obstetric, and postnatal care for working women is provided in most countries under the medical services program. Obstetric care is sometimes limited to the services of a midwife, although a doctor is usually available in case of complications. Care in a maternity home or hospital, as well as essential drugs, are ordinarily furnished where necessary.

Medical Care for Dependents. When medical benefits for insured workers are provided through social insurance, similar services are typically furnished to their spouse and young children (and, in some cases, other adults or young relatives living with and dependent on the insured). Maternity care is generally provided to the wife of an insured man.

In some countries, however, medical services available to dependents are more limited than those provided to insured workers or heads of families. Dependents may be subject to a shorter maximum duration for hospital stays, for example, and may have to pay a larger percentage of the cost of certain services such as medicines.

Administrative Organization. The administrative organization for the sickness and maternity program is similar to that of the old-age, disability, and survivor program in many countries. Most commonly, such programs are administered by some form of national social security institution. Under some systems, social security agencies own and operate their own medical facilities, furnishing at least part of the services available under their programs.

In most countries with a national health insurance program, responsibility for detailed administration lies with semiautonomous, nongovernment health funds or associations. All workers covered by the program must join one of these funds.

Each health fund usually requires government approval and must satisfy certain requirements. Workers and, in some countries, employers participate in the election of governing bodies. The funds normally collect contributions within minimum and maximum limits. Funds may also receive government subsidies related to their expenditures or to the number of affiliated members.

National law usually prescribes the minimum (and, in some cases, the maximum) cash benefits and medical services the health funds may provide. In a few countries, individual funds may determine what specific health care benefits and services to provide and arrange to furnish medical care to their members. This arrangement can involve delivery through contracts with care and service providers in the region.

Less commonly, government departments are responsible for the actual provision of medical services, usually through a national health service program. The administrative responsibility for delivering medical services in some countries is often separated from the administration of cash benefit programs, which tend to be linked with other types of social security benefits.

Work Injury

The oldest type of social security—the work injury program—provides compensation for work-connected injuries and occupational illnesses. Such programs usually furnish short- and long-term benefits, depending on both the duration of the incapacity and the age of survivors. Work injury benefits nearly always include cash benefits and medical services. Most countries attempt to maintain separate work injury programs that are not linked directly with other social security measures. In some countries, however, work injury benefits are paid under special provisions of the general social security programs. Both types of programs are dealt with under Work Injury.

Types of Systems. There are two basic types of work injury systems: social insurance systems that use a public fund, and various forms of private or semipri-

vate arrangements required by law. In most countries, work injury programs operate through a central public fund, which may or may not be part of the general social insurance system. All employers subject to the program must pay contributions to the public carrier, which in turn pays the benefits.

Countries that rely primarily on private arrangements require employers to insure their employees against the risk of employment injury. However, in some of these countries, only private insurance is available. In the remainder, a public fund does exist, but employers are allowed the option of insuring with either a private carrier or the public fund.

The premiums charged by private or mutual insurance companies for work injury protection usually vary according to the experience of work accidents in different undertakings or industries, and the cost of protection may vary widely. In some countries, however, experience rating has been eliminated, and all employers contribute to the program at one rate.

In other instances, workers' compensation laws simply impose on employers a liability to pay direct compensation to injured workers or their survivors. Employers covered under such laws may simply pay benefits from their own funds as injuries occur or may voluntarily purchase a private or mutual insurance contract to protect themselves against risk.

Coverage. Work injury programs commonly cover wage and salary workers and exclude the self-employed. The programs of some of the more highly industrialized nations cover practically all employees. However, many countries either exclude all agricultural employees or cover only those who operate power-driven machinery. Some programs also exclude employees of small enterprises.

Source of Funds. Work injury benefits are financed primarily by employer contributions, reflecting the traditional assumption that employers should be liable when their employees suffer work injuries. Where certain elements of the work injury program are meshed with one or more of the other branches of the social insurance system, however, financing usually involves contributions from employees, employers, and the government. Another exception occurs in countries that provide medical treatment for work-connected illnesses under their ordinary public medical care programs.

Work Injury Benefits. Work injury programs provide cash benefits and medical benefits. Cash benefits under work injury programs may be subdivided into three types: benefits for temporary disability, those for permanent total disability, and those for permanent partial disability. No qualifying period of coverage or employment is ordinarily required for entitlement to work injury benefits. The concept of work-connected injury has gradually been liberalized in a number of countries to cover injuries occurring while commuting to and from work.

Temporary disability benefits are usually payable from the start of an incapacity caused by a work injury, though some programs require a waiting period of 1 to 3 days. Benefits normally continue for a limited period, such as 26 to 52 weeks, depending on the duration of incapacity. If incapacity lasts longer, the temporary disability benefit may be replaced by a permanent disability benefit. In some systems, temporary benefits may continue for an extended period, particularly if the temporary and permanent benefit amounts are identical.

The temporary benefit is nearly always a fraction of the worker's average earnings during a period immediately before injury, usually at least one-third to one-half. A ceiling may be placed on the earnings considered in computing a benefit. Temporary benefits under work injury programs may be significantly higher than in the case of ordinary sickness. Benefits are reduced under some programs when a worker is hospitalized.

The second type of cash work injury benefit is provided in cases of permanent total disability. Generally, it becomes payable immediately after the temporary disability benefit ceases, based on a medical evaluation that the worker's incapacity is both permanent and total. The permanent total disability benefit is usually payable for life, unless the worker's condition changes. A minority of programs, however, pay only a single lump-sum grant equal to several years' wages.

The permanent total disability benefit usually amounts to two-thirds to three-fourths of the worker's average earnings before injury, somewhat higher than for ordinary disability benefits. In addition, unlike ordinary disability benefits, the rate usually does not vary based on the length of employment before the injury. Supplements may be added for dependents and for pensioners requiring the constant attendance of another person, in which case benefits may exceed former earnings. In some countries, the benefits of apprentices or new labor force entrants who become permanently disabled as a result of work-connected injury or disease are based on hypothetical lifetime wages or on the wage of an average worker in the particular industry. This mechanism overcomes the problem of establishing a lifetime benefit based on a very low starting wage.

The third type of cash work injury benefit is provided when permanent partial disability results in a worker's loss of partial working or earning capacity. It is usually equal to a portion of the full benefit corresponding to the percentage loss of capacity. Alternatively, permanent partial disability benefits may be paid in the form of a lump-sum grant. Partial disability payments are generally smaller and are usually stipulated in a schedule of payments for particular types of injuries. Some systems pay the benefit as a lump sum when the extent of disability is below a stated percentage, such as 20 percent.

Medical and hospital care and rehabilitation services are also provided to injured workers. Nearly always free, they may include a somewhat wider range of services than the general sickness program. Ordinarily, they are available until the worker recovers or the condition stabilizes. In some countries, however, free care is limited, the amount being based on the duration of services or their total cost.

Survivor Benefits. Most work injury programs also provide benefits to survivors. These benefits are customarily payable to a widow, regardless of her age, until her death or remarriage; to a disabled widower; and to orphans below specified age limits. If the benefit is not exhausted by the immediate survivors' claims, dependent parents or other relatives may be eligible for small benefits. No minimum period of coverage is required.

Survivor benefits are computed as a percentage of either the worker's average earnings immediately before death or the benefit payable (or potentially payable) at death. These percentages are typically larger than those for survivor benefits under the general program and do not normally vary with the length of covered employment. They are usually about one-third to one-half of the worker's average earnings for a widow, about half as much for each half orphan, and about two-thirds as much for each full orphan. A limit is commonly placed on the combined total of survivor benefits.

Not all countries, however, provide work injury benefits to survivors, and some do not differentiate between survivors in this category and survivors entitled to benefits under other social insurance programs. Some schemes pay only a lump sum equal to the worker's earnings over a specified number of years. Most systems also pay a funeral grant equivalent to a fixed sum or a percentage of the worker's earnings.

Administrative Organization. The functions involved in administering work injury programs differ widely between countries in which employers are not required to insure or can insure with private carriers and those in which a public agency or fund has sole responsibility for both collecting contributions and paying benefits.

Unemployment

Benefits in this category provide compensation for the loss of income resulting from involuntary unemployment. In some countries, these programs are independent of other social security measures and may be closely linked with employment services. In other countries, the unemployment programs are included with social security measures covering other short-term risks, although employment services may continue to verify unemployment and assist in a job search.

Unemployment programs, which exist mainly in industrialized countries, are compulsory and fairly broad in scope in many countries. Some countries restrict benefits to those who satisfy a means or income test. In addition to the programs offering scheduled payments, a number of countries provide lump-sum grants, payable by either a government agency or the employer; other countries provide mandatory individual severance accounts, providing total benefits equal to the value of accumulated capital in the individual account. In addition, employers in many instances are required to pay lump-sum severance indemnities to discharged workers.

Coverage. About half of the compulsory unemployment programs cover the majority of employed persons, regardless of the type of industry. Coverage under the remaining programs is limited to workers in industry and commerce. A few exclude salaried employees earning more than a specified amount. Some have special provisions covering temporary and seasonal employees. Several countries have special occupational unemployment programs, most typically for workers in the building trades, dockworkers, railway employees, and seafarers.

Voluntary insurance systems are limited to industries in which labor unions have established unemployment funds. Membership in these funds is usually compulsory for union members in a covered industry and may be open on a voluntary basis to nonunion employees. Noninsured workers, such as recent school graduates or the self-employed, for example, may be eligible for a government-subsidized assistance benefit when they become unemployed.

Source of Funds. The methods used to finance unemployment insurance are usually based on the same contributory principles as for other branches of social insurance—contributions amounting to a fixed percentage of covered wages are paid on a scheduled basis. In many cases, the government also grants a subsidy, particularly for extended benefits.

Unemployment insurance contributions are shared equally between employees and employers in many countries. Alternatively, the entire contribution may be made by the employer. However, government subsidies may be quite large, amounting to as much as two-thirds of the program's expenditures. Means-tested unemployment assistance programs are financed entirely by governments, with no employer or employee contribution.

Qualifying Conditions. To be entitled to unemployment benefits, a worker must be involuntarily unemployed and have completed a minimum period of contributions or covered employment. The most common qualifying period is 6 months of coverage within the year before employment ceased. In a number of industrialized countries, however, students recently out of school who are unable to find jobs may be eligible for unemployment benefits, even without a work record. This benefit provides a transition from school to work, particularly in periods of recession.

Nearly all unemployment insurance programs, as well as those providing unemployment assistance, require that applicants be capable of, and available for, work. An unemployed worker, therefore, is usually ineligible for unemployment benefits when incapacitated or otherwise unable to accept a job offer. Usually, the unemployed worker must register for work at an employment office and report regularly for as long as payments continue. This close linkage between unemployment benefits and placement services ensures that benefits will be paid only after the person has been informed of any current job opportunities and been found unsuitable.

An unemployed worker who refuses an offer of a suitable job without good cause usually will have benefits temporarily or permanently suspended. Most programs stipulate that the job offered must have been suitable for the worker. The definitions of suitable employment vary considerably. Generally, the criteria include the rate of pay for the job being offered in relation to previous earnings; distance from the worker's home; relationship to the worker's previous occupation, capabilities, and training; and the extent to which the job may involve dangerous or unhealthy work. In some countries, long-term unemployed workers may also be obliged to undertake employment retraining programs. Some countries also provide the unemployed with access to educational placements. If an unemployed worker refuses a place on a retraining program or fails, without good cause, to attend an educational placement, benefits can be temporarily or permanently suspended.

An unemployed worker may satisfy all of the qualifying conditions for a benefit but still be temporarily or permanently disqualified. Nearly all unemployment systems disqualify a worker who left voluntarily without good cause, was dismissed because of misconduct, or participated in a labor dispute leading to a work stoppage that caused the unemployment. The period of disqualification varies considerably, from a few weeks to permanent disqualification.

Unemployment Benefits. Weekly benefits are usually a percentage of average wages during a recent period. A system of wage classes rather than a single fixed percentage is used in some countries. The basic rate of unemployment benefits is usually between 40 percent and 75 percent of average earnings. However, a ceiling on the wages used for benefit computations or maximum benefit provisions may considerably narrow the range within which the basic percentage of wages applies.

Flat-rate amounts are sometimes payable instead of graduated benefits that vary with past wages and customarily differ only according to the family status or, occasionally, the age of the worker. Supplements for a spouse and children are usually added to the basic benefit of unemployed workers who are heads of families. These supplements are either flat-rate amounts or an additional percentage of average earnings.

Most countries have a waiting period of several days before unemployment benefits become payable to reduce the administrative burden of dealing with a very large number of small claims. Most waiting periods are between 3 and 7 days. Some programs have a waiting period for each incident of unemployment, and others limit eligibility to once a year. Longer waiting periods may be prescribed for certain workers, such as the seasonally employed.

Most countries place a limit on the period during which unemployment benefits may be continuously drawn. Typically, this limit varies from 8 to 36 weeks but may be longer in certain cases.

Duration of benefits may also depend on the length of the preceding period of contribution or coverage under the program. That criterion may reduce the maximum duration of unemployment benefits for workers with brief work histories. However, workers with a long history of coverage may, under some programs, have their benefit period extended well beyond the ordinary maximum.

Many unemployed workers who exhaust the right to ordinary benefits continue to receive some assistance, provided their means or incomes are below specified levels. Recipients are usually required to continue registering and reporting at an employment exchange. Some countries that have unemployment assistance but no insurance program do not place any limit on the duration of payments. A number of countries require that insured workers approaching retirement age who have been out of work for a specified period be removed from the unemployment rolls and granted a regular old-age benefit.

Administrative Organization. Unemployment insurance systems may be administered by government departments or self-governing institutions that are usually managed by representatives of insured persons, employers, and the government.

Unemployment insurance and placement service programs usually maintain a close administrative relationship that ensures that benefits are paid only to workers who are registered for employment. At the same time, this liaison increases the effectiveness of the placement services by providing an incentive, through payment of benefits, for unemployed persons to register and report regularly.

Some countries have merged the administration of unemployment insurance and employment service programs, especially at the lower administrative levels where claims are received and benefits are paid by the local employment office. Other countries require persons to register with a local employment office, but the receipt of claims and payment of benefits are handled by a separate insurance office.

In addition to providing an income for the unemployed, many governments have elaborate measures to prevent or counteract unemployment. The typical procedure is for government employment services to work with industry to promote occupational and geographic mobility of labor and to minimize unemployment caused by economic or technological developments; they do that by subsidizing the retraining and relocation of workers in industries that are declining or being restructured. Governments may grant tax and other incentives to industry to locate in areas of high unemployment, or they may allocate funds to create jobs in anticipation of periods of seasonal unemployment.

Family Allowances

The general purpose of family allowance programs is to provide additional income for families with young children in order to meet at least part of the added costs of their support. These programs may either be integrated with other social security measures or kept entirely separate. In this report, family allowances primarily include regular cash payments to families with children. In some countries, they also include school grants, birth grants, maternal and child health services, and allowances for adult dependents.

Most industrialized countries have family allowance programs that originated in Europe in the 19th century when some large companies began paying premiums to workers with large families. The idea spread gradually, and several European countries enacted programs during the 1920s and 1930s. Most programs in operation today, however, have been in place since 1945.

Types of Systems and Coverage. Family allowance programs are of two types: universal and employment-related. The first category, in principle, provides allowances to all resident families with a specified number of children. The second category provides allowances to all wage and salary workers and, in some cases, the self-employed. A few systems cover some categories of nonemployed persons as well. Most employment-related programs continue to pay family allowances to insured persons with dependent children in their care when they retire or are temporarily off the job and receiving sickness, unemployment, work injury, disability, or other benefits. Employment-related family programs also pay allowances to widows of social security beneficiaries.

Source of Funds. The differences in family allowance programs are reflected in the methods used for financing. In universal systems, the entire cost is usually covered by general revenue. By contrast, countries linking eligibility with employment meet the cost of allowances entirely or in considerable part from employer contributions, usually at a uniform percentage-of-payroll rate. If employer contributions do not cover the entire cost, the remainder is usually met from a government subsidy. Few countries require an employee contribution toward family allowances, although some require self-employed persons to contribute.

Eligibility. Eligibility is commonly related to the size of the family and, in some cases, to family income. Many countries pay allowances beginning with the first child. In addition, some countries pay an allowance for a nonemployed wife or other adult dependent, even if there are no children.

In some countries, families with only one child are ineligible. Age requirements vary but are usually tied to the last year of school or the minimum working age, which are often the same and fall somewhere between ages 14 and 18. Under most programs, the continuation of schooling, apprenticeship, or vocational training qualifies a child for an extension of the age limit. In the case of disabled children, many countries extend the age limit beyond that for continued education or pay allowances indefinitely.

Benefits. Whether a program pays a uniform rate for all children or an increasing or decreasing amount for each additional child may reflect the history or the intent of the program. The allowance structure may vary, for example, depending on whether the primary intent is to provide assistance or stimulate population growth. The allowance in most countries is a uniform amount for every child, regardless of the number of children in a family. The allowance in most of the other countries increases for each additional child; the payment for a fifth child, for example, may be considerably larger than that for the first or second child. In a few countries, the allowance per child diminishes or ceases with the addition of children beyond a certain number. In some countries, family allowances (and tax exemptions for dependent family members) have been replaced or supplemented by credits or other forms of a negative income tax.

Administrative Organization. In countries where family allowances are available to all families and financed from general revenues, the program is usually administered by a government department. Where allowances are payable mainly to families of employed persons and financed primarily from employer contributions, the administration may be by a semiautonomous agency under public supervision. Equalization funds may handle the program's financial operations. Each employer pays family allowances to its employees with their wages. The firm then settles with the local fund only the surplus or deficit of contributions due, after deducting allowances the firm has paid. A similar procedure of settling only surpluses or deficits is followed by the local funds in relation to the regional equalization funds under whose supervision they operate. The equalization process makes it possible to fix a uniform contribution rate for all employers, regardless of the number of children in their employees' families. It also eliminates any effect allowances might have in inducing employers to discriminate in hiring workers with children.

Table 1.
Types of social security programs

Country	Old age, disability, and survivors	Sickness and maternity		Work injury	Unemployment	Family allowances
		Cash benefits for both	Cash benefits plus medical care [a]			
Antigua and Barbuda	X	X	b	b	b	b
Argentina	X	X	X	X	X	X
Bahamas	X	X	b	X	b	b
Barbados	X	X	b	X	X	b
Belize	X	X	b	X	b	b
Bermuda	X	b	c	X	b	b
Bolivia	X	X	X	X	b	X
Brazil	X	X	X	X	X	X
British Virgin Islands	X	X	b	X	b	b
Canada	X	X	X	X	X	X
Chile	X	X	X	X	X	X
Colombia	X	X	X	X	X	X
Costa Rica	X	X	X	X	b	X
Cuba	X	X	X	X	b	X
Dominica	X	X	b	X	b	b
Dominican Republic	X	X	X	X	b	X
Ecuador	X	X	X	X	X	b
El Salvador	X	X	X	X	b	b
Grenada	X	X	b	X	b	b
Guatemala	X	X	X	X	b	b
Guyana	X	X	b	X	b	b
Haiti	X	b	b	X	b	b
Honduras	X	X	X	X	b	b
Jamaica	X	d	X	X	b	X
Mexico	X	X	X	X	X	X
Nicaragua	X	X	X	X	b	X
Panama	X	X	X	X	b	b
Paraguay	X	X	X	X	b	b
Peru	X	X	X	X	b	b
Saint Kitts and Nevis	X	X	b	X	b	b
Saint Lucia	X	X	b	X	b	b

(Continued)

Table 1.
Continued

Country	Old age, disability, and survivors	Sickness and maternity		Work injury	Unemployment	Family allowances
		Cash benefits for both	Cash benefits plus medical care [a]			
Saint Vincent and the Grenadines	X	X	b	X	b	b
Trinidad and Tobago	X	X	X	X	b	X
United States	X	X	X	X	X	X
Uruguay	X	e	e	X	X	X
Venezuela	X	X	X	X	X	e

SOURCE: Based on information in the country summaries in this volume.

a. Coverage is provided for medical care, hospitalization, or both.
b. Has no program or information is not available.
c. Medical benefits only.
d. Maternity benefits only.
e. Coverage is provided under other programs.

Table 2.
Types of mandatory systems for retirement income

Country	Flat-rate	Earnings-related	Means-tested	Flat-rate universal	Provident funds	Occupational retirement schemes	Individual retirement schemes
Antigua and Barbuda		X	X				
Argentina		X	X				X
Bahamas		X	X				
Barbados		X	X				
Belize		X	X				
Bermuda	X [a]		X			X	
Bolivia				X			X
Brazil		X	X				
British Virgin Islands		X					
Canada		X		X [b]			
Chile		X [c]	X				X [d]
Colombia		X					X [d]
Costa Rica		X	X				X
Cuba		X					
Dominica		X					
Dominican Republic		X [c]	X [e]				X
Ecuador		X					
El Salvador		X [c]					X [d]
Grenada		X					
Guatemala		X					
Guyana		X					
Haiti		X					
Honduras		X					
Jamaica	X [f]	X [f]					
Mexico		X [c]					X [d]
Nicaragua		X	X				
Panama		X					
Paraguay		X					
Peru		X					X [d]
Saint Kitts and Nevis		X	X				
Saint Lucia		X					

(Continued)

Table 2.
Continued

Country	Flat-rate	Earnings-related	Means-tested	Flat-rate universal	Provident funds	Occupational retirement schemes	Individual retirement schemes
Saint Vincent and the Grenadines		X					
Trinidad and Tobago		X	X				
United States		X	X				
Uruguay		X	X				X
Venezuela	X [f]	X [f]					

SOURCE: Based on information in the country summaries in this volume.

NOTE: The types of mandatory systems for retirement income are defined as follows:

Flat-rate pension: A pension of uniform amount or based on years of service or residence but independent of earnings. It is financed by payroll tax contributions from employees, employers, or both.

Earnings-related pension: A pension based on earnings. It is financed by payroll tax contributions from employees, employers, or both.

Means-tested pension: A pension paid to eligible persons whose own or family income, assets, or both fall below designated levels. It is generally financed through government contributions, with no contributions from employers or

Flat-rate universal pension: A pension of uniform amount normally based on residence but independent of earnings. It is generally financed through government contributions, with no contributions from employers or employees.

Provident funds: Employee and employer contributions are set aside for each employee in publicly managed special funds. Benefits are generally paid as a lump sum with accrued interest.

Occupational retirement schemes: Employers are required by law to provide private occupational retirement schemes financed by employer and, in some cases, employee contributions. Benefits are paid as a lump sum, annuity, or pension.

Individual retirement schemes: Employees and, in some cases, employers must contribute a certain percentage of earnings to an individual account managed by a public or private fund manager chosen by the employee. The accumulated capital in the individual account is used to purchase an annuity, make programmed withdrawals, or a combination of the two and may be paid as a lump sum.

a. The benefit increases with the length of the contribution period.
b. The universal pension is increased by an income-tested supplement.
c. The earnings-related social insurance system is closed to new entrants and is being phased out.
d. The government provides a guaranteed minimum pension.
e. The means-tested pension has not been implemented.
f. The pension formula contains a flat-rate component as well as an earnings-related element.

Table 3.
Demographic and other statistics related to social security, 2005

Country	Total population (millions)	Per-centage 65 or older	Dependency ratio[a]	Life expectancy at birth (years)		Statutory pensionable age		Early pensionable age[b]		GDP per capita (US$)
				Men	Women	Men	Women	Men	Women	
Antigua and Barbuda	0.081	4.5	48.3	68.9	73.7	60	60	c	c	10,294
Argentina	38.7	10.2	58	71.6	79.1	65	60	60	55	12,106
Bahamas	0.323	6.2	53	69	75.3	65	65	60	60	17,159
Barbados	0.27	10	41	73.1	79.2	65.5	65.5	62	62	15,720
Belize	0.27	4.3	70	69.5	74.1	65	65	60	60	6,950
Bermuda	0.064	11.5	44.3	75.3	79.4	65	65	c	c	36,000
Bolivia	9.1	4.5	74	63.4	67.7	65	65	c	c	2,587
Brazil	186.4	6.1	51	68.2	75.7	65 [d]	60 [d]	c	c	7,790
British Virgin Islands	0.022	5	36.7	75	77.1	65	65	c	c	38,500
Canada	32.2	13.1	44	78.2	83.1	65	65	c	c	30,677
Chile	16.2	8.1	49	75.5	81.5	65	60	c	c	10,274
Colombia	45.6	5.1	57	70.3	76.3	60	55	c	c	6,702
Costa Rica	4.3	5.8	52	76.5	81.2	61	59	c	c	9,606
Cuba	11.2	10.8	43	76.8	80.3	60	55	c	c	3,000
Dominica	0.079	7.9	55.5	71.2	77.1	60	60	c	c	5,448
Dominican Republic	8.9	4.1	58	65.4	72.3	60	60	57	57	6,823
Ecuador	13.2	5.8	62	72.1	78	55	55	c	c	3,641
El Salvador	6.8	5.4	65	68.8	74.9	60	55	c	c	4,781
Grenada	0.103	3.6	63.1	62.7	66.3	60	60	c	c	7,959
Guatemala	12.6	4.3	91	64.9	72.1	60	60	c	c	4,148
Guyana	0.75	5.2	53	62.3	68.4	60	60	c	c	4,230
Haiti	8.5	4	71	52.9	54	55	55	c	c	1,742
Honduras	7.2	3.9	76	67.2	71.4	65	60	c	c	2,665
Jamaica	2.6	7.6	63	69.4	72.7	65	60	c	c	4,104
Mexico	107	5.3	57	73.7	78.6	65	65	60	60	9,168
Nicaragua	5.4	3.3	73	68.7	73.5	60	60	c	c	3,262
Panama	3.2	6	57	73	78.2	62	57	c	c	6,854
Paraguay	6.1	3.7	70	69.7	74.2	60	60	55	55	4,684
Peru	27.9	5.3	60	68.7	73.9	65	65	55	50	5,260
Saint Kitts and Nevis	0.043	8.5	60	68.7	74.5	62	62	c	c	12,404
Saint Lucia	0.161	7.2	56	71.6	74.6	62	62	60	60	5,709

(Continued)

Table 3.
Continued

Country	Total population (millions)	Per- centage 65 or older	Dependency ratio [a]	Life expectancy at birth (years)		Statutory pensionable age		Early pensionable age [b]		GDP per capita (US$)
				Men	Women	Men	Women	Men	Women	
Saint Vincent and the Grenadines	0.119	6.5	56	69.3	74.8	60	60	c	c	6,123
Trinidad and Tobago	1.3	7.4	41	67.7	72.5	60	60	c	c	10,766
United States	298.2	12.3	49	75.2	80.6	65.5	65.5	62	62	37,562
Uruguay	3.4	13.2	60	72.7	79.8	60	60	c	c	8,280
Venezuela	26.7	5.1	57	70.9	76.8	60	55	c	c	4,919

SOURCES: United Nations Population Division, Department of Economic and Social Affairs, *World Population Prospects: The 2004 Revision Population Database*, available at http://esa.un.org/unpp/index.asp?panel=1; *Human Development Report 2005*, prepared for the United Nations Development Programme (New York: Oxford University Press, 2005); U.S. Central Intelligence Agency, *The World Factbook, 2005* (Washington, DC: Central Intelligence Agency, 2005). Information on statutory and pensionable ages is taken from the country summaries in this volume.

NOTES: This edition of the current four-volume series uses updated demographic statistics.

GDP = gross domestic product.

a. Population aged 14 or younger plus population aged 65 or older, divided by population aged 15–64.

b. General early pensionable age only; excludes early pensionable ages for specific groups of employees.

c. The country has no early pensionable age, has one only for specific groups, or information is not available.

d. Urban workers.

Table 4.
Contribution rates for social security programs, 2005 (in percent)

Country	Old age, disability, and survivors			All social security programs [a]		
	Insured person	Employer	Total	Insured person	Employer	Total
Antigua and Barbuda	3 [b]	5 [b]	8 [b]	3	5	8 [c]
Argentina	7 [d]	10.17	17.17 [d]	13	22.7 [e]	35.7 [c]
Bahamas	1.7 [b]	7.1 [b]	8.8 [b]	1.7	7.1 [e]	8.8 [c]
Barbados	7.43	7.43	14.86	8.18	8.18	16.36 [c]
Belize	f	f	f	f	f	f
Bermuda	5 [d,g]	5 [d,g]	10 [d,g]	5 [g]	5 [e,g]	10 [c,g]
Bolivia	10 [d]	1.71	11.71 [d]	10	11.71 [e,h]	21.71 [c]
Brazil	7.65 [b]	20 [b]	27.65 [b]	7.65	20 [e]	27.65 [c,i]
British Virgin Islands	3.25	3.25	6.5	4	4.5	8.5 [c]
Canada	4.95	4.95	9.9	6.9 [j]	8.68 [e,j]	15.58 [c,j,k]
Chile	10 [d]	0	10 [d]	17.6	2.4 [e]	20 [c,k]
Colombia	3.75	11.25	15	7.75	31.55 [e]	39.3 [c]
Costa Rica	3.5 [d]	6.25	9.75 [d]	9	20.5 [e]	29.5
Cuba	0	14 [b]	14 [b]	0	14	14
Dominica	3 [b]	6.75 [b]	9.75 [b]	3	6.75 [e]	9.75 [c]
Dominican Republic	2.28	5.72	8	4.98	12.02 [e]	17 [c]
Ecuador	9.15 [b]	9.15 [b]	18.3 [b]	11.15	10.15	21.3 [c]
El Salvador	3.25 [d]	6.75	10 [d]	6.25	14.25	20.5 [c]
Grenada	4 [b]	5 [b]	9 [b]	4	5	9 [c]
Guatemala	1.83	3.67	5.5	4.83	10.67	15.5 [c]
Guyana	5.2 [b]	7.8 [b]	13 [b]	5.2	7.8	13 [c]
Haiti	6	6	12	6	6 [e]	12
Honduras	1	2	3	3.5	7	10.5 [c]
Jamaica	2.5 [b]	2.5 [b]	5 [b]	2.5	2.5	5 [c]
Mexico	1.125 [d]	5.15	6.275 [d]	1.375	6.85 [e,l]	8.225 [c]
Nicaragua	4 [b]	6 [b]	10 [b]	10.25	24	34.25
Panama	6.75	2.75	9.5	7.25	10.75 [e]	18
Paraguay	9 [b]	14 [b]	23 [b]	9	14	23 [c]
Peru	8 [d]	0	8 [d]	8	9 [e]	17 [c]
Saint Kitts and Nevis	5 [b]	5 [b]	10 [b]	5	6	11 [c]
Saint Lucia	5 [b]	5 [b]	10 [b]	5	5	10 [c]

(Continued)

Table 4.
Continued

Country	Old age, disability, and survivors			All social security programs [a]		
	Insured person	Employer	Total	Insured person	Employer	Total
Saint Vincent and the Grenadines	2.5 [b]	3.5 [b]	6 [b]	2.5	4	6.5 [c]
Trinidad and Tobago	2.8	5.6	8.4	3.3	6.6	9.9 [c,k]
United States	6.2	6.2	12.4	7.65	8.45 [e]	16.1 [c,k,m]
Uruguay	15 [d]	12.5 [d]	27.5 [d]	18	17.5 [e]	35.5 [c,i,k]
Venezuela	1.93	4.82	6.75	4.22	9.98	14.2 [c]

SOURCE: Based on information in the country summaries in this volume.

a. Includes old age, disability, and survivors; sickness and maternity; work injury; unemployment; and family allowances. In some countries, the rate may not cover all of these programs. In some cases, only certain groups, such as wage earners, are represented. When the contribution rate varies, or the country has a dual system with different contribution rates, either the average or the lowest rate in the range is used.

b. Also includes the contribution rates for other programs.

c. Contributions are subject to an upper earnings limit for some benefits.

d. The contribution rate is for old-age benefits only. Additional contributions are required for survivor and disability

e. Employers pay the total cost of Work Injury.

f. A flat-rate weekly contribution to finance all benefits is paid according to eight earnings classes.

g. Plus flat-rate social insurance contributions.

h. Employers pay the cost of Family Allowances.

i. Government pays the cost of Unemployment Benefits.

j. Contribution rates may be higher in some provinces.

k. Government pays the cost of Family Allowances.

l. Plus flat-rate contributions for medical benefits.

m. Contribution rates may be higher or lower in some states.

Table 4.
Continued

Country
Summaries

Antigua and Barbuda

Exchange rate: US$1.00 equals
2.70 East Caribbean dollars (EC$).

Old Age, Disability, and Survivors

Regulatory Framework

First and current laws: 1972 (social insurance), 1973 (old age), 1977 (disability), and 1993 (social assistance).

Type of program: Social insurance and social assistance system.

Coverage

Social insurance: Employees and self-employed persons aged 16 to 59.

There is no voluntary insurance.

Exclusions: A married woman working for her husband, certain family members working for a family business, and casual workers with weekly earnings less than EC$7.50; employed persons with any earnings paid on the basis of commissions, fees, or profit sharing.

There are no special systems for any specified groups of employees.

Social assistance: Persons who were aged 65 or older in 1993; age 60 or older and blind with annual income up to EC$5,000.

Source of Funds

Insured person: 3% of monthly earnings (private sector) or 2% of monthly earnings (public sector).

The minimum weekly earnings for contribution purposes are EC$7.50.

The maximum annual earnings for contribution purposes are EC$54,000.

The insured's (private sector) contributions also finance sickness and maternity benefits.

Self-employed person: 8% of monthly earnings.

The minimum monthly earnings for contribution purposes are EC$450.

The maximum annual earnings for contribution purposes are EC$54,000.

The self-employed person's contributions also finance sickness and maternity benefits.

Employer: 5% of monthly payroll.

The minimum earnings for contribution purposes are EC$7.50 a week; EC$32.50 a month.

The maximum annual earnings for contribution purposes are EC$54,000.

The employer's contributions also finance sickness and maternity benefits.

Government: None; contributes as an employer.

Note: The Social Security Board finances social assistance benefits.

Qualifying Conditions

Old-age pension: Age 60 with at least 500 weeks of contributions for a full pension.

Partial pension: A reduced pension is paid at age 60 with 350 to 499 weeks of contributions.

Transitional pension: A reduced pension is paid at age 60 with 156 weeks of contributions starting before 1975.

Early pension: There is no early pension.

Deferred pension: There is no deferred pension.

Old-age settlement: Age 60 or older and does not meet the qualifying conditions for the old-age pension, but has at least 26 paid contributions starting before 1975 or at least 52 contributions starting after 1974.

Old-age benefits are payable abroad.

Old-age assistance: Age 77 or older; age 60 if blind or disabled.

Disability pension: Younger than age 60 with at least 156 weeks of contributions.

The degree of disability is assessed by the insured's doctor and a Social Security Board doctor.

Disability settlement: Younger than age 60 and does not meet the qualifying conditions for the disability pension, but has at least 52 weeks of contributions.

The degree of disability is assessed by the insured's doctor and a Social Security Board doctor.

Disability benefits are payable abroad.

Survivor pension: Payable if the deceased was eligible for or was receiving a disability pension or an old-age pension at the time of death.

Eligible survivors are a widow or a dependent disabled widower and children younger than age 16 (age 18 if a student).

Survivor settlement: Payable if the deceased was eligible for or was receiving an old-age grant or a disability grant.

Eligible survivors are a widow or a dependent disabled widower and children younger than age 16 (age 18 if a student).

Survivor benefits are payable abroad.

Funeral grant: The deceased had at least 26 weeks of paid contributions in the last 12 months or was eligible for or was receiving sickness benefits, maternity benefits, an old-age pension, or a disability pension.

Old-Age Benefits

Old-age pension: The full pension is equal to 25% of the insured's average earnings, plus 1% for every 50-week period of contributions above 500 contributions, up to a maximum of 50%.

Average earnings are based on earnings in the best-paid 5 years in the last 10 years of work; if the number of years worked is less than 5 years, the average is based on total earnings.

Partial pension: The full pension is reduced in proportion to the number of weeks of contributions.

Transitional pension: 25% of average earnings in the best-paid 5 years in the last 10 years of work.

Early pension: There is no early pension.

Deferred pension: There is no deferred pension.

The minimum monthly pension is EC$350.

The maximum monthly pension is EC$2,250.

Old-age settlement: EC$1,200 or 75% of the combined employer and employee contributions, whichever is higher.

Benefit adjustment: Benefits are adjusted according to actuarial reviews, subject to economic conditions.

Old-age assistance: EC$255 a month.

Permanent Disability Benefits

Disability pension: The pension is equal to 25% of the insured's average earnings, plus 1% for every 50-week period of contributions above 500 contributions, up to a maximum of 50%.

Average earnings are based on earnings in the best-paid 5 years in the last 10 years of work; if the insured has less than 5 years of work, the average is based on earnings in the total period.

The minimum monthly pension is EC$350.

The maximum monthly pension is EC$2,250.

Disability settlement: EC$1,200 or 75% of the combined employer and employee contributions, whichever is higher.

Benefit adjustment: Benefits are adjusted according to actuarial reviews, subject to economic conditions.

Survivor Benefits

Survivor pension: 50% of the pension paid or payable to the deceased is payable to a widow aged 50 or older or a dependent disabled widower. A limited pension is paid for a year if the widow is younger than age 50 and employed at the time of the insured's death.

The pension ceases on remarriage.

Orphan's pension: 25% of the deceased's pension (40% if a full orphan) is payable to an orphan younger than age 16 (age 18 if a student).

Survivor settlement: The grant must not exceed the value of the old-age settlement or disability settlement.

Benefit adjustment: Benefits are adjusted according to actuarial reviews, subject to economic conditions.

Funeral grant: EC$2,500 is payable to the person who paid for the funeral.

Administrative Organization

Ministry of Finance provides general supervision.

Social Security Board (http://www.socialsecurity.gov.ag) administers the program.

Sickness and Maternity

Regulatory Framework

First and current laws: 1972 (social insurance), 1973 (sickness), and 1973 (maternity).

Type of program: Social insurance system. Cash benefits only.

Coverage

Private-sector employees and self-employed persons aged 16 to 59.

There is no voluntary insurance.

Exclusions: A married woman working for her husband, certain family members working for a family business, and casual workers with weekly earnings less than EC$7.50; employed persons with any earnings paid on the basis of commissions, fees, or profit sharing.

There are no special systems for any specified groups of employees.

Source of Funds

Insured person: See source of funds under Old Age, Disability, and Survivors, above.

Self-employed person: See source of funds under Old Age, Disability, and Survivors, above.

Employer: See source of funds under Old Age, Disability, and Survivors, above.

Government: None.

Qualifying Conditions

Cash sickness benefits: Must be insured for at least 26 weeks; worked at least 8 weeks in the 3 calendar months immediately before the onset of incapacity and was employed the day before the onset of incapacity. The incapacity is not the result of an occupational injury.

Cash maternity benefits: Must have 26 weeks of contributions in the year before the expected date of childbirth.

Maternity grant: The grant is payable to an insured woman or the wife of an insured man, with at least 26 weeks of paid contributions in the year before the expected date of childbirth.

Sickness and Maternity Benefits

Sickness benefit: The benefit is equal to 60% of the insured's average weekly earnings and is payable after a 3-day waiting period. The benefit is payable for up to 26 weeks; may be extended for an additional 13 weeks.

Average insurable weekly earnings are based on earnings in the 3 calendar months before the onset of incapacity.

Maternity benefit: The benefit is equal to 60% of the insured's average weekly earnings and is payable for a maximum of 13 weeks beginning not earlier than 6 weeks before the expected date of childbirth or later than the expected week of childbirth.

Average insurable weekly earnings are based on earnings in the 52 weeks before the last 6 weeks before the expected week of childbirth.

Maternity grant: A lump sum of EC$560.

Workers' Medical Benefits

No statutory benefits are provided.

Medical services are provided by the Ministry of Health directly through public health facilities. Necessary medical treatment is permitted abroad, up to a maximum of EC$2,000.

Dependents' Medical Benefits

No statutory benefits are provided.

Medical services are provided by the Ministry of Health directly through public health facilities. Necessary medical treatment is permitted abroad, up to a maximum of EC$2,000.

Administrative Organization

Ministry of Finance provides general supervision.

Social Security Board (http://www.socialsecurity.gov.ag) administers the program.

Argentina

Exchange rate: US$1.00 equals 2.88 pesos.

Old Age, Disability, and Survivors

Regulatory Framework

First laws: 1904 to 1958 (various laws on special categories), 1944 (commerce), 1946 (industry), and 1954 (rural workers).

Current laws: 1993 (pensions), implemented in 1994; 1995; 1998 (small contributors), implemented in 1999, with 2004 amendment; 1999 (domestic workers), implemented in 2000; 2004 (early retirement), implemented in 2005; and 13 national social assistance laws approved between 1952 and 1994.

Type of program: Social insurance, individual account, and social assistance system.

Note: Beginning in 1994, the insured, including new entrants, can opt to direct part of the contribution to an individual account or to remain only in the social insurance system.

Coverage

Social insurance and individual account: Employed and self-employed persons; occasional workers with declared earnings of 12,000 pesos or less in the previous year.

Voluntary coverage for some clergy, domestic workers, and persons insured under professional provincial systems.

Exclusions: Armed forces, security forces, and police force personnel; technical workers hired abroad who work in the country for less than 2 years and are insured in another country; and persons younger than age 18.

Special systems for civil servants of some provinces and municipalities; armed forces, security forces, and police force personnel; and certain other groups.

Social assistance: The needy elderly and disabled.

Source of Funds

Insured person: 11% of gross earnings if opting for social insurance only; 7% of earnings, including an average 1.27% of gross earnings for disability and survivor insurance and an average 1.25% of gross earnings for administrative fees, if opting into the individual account system.

Voluntary contributions are the same as those for the insured person.

The minimum monthly earnings for contribution purposes are equal to three MOPREs.

The maximum monthly earnings for contribution purposes are equal to 60 MOPREs.

The MOPRE is an indexed figure determined once a year. The value of the MOPRE is 80 pesos in 2005.

Contributions are paid monthly.

Self-employed person: 27% of earnings, according to a fixed earnings reference scale. (Self-employed persons who opt for the individual account also contribute an average 1.27% of earnings for disability and survivor insurance and an average 1.25% of earnings for administrative fees.)

Occasional workers contribute 5% of each declared invoice. Small contributors contribute a monthly lump sum between 92.44 pesos and 564.44 pesos (according to annual declared earnings). The contribution includes value-added taxes and income taxes, as well as the contributions for old-age, disability, and survivor benefits and sickness benefits. (Small contributors are persons who sell goods, rent goods, provide services, or who are members of workers' cooperatives or certain enterprises specified by law with less than three members.)

Contributions are paid monthly.

Employer: 10.17% or 12.71% of payroll, according to the type of enterprise. (Additional contributions are made on behalf of workers in hazardous or unhealthy occupations.)

The minimum monthly earnings for contribution purposes are equal to three MOPREs.

The MOPRE is an indexed figure determined once a year. The value of the MOPRE is 80 pesos in 2005.

There are no maximum monthly earnings for contribution purposes after October 2005.

Employers of domestic workers contribute a monthly lump sum of 20, 39, or 55 pesos (according to hours worked).

Contributions are paid monthly.

Government: Contributes through general revenue, investment income, and certain earmarked taxes to the cost of social insurance pensions; finances the total cost of social assistance pensions; and contributes to the cost of the disability and survivor pensions for insured persons born before 1963 (men) or 1968 (women) who have opted for the individual account.

Qualifying Conditions

Old-age pension

Basic universal old-age pension (social insurance and individual account): Age 65 (men) or age 60 (women) with at least 30 years of contributions and service, up to a maximum of 45 years. (In order to meet the contribution qualifying condition, the insured may substitute 2 years of age after the retirement age for 1 year of contributions.)

The retirement age and contribution conditions are reduced by up to 10 years for hazardous or unhealthy occupations.

Compensatory pension (social insurance): Age 65 (men) or age 60 (women) with at least 30 years of contributions and service, up to a maximum of 45 years. The benefit is paid only if the insured has credited contributions to the social insurance system before June 1994.

Additional pension (social insurance): Age 65 (men) or age 60 (women) with at least 30 years of contributions and service, up to a maximum of 45 years. The additional pension is paid if the insured has been credited with contributions to the social insurance system since June 1994.

Early pension (social insurance): Age 60 (men) or age 55 (women) with at least 30 years of contributions and service and unemployed since November 30, 2004. Persons receiving the early pension must cease all gainful activity. (No new claims for an early pension will be awarded as of February 2007; thereafter, an existing claim will continue to be paid until the beneficiary reaches the normal pensionable age.)

Advanced-age old-age pension (social insurance and individual account): Aged 70 or older (men and women) with at least 10 years of service with contributions paid while employed or self-employed, including 5 of the last 8 years before leaving employment. A self-employed person must have been insured for at least 5 years.

Old-age pension (individual account): Age 65 (men) or age 60 (women).

Early pension (individual account): Payable only if the individual account balance is sufficient to finance a minimum monthly benefit specified by law.

Noncontributory old-age pension (social assistance): Indigent residents aged 70 or older.

Disability pension

Disability pension (social insurance and individual account): Payable for the loss of at least 66% of earning capacity. The insured must be younger than the normal retirement age, have paid contributions on a regular or nonregular basis, and not be receiving early retirement benefits.

Regular contributors must meet the minimum contribution requirement for the old-age pension (basic universal) or have paid 30 months of contributions in the last 36 months before the onset of disability.

Nonregular contributors must meet 50% of the minimum contribution requirement for the old-age pension (basic universal) or have paid 12 months of contributions in the 60 months before the onset of disability or have paid 18 months of contributions in the 36 months before the onset of disability.

District medical commissions assess the degree of disability. Three years after the initial assessment, the commission can certify permanent disability, extend the disability certification for 2 years, or determine that the person is no longer disabled.

Advanced-age disability pension (social insurance and individual account): The loss of at least 66% of earning capacity and aged 70 or older (men and women) with at least 10 years of service with contributions paid while employed or self-employed, including 5 of the last 8 years before leaving employment. A self-employed person must have been insured for at least 5 years.

Noncontributory disability pension (social assistance): Indigent disabled residents.

Survivor pension

Survivor pension (social insurance and individual account): The deceased was a pensioner or had paid contributions on a regular or nonregular basis.

Regular contributors must meet the minimum contribution requirement for the old-age pension (basic universal) or have paid 30 months of contributions in the last 36 months before the onset of disability.

Nonregular contributors must meet 50% of the minimum contribution requirement for the old-age pension (basic universal) or have paid 12 months of contributions in the 60 months before the onset of disability or have paid 18 months of contributions in the 36 months before the onset of disability.

Eligible survivors include a widow(er) or partner who lived with the deceased for at least 5 years (2 years if they had children); an unmarried child younger than age 18 who is not receiving benefits; a widowed daughter younger than age 18 who is not receiving benefits; and a disabled child (regardless of age) who was dependent on the deceased.

Old-Age Benefits

Old-age pension

Note: Insured persons who have set up an individual account may receive different combinations of social insurance and individual account benefits.

Basic universal old-age pension (social insurance and individual account): The monthly pension is equal to 2.5 MOPREs, plus 1% of 2.5 MOPREs for each year of contributions exceeding 30 years, up to a maximum of 45 years.

The value of the MOPRE is 80 pesos in 2005.

Compensatory pension (social insurance): The monthly pension is equal to 1.5% of the insured's average adjusted monthly salary in the last 10 years (weighted average adjusted amounts for all periods if self-employed) with contributions paid before July 1994, up to a maximum of 35 years.

The maximum compensatory pension is equal to one MOPRE for each year of contributions used to calculate the compensatory pension.

The value of the MOPRE is 80 pesos in 2005.

Additional pension (social insurance): The monthly pension is equal to 0.85% of the insured's average adjusted monthly salary in the last 10 years (weighted average adjusted amounts for all periods if self-employed) with contributions paid after July 1994, up to a maximum of 35 years.

The maximum additional pension is 1,428 pesos a month.

Early pension (social insurance): The monthly pension is equal to 50% of the full old-age pension (including all pension entitlements). The early pension is commuted to a full old-age pension (including all pension entitlements) at age 65 (men) or age 60 (women).

An early pensioner is not entitled to receive other benefits.

The minimum monthly early pension is 390 pesos.

Advanced-age old-age pension (social insurance and individual account): The monthly pension is equal to 70% of the basic universal old-age pension, plus the compensatory pension, the additional pension, and the value of any pension received from an individual account.

The minimum monthly advanced-age pension is 390 pesos.

The combined minimum monthly advanced-age pension (the sum of all contributory pensions) is 390 pesos.

The maximum monthly advanced-age pension (the sum of the basic universal and social insurance pensions) is 3,100 pesos.

Schedule of payments: Pensions are payable monthly, with a 13th payment equal to the regular monthly payment divided in half and paid in June and December.

Pensions are payable abroad under bilateral or multilateral agreement.

Benefit adjustment: Pensions are adjusted annually by government, according to changes made to the MOPRE.

Old-age pension (individual account): The pension depends on the value of the insured's contributions plus accrued interest. The pension is payable as a life pension annuity, as programmed withdrawals, or as partial withdrawals.

The combined minimum old-age pension of 390 pesos does not apply to insured persons who are eligible only for an old-age pension based on an individual account.

Early pension (individual account): The insured may receive an early pension, regardless of age, if the individual account balance is sufficient to finance a monthly benefit that, when paid under the life pension annuity or programmed withdrawal method, provides at least 50% of the base salary or 460 pesos a month, whichever is greater.

Schedule of payments: The pension is paid monthly, with a 13th payment equal to the regular monthly payment divided in half and paid in June and December.

Pensions are payable abroad under bilateral or multilateral agreement.

Noncontributory old-age pension (social assistance): The monthly pension is equal to 273 pesos (70% of the minimum pension of 390 pesos). Additional benefits may be paid for dependents under Family Allowances, below.

Schedule of payments: The noncontributory pension is paid monthly, with a 13th payment equal to the regular monthly payment divided in half and paid in June and December.

Social assistance pensions are not payable abroad.

Benefit adjustment: Pensions are adjusted annually by government, according to changes made to the MOPRE.

Permanent Disability Benefits

Disability pension

Disability pension (social insurance and individual account): The pension is equal to 70% of the insured's average salary (regular contributor) or 50% of the insured's average salary (nonregular contributor) during the 5 years before the onset of disability. (Disability insurance tops up the accumulated capital in the individual account if the balance is less than the required minimum to finance the permanent disability pension.)

The pension payable to insured persons who opted for the individual account is subject to review after 3 years.

The minimum monthly disability pension is 390 pesos.

The maximum monthly disability pension is 3,100 pesos.

Schedule of payments: The disability pension is paid monthly, with a 13th payment equal to the regular monthly payment divided in half and paid in June and December.

The pension is payable abroad under bilateral or multilateral agreement.

Advanced-age disability pension (social insurance and individual account): The monthly pension is equal to 70% of the basic universal old-age pension, plus the insured's compensatory pension, additional pension, and the value of any pension received from an individual account.

The minimum monthly advanced-age disability pension is 390 pesos.

The maximum monthly advanced-age disability pension is 3,100 pesos.

Schedule of payments: The advanced-age disability pension is paid monthly, with a 13th payment equal to the regular monthly payment divided in half and paid in June and December.

The pension is payable abroad under bilateral or multilateral agreement.

Benefit adjustment: Pensions are adjusted annually by government, according to changes made to the MOPRE.

Noncontributory disability pension (social assistance): The monthly pension is equal to 273 pesos (70% of the minimum pension of 390 pesos). Additional benefits may be paid for dependents under Family Allowances, below.

The noncontributory disability pension is not payable abroad.

Benefit adjustment: Pensions are adjusted annually by government, according to changes made to the MOPRE.

Survivor Benefits

Survivor pension

Survivor pension (social insurance and individual account): A widow(er) or partner without dependents receives 70% of the reference payment or, if the deceased was a pensioner, the pension; a widow(er) or partner with children receives 50%. (Life insurance tops up the accumulated capital in the deceased's individual account if the balance is less than the required minimum to finance the survivor pension.)

In certain cases, both the deceased's widow(er) and a partner may be entitled to survivor benefits. A widow(er) or partner without dependents receives 35% of the reference payment or, if the deceased was a pensioner, the pension; a widow(er) or partner with children receives 25%.

The reference payment is equal to 70% of the deceased's average salary (regular contributor) or 50% of the deceased's average salary (nonregular contributor) during the 5 years before death.

The amount payable may be recalculated if the number of eligible survivors changes.

The minimum monthly survivor pension is 390 pesos.

The maximum monthly survivor pension is 3,100 pesos.

Orphan's pension (social insurance and individual account): Each eligible child receives 20% of the deceased's pension or reference payment. In the absence of an eligible widow(er) or partner, the survivor pension is also split equally among the surviving children. (Life insurance tops up the accumulated capital in the deceased's individual account if the balance is less than the required minimum to finance the survivor pension.)

The maximum total survivor pension is equal to 100% of the reference payment or 100% of the deceased's pension.

The reference payment is equal to 70% of the deceased's average salary (regular contributor) or 50% of the deceased's average salary (nonregular contributor) during the 5 years before death.

The amount payable may be recalculated if the number of eligible survivors changes.

Schedule of payments: Survivor pensions are paid monthly, with a 13th payment equal to the regular monthly payment divided in half and paid in June and December.

Survivor pensions are payable abroad under bilateral or multilateral agreement.

Benefit adjustment: Pensions are adjusted annually by government, according to changes made to the MOPRE.

Funeral grant (social insurance and individual account): A lump sum of 450 pesos is paid to survivors.

Administrative Organization

Secretariat for Social Security (http://www.seguridadsocial .gov.ar) is responsible for policy development for all areas of social security except health insurance.

National Social Security Administration (http://www.anses .gov.ar) provides supervision and administers the social insurance program.

Superintendent of Retirement and Pension Fund Administrators (http://www.safjp.gov.ar) provides general supervision of the pension funds.

Retirement and Pension Fund Administrators (AFJPs) administer the pension funds and benefits.

National Assistance Pension Commission (http://www.cnpa .gov.ar) administers the social assistance pension program.

Sickness and Maternity

Regulatory Framework

First laws: 1934 (maternity) and 1944 (sickness).

Current laws: 1996 (family allowances); 1988 (health institutions), implemented in 1989; 1988 (health insurance), implemented in 1989; and 2000 (health institutions deregulation), implemented in 2001.

Type of program: Social insurance (medical benefits), employer-liability (cash sickness benefits), and employment-related (maternity benefits) system.

Coverage

Cash sickness benefits: No statutory benefits are provided. (Under employment law, the employer is required to pay monthly cash sickness benefits to employees.)

Cash maternity benefits: Employed women (including temporary workers).

Exclusions: Domestic workers and the self-employed.

Medical benefits: Employed persons, small contributors, the unemployed, and pensioners.

Voluntary coverage for other persons and domestic workers.

Exclusions: Military police, provincial and municipal public-sector employees, and beneficiaries of noncontributory or social assistance benefits.

Source of Funds

Cash sickness benefits: No statutory benefits are provided.

Cash maternity benefits

Insured person: None.

Self-employed person: None.

Employer: See source of funds under Family Allowances, below.

Government: See source of funds under Family Allowances, below.

Medical benefits

Insured person: 6% of gross earnings, plus 1.5% of gross earnings for each covered dependent other than the spouse or children. Pensioners contribute 3% of the pension.

The minimum monthly earnings for contributions purposes are equal to three MOPREs.

The maximum monthly earnings for contributions purposes are equal to 60 MOPREs.

The MOPRE is an indexed figure determined once a year. The value of the MOPRE is 80 pesos in 2005.

Self-employed person: Small contributors pay a monthly lump sum of 24.44 pesos, plus 24.44 pesos for a spouse and children. Domestic workers pay a monthly lump sum of 20 pesos, plus 20 pesos for a spouse and children.

Employer: The average contribution is 7.2% of payroll (including 1.5% or 1.62% of payroll for retired persons).

The minimum monthly earnings for contributions purposes are equal to three MOPREs.

The MOPRE is an indexed figure determined once a year. The value of the MOPRE is 80 pesos in 2005.

There are no maximum monthly earnings for contribution purposes after October 2005.

Government: Provides subsidies for persons who would not otherwise qualify and provides tax incentives for self-employed persons.

Qualifying Conditions

Cash sickness benefits: No statutory benefits are provided. (Under employment law, the employer is required to pay monthly cash sickness benefits to employees. The duration of benefits depends on the length of the employment period.)

Cash maternity benefits: Must have at least 3 months of continuous employment before the expected date of childbirth; temporary workers must be in employment immediately before the start of the maternity leave period.

Medical benefits: Must be currently employed or a pensioner. Coverage may be extended for 3 months if the insured has more than 3 months of continuous service.

Sickness and Maternity Benefits

Sickness benefit: No statutory benefits are provided. (Under employment law, employers are required to provide 100% of salary for up to 3 months to employees with less than 5 years of service; up to 6 months with at least 5 years of service. The maximum duration of cash benefits is doubled for workers with dependents.)

Maternity benefit: The benefit is equal to 3 months of average gross earnings before the maternity leave period and is paid for 45 days before and 45 days after the expected date of childbirth; the benefit is extended for 6 months if the child suffers from Down's syndrome.

The benefit is also paid if the pregnancy ends after at least 180 days of gestation or if the child is stillborn.

Workers' Medical Benefits

Benefits include medical, hospital, dental, and palliative care; rehabilitation; prostheses; and transportation. Benefits are defined by the schedule in law issued by the Ministry of Health and Environment.

There is no limit to duration, except in cases of hospitalization for psychiatric treatment.

Pharmaceutical products for chronic diseases are either free or require a 30% copayment; 60% for other diseases.

Pharmaceutical products are free during pregnancy, childbirth, and for postnatal care; for the child until age 1; and in cases of hospitalization.

Cost sharing: Up to 4 pesos for an outpatient visit, up to 5 pesos for medical examinations, and up to 7 pesos for outpatient dental treatment.

There is no cost sharing for pregnancy, childbirth, or postnatal care; for the child up to age 1; in case of hospitalization; and for the treatment of tumors.

Dependents' Medical Benefits

Eligible dependents include a spouse or cohabiting partner and single children younger than age 21 (up to age 25 if a student, no limit if disabled and dependent).

Other dependents are eligible only with the payment of additional contributions.

Benefits include medical, hospital, dental, and palliative care; rehabilitation; prostheses; and transportation. Benefits are defined by the schedule in law issued by the Ministry of Health and Environment.

There is no limit to duration, except in cases of hospitalization for psychiatric treatment.

Pharmaceutical products for chronic diseases are either free or require a 30% copayment; 60% for other diseases.

Pharmaceutical products are free during pregnancy, childbirth, and for postnatal care; for the child until age 1; and in cases of hospitalization.

Cost sharing: Up to 4 pesos for an outpatient visit, up to 5 pesos for medical examinations, and up to 7 pesos for outpatient dental treatment.

There is no cost sharing for pregnancy, childbirth, or postnatal care; for the child up to age 1; in cases of hospitalization; and for the treatment of tumors.

Administrative Organization

Ministry of Health and Environment (http://www.minsal .gov.ar) provides general supervision.

Superintendent of Health Services (http://www.sssalud .gov.ar) controls, coordinates, and administers the program.

Authorized health insurance institutions provide medical services. Insured persons are free to choose between health insurance institutions.

Work Injury

Regulatory Framework

First law: 1915.

Current law: 1995 (work injury), implemented in 1996.

Type of program: Employer-liability system.

The employer and public institutions (other than national institutions), may self-insure if solvency requirements are met and medical care services can be guaranteed. If the employer does not meet both conditions, mandatory insurance must be taken with a work injury insurer (ART).

Coverage

Employed persons in the private and public sectors (including provinces and municipalities).

There is no voluntary coverage.

Exclusions: Domestic workers, the self-employed, and firemen.

Source of Funds

Insured person: None.

Self-employed person: None.

Employer: Total cost, met through a work injury insurer (ART) or through self-insurance.

Government: None.

Qualifying Conditions

Work injury benefits: There is no minimum qualifying period. Accidents that occur while commuting to and from work are covered.

Temporary Disability Benefits

The monthly benefit is equal to the insured's average earnings in the 12 months before the onset of disability and is payable from the day after the onset of disability. The employer pays the benefit for the first 10 days, with the remaining period covered by the ART. The benefit is payable until recovery or certification of permanent disability.

The minimum monthly earnings for benefit calculation purposes are equal to three MOPREs.

The maximum monthly earnings for benefit calculation purposes are equal to 60 MOPREs.

The MOPRE is an indexed figure determined once a year. The value of the MOPRE is 80 pesos in 2005.

The disability is presumed to be permanent if it continues beyond a year.

A medical commission assesses the degree of disability.

Permanent Disability Benefits

For an assessed degree of loss of earning capacity of 66% or more, the benefit is equal to 70% of the insured's average earnings in the 12 months before the onset of disability, plus family allowances.

The minimum monthly earnings for benefit calculation purposes are equal to three MOPREs.

The maximum monthly earnings for benefit calculation purposes are equal to 60 MOPREs.

The MOPRE is an indexed figure determined once a year. The value of the MOPRE is 80 pesos in 2005.

An initial benefit is paid for 36 months (extended for 24 months if there is uncertainty about the final degree of loss of earning capacity). When the disability is assessed as permanent, the monthly disability benefit—70% of average salary (regular contributor) or 50% of average salary (nonregular contributor) during the 5 years before the onset of disability—is paid, plus an annuity based on 53 times the insured's average earnings in the 12 months before the onset of disability multiplied by a coefficient resulting from dividing 65 by the age of the worker at the date of the onset of disability. The amount must not exceed 180,000 pesos, plus a lump-sum benefit of 40,000 pesos.

Constant-attendance allowance: For a severe permanent total disability, an additional monthly benefit equal to three MOPREs is paid by the ART for the assistance of another person.

Permanent partial disability benefit: For an assessed degree of loss of earning capacity lower than 66%, the benefit is 70% of the insured's average earnings in the 12 months before the onset of disability multiplied by the assessed degree of loss of earning capacity, plus family allowances.

The minimum monthly earnings for benefit calculation purposes are equal to three MOPREs.

The maximum monthly earnings for benefit calculation purposes are equal to 60 MOPREs.

The MOPRE is an indexed figure determined once a year. The value of the MOPRE is 80 pesos in 2005.

A preliminary partial permanent benefit is paid for 36 months; the period may be reduced if there is uncertainty about the final degree of loss of earning capacity.

When the partial disability is assessed as permanent with an assessed degree of loss of earning capacity from 50% to 66%, the benefit is equal to the insured's average earnings in the 12 months before the onset of disability (up to a maximum of 180,000 pesos), plus a lump-sum benefit of 30,000 pesos.

When the partial disability is assessed as permanent with an assessed degree of loss of earning capacity lower than 50%, a lump-sum benefit is paid equal to 53 times the insured's average earnings in the 12 months before the onset of disability multiplied by the assessed degree of loss of earnings capacity and a coefficient resulting from dividing 65 by the age of the worker at the date of the onset of disability. The amount must not exceed 180,000 pesos multiplied by the assessed degree of disability.

A medical commission assesses the degree of disability.

Benefit adjustment: Pensions are adjusted annually by the government, according to changes made to the MOPRE.

Workers' Medical Benefits

Benefits include medical, pharmaceutical, and orthopedic care; prostheses; rehabilitation; and professional training.

Survivor Benefits

Survivor pension: A widow(er) or partner without dependents receives 70% of the reference payment; a widow(er) or partner with children receives 50%.

In certain cases, both the deceased's widow(er) and a partner may be entitled to survivor benefits. A widow(er) or partner without dependents receives 35% of the reference payment; a widow(er) or partner with children receives 25%.

The reference payment is equal to 70% of average salary (regular contributor) or 50% of average salary (nonregular contributor) in the 5 years before the insured's death.

Nonregular contributors must fulfill 50% of the minimum contribution requirement for the old-age pension (basic universal) or have paid 12 months of contributions in the 60 months before the date of the onset of disability or have paid 18 months of contributions in the 36 months before the onset of disability.

The amount payable may be recalculated if the number of eligible survivors changes.

The minimum monthly survivor pension is 390 pesos.

The maximum monthly survivor pension is 3,100 pesos.

Schedule of payments: The survivor pension is paid monthly, with a 13th payment equal to the regular monthly payment divided in half and paid in June and December.

Pensions are payable abroad under bilateral or multilateral agreement.

Benefit adjustment: Pensions are adjusted annually by the government, according to changes made to the MOPRE.

Orphan's pension: Each eligible child younger than age 21 (age 25 if a student, no limit if disabled) receives 20% of the deceased's pension or reference payment. In the absence of an eligible widow(er) or partner, the survivor pension is also split equally among the surviving children.

The maximum total survivor pension is equal to 100% of the reference payment.

The amount payable may be recalculated if the number of eligible survivors changes.

Benefit adjustment: Pensions are adjusted annually by the government, according to changes made to the MOPRE.

Survivors also receive an annuity based on 53 times the insured's average earnings in the 12 months before the onset of disability multiplied by a coefficient resulting from dividing 65 by the age of the worker at the date of the onset of disability. The sum must not exceed 180,000 pesos, plus a lump-sum benefit of 50,000 pesos.

The lump sum is split equally among eligible survivors.

Other eligible survivors (in the absence of the above): In order of priority, parents or relatives who were dependent on the deceased receive the full pension.

Benefit adjustment: Pensions are adjusted annually by the government, according to changes made to the MOPRE.

Administrative Organization

Secretariat for Social Security (http://www.seguridadsocial.gov.ar) is responsible for policy development for all areas of social security except health insurance.

Superintendent of Work Injury provides general supervision.

Work injury insurers (ART) are responsible for work injury prevention and the management of benefits.

Unemployment

Regulatory Framework

First law: 1967.

Current laws: 1991 (unemployment insurance), implemented in 1992; 1999 (agricultural workers), implemented in 2004; and 2000 (construction workers), implemented in 2001.

Type of program: Social insurance system.

Coverage

Private-sector employees, including temporary and occasional workers.

There is no voluntary coverage.

Exclusions: The self-employed, domestic workers, public-sector employees, and teachers in private institutions.

Special systems for agricultural and construction workers.

Source of Funds

Insured person: None.

Self-employed person: None.

Employer: 0.89% or 1.11% of payroll, according to the enterprise type.

The minimum monthly earnings for contribution purposes are equal to three MOPREs.

The MOPRE is an indexed figure determined once a year. The value of the MOPRE is 80 pesos in 2005.

There are no maximum monthly earnings for contribution purposes after October 2005.

Government: Any deficit.

Qualifying Conditions

Unemployment benefits: Twelve months of contributions before the date of unemployment; 12 months of contributions in the 3 years before or 90 days in the 12 months before the date of unemployment for temporary workers; 90 days of contributions in the 12 months before the date of unemployment for occasional workers.

Extended unemployment benefit: The benefit may be extended for 6 months if the unemployed person is at least age 45 (men and women) and has children who are eligible for family allowances.

Single-payment benefit: The benefit is paid to an unemployed person who intends to create an enterprise. The unemployed person must present a business plan to the Ministry of Labor, Employment, and Social Security for approval.

The unemployed person must be registered and available for suitable employment and not be receiving any other social security benefit.

Unemployment Benefits

The monthly benefit is equal to 41.5% of the insured's best wage in the 6 months before the date of unemployment. The benefit is paid for 4 months if the insured has 12 to 23 months of contributions; for 8 months with 24 to 35 months; for 12 months with 36 months or more.

The benefit is equal to 100% of the calculated amount for the first 4 months; thereafter, the benefit declines to 85% of the calculated amount for the fifth to the eighth month and to 75% for the ninth to the twelfth month.

The minimum monthly unemployment benefit is 150 pesos.

The maximum monthly unemployment benefit is 300 pesos.

Extended unemployment benefit: The benefit is equal to 70% of the first monthly unemployment benefit paid.

Single-payment benefit: Payable after the first monthly payment has been paid and there remains at least 3 monthly payments before entitlement ceases. The benefit is equal to twice the total amount of the remaining monthly payments.

Unemployment beneficiaries may receive family allowances.

Administrative Organization

Ministry of Labor, Employment, and Social Security (http://www.trabajo.gov.ar) provides general supervision.

National Social Security Administration (http://www.anses.gov.ar) administers the social insurance program.

National Registry of Agricultural Workers and Employers (http://www.renatre.org.ar) administers the agricultural social insurance program.

Family Allowances

Regulatory Framework

First law: 1957.

Current law: 1996 (family allowances), implemented in 1996.

Type of program: Social insurance and social assistance system.

Coverage

Social insurance: Employed persons in the private sector and beneficiaries of work injury and unemployment programs.

Social assistance: Beneficiaries of the social insurance, individual account, or social assistance programs.

Exclusions: Self-employed persons and domestic workers.

Source of Funds

Insured person: None.

Self-employed person: None.

Employer: 4.44% or 5.56% of payroll, according to the enterprise type. Contributions also finance maternity benefits (see Sickness and Maternity, above).

The minimum monthly earnings for contribution purposes are equal to three MOPREs.

The MOPRE is an indexed figure determined once a year. The value of the MOPRE is 80 pesos in 2005.

There are no maximum monthly earnings for contribution purposes after October 2005.

Government: The cost of benefits for pensioners and other recipients of noncontributory benefits.

Qualifying Conditions

Family allowances: The monthly income of employed persons or beneficiaries of work injury and unemployment benefits must be between 100 pesos and 3,000 pesos (lower than 3,100 pesos for other beneficiaries), depending on the allowance. Income limits and benefit amounts vary by region.

Child benefit (means-tested): A monthly benefit is paid to an employed person or to a pensioner who qualifies for family allowances or to an ART beneficiary for every unmarried child younger than age 18. The benefit is paid to one of the parents or to the guardian.

Disabled child benefit (not means-tested): A monthly benefit is paid to an employed person or to a pensioner who qualifies for family allowances or to an ART beneficiary for every disabled child of any age. The benefit is paid to one of the parents or to the guardian.

Prenatal grant (means-tested): A monthly benefit is paid to an employed person or to an ART beneficiary from the time of conception to the expected date of childbirth or end of the pregnancy. The insured must have current continuous employment for 3 months.

School allowance (means-tested): An annual benefit is paid to an employed person or to a pensioner who qualifies for family allowances or to an ART beneficiary who qualifies for a child benefit or a disabled child benefit. Certification of school enrollment must be provided at the beginning of the year.

Birth grant (means-tested): A benefit is paid to an employed person or to an ART beneficiary for the birth of a child. The grant is paid to one of the parents or to the guardian. The insured must have current continuous employment for 6 months.

Adoption grant (means-tested): A benefit is paid to an employed person or to an ART beneficiary for the adopted child. The grant is paid to one of the adopting parents. The insured must have current continuous employment for 6 months.

Marriage grant (means-tested): A benefit is paid to both spouses if they are employed or are ART beneficiaries who qualify for family allowances. The insured must have current continuous employment for 6 months.

Spouse benefit (means-tested): A monthly benefit is paid to a pensioner for a legal spouse who resides in the country.

Family Allowance Benefits

Family allowances

Child benefit (means-tested): The monthly child benefit allowance is between 30 pesos and 129 pesos, depending on the insured's income (in some cases, including cash benefits) and region.

Disabled child benefit (not means-tested): The monthly benefit is between 120 pesos and 480 pesos, depending on the region.

Prenatal allowance (means-tested): The monthly allowance is between 30 pesos and 129 pesos, depending on the insured's income (in some cases, including cash benefits) and region.

School allowance (means-tested): The annual allowance is between 130 pesos and 520 pesos, depending on the insured's income (in some cases, including cash benefits) and region.

Birth grant (means-tested): A lump sum of 200 pesos.

Adoption grant (means-tested): A lump sum of 1,200 pesos.

Marriage grant (means-tested): A lump sum of 300 pesos.

Spouse benefit (means-tested): The monthly benefit is between 15 pesos and 30 pesos, depending on the beneficiary's income and region.

Administrative Organization

Secretariat for Social Security (http://www.seguridadsocial .gov.ar) is responsible for policy development for all areas of social security except health insurance.

National Social Security Administration (http://www.anses .gov.ar) provides supervision and administers the social insurance program.

Bahamas

Exchange rate: US$1.00 equals
1.00 Bahamian dollar (B$).

Old Age, Disability, and Survivors

Regulatory Framework

First laws: 1956 (old-age noncontributory pensions) and 1967 (public assistance for disability).

Current law: 1972 (national insurance), with 1999 amendment.

Type of program: Social insurance and social assistance system.

Coverage

Social insurance: Employed persons, self-employed persons, and the voluntarily insured.

Social assistance: Residents who do not qualify under the National Insurance Act.

Source of Funds

Social insurance

Insured person: 1.7% of earnings, if weekly insurable earnings are less than B$60; 3.4% for earnings greater than B$60. Voluntarily insured persons contribute 5% of weekly average wages or income, based on the insured's wages or income of the previous year before registration.

The maximum annual earnings for contribution and benefit purposes are B$20,800.

The above mandatory contributions also finance cash sickness, maternity, and work injury benefits. The contributions of the voluntarily insured finance old-age, disability, and survivor pensions and funeral and maternity grants.

Self-employed person: 8.8% of earnings if also covered for work injury benefits; 6.8% or earnings if not covered for work injury benefits.

The maximum annual earnings for contribution and benefit purposes are B$20,800.

The above contributions also finance cash sickness, maternity, and work injury benefits (except for certain categories of self-employed persons).

Employer: 7.1% of payroll for weekly insurable wages less than B$60; 5.4% for wages greater than B$60. (0.75% of the employer's contribution is earmarked for work injury benefits.)

The maximum annual earnings for contribution and benefit purposes are B$20,800.

The above contributions also finance cash sickness, maternity, and work injury benefits.

Government: None.

Social assistance

Insured person: None.

Self-employed person: None.

Employer: None.

Government: Total cost of all income-tested allowances in force before October 1974.

Qualifying Conditions

Social insurance

Retirement pension: Age 65 with 150 weeks of paid contributions. Employees who were older than age 35 in 1974 (self-employed older than age 35 in 1976) receive a 25-week credit for each year that they were older than age 35, up to a maximum of 600 weeks, provided that contributions were paid for 150 weeks during the first 3 years that the program was in operation.

Entitlement ceases if the insured person earns B$200 or more a week.

Early pension: An early pension is payable between ages 60 and 64.

Deferred pension: The pension can be deferred up to age 69.

Benefit is paid locally for insured persons who live abroad.

Disability pension: Younger than age 65 and permanently incapable of any work. Employees who were older than age 35 in 1974 (self-employed older than age 35 in 1976) receive a 25-week credit for each year that they were older than age 35, up to a maximum of 600 weeks, provided that contributions were paid for 150 weeks during the first 3 years that the program was in operation.

Survivor pension: The deceased was a pensioner or had made 150 contributions at the time of death.

Eligible survivors are a widow aged 40 or older who is incapable of gainful employment or is caring for a child eligible for survivor benefits. The pension is also payable to a dependent disabled widower with weekly income less than B$46.15 and a dependent child younger than age 16 (age 21 if a student).

Funeral grant: Payable for the death of an insured person or the spouse of an insured person. The insured must have at least 50 paid contributions.

Social assistance

Noncontributory old-age pension (income-tested): For resident retired workers aged 65 or older who do not qualify under the National Insurance Act.

Disability assistance (income-tested): For residents who are assessed as disabled and who do not qualify under the National Insurance Act.

Survivor assistance (income-tested): Payable if the deceased did not qualify under the National Insurance Act.

Old-Age Benefits

Social insurance

Retirement pension: The pension is equal to 40% of the covered wage with 750 weeks of paid or credited contributions; 15% to 38% of the covered wage with between 150 and 749 weeks of paid or credited contributions. The pension is increased by 1% of the covered wage for each 50-week period of paid or credited contributions exceeding 750 weeks, up to a maximum of 60%.

The covered wage is based on average weekly earnings in the best 3 years in the 10 years before the contribution year in which the insured reaches age 65.

Early pension: The benefit is reduced by between 20% and 4%, depending on the age at which the pension is taken between ages 60 and 64.

Deferred pension: Calculated in the same way as the retirement pension, above.

The minimum pension is B$53.07 a week.

Social assistance

Noncontributory old-age pension (income-tested): B$46.15 a week.

Permanent Disability Benefits

Social insurance

Disability pension: The pension is equal to 40% of the covered wage, according to wage class, with 750 weeks of paid or credited contributions; 15% to 38% of covered wage with between 150 and 749 weeks of paid or credited contributions. The pension is increased by 1% of the covered wage for each 50-week period of paid or credited contributions exceeding 750 weeks, up to a maximum of 60%.

The covered wage is based on average weekly earnings in the best 3 years in the 10 years before the contribution year in which the onset of disability occurs.

The maximum annual wage for benefit calculation purposes is B$20,800.

The minimum pension is B$53.07 a week.

Social assistance

Disability assistance (income-tested): B$46.15 a week.

Survivor Benefits

Social insurance

Survivor pension: 50% of the deceased's pension is payable to a widow aged 40 or older who is incapable of gainful employment or is caring for a child eligible for survivor benefits. The pension is also payable to a dependent disabled widower with weekly income less than B$46.15.

Other eligible survivors (in the absence of the above): The full pension is awarded to a dependent mother older than age 40 or a disabled father with weekly income less than B$46.15.

The minimum survivor pension is B$53.07 a week.

Orphan's pension: Each dependent child younger than age 16 (age 21 if a full-time student) receives 10% of the deceased's pension, up to a family maximum of 100%.

Full orphans receive B$21.92 a week each; up to B$25.50 a week each if older than age 12, a student, or disabled.

The minimum orphan's pension is B$21.92 a week.

Funeral grant: A lump sum of B$1,500 is payable to the person who pays for the funeral. If the funeral costs less than B$1,500, the remaining balance is payable at the discretion of the National Insurance Board.

Social assistance

Survivor assistance (income-tested): Adults receive B$46.15 a week; children receive B$18.46 a week each.

Administrative Organization

Ministry of Housing and National Insurance provides general supervision.

National Insurance Board (http://www.nib-bahamas.com) administers the program.

Sickness and Maternity

Regulatory Framework

First and current law: 1972 (national insurance), with 1999 amendment.

Type of program: Social insurance system. Cash benefits only.

Coverage

Employed and self-employed persons.

Source of Funds

Insured person: See source of funds under Old Age, Disability, and Survivors, above.

Self-employed person: See source of funds under Old Age, Disability, and Survivors, above.

Employer: See source of funds under Old Age, Disability, and Survivors, above.

Government: None.

Qualifying Conditions

Cash sickness benefits: Must have 40 weeks of paid contributions with 26 weeks paid or credited contributions in the year immediately before the onset of incapacity, or in the last contribution year, or 13 weeks paid or credited contributions in the 26 weeks immediately before the onset of incapacity.

Cash maternity benefits: Must have 50 weeks of contributions since entry into the system with 26 weeks of paid or credited contributions in the last contribution year, or 26 weeks of contributions in the 40 weeks before benefit is due.

Maternity grant: Must have at least 50 paid contributions.

Funeral benefit: Payable for the death of an insured person or the spouse of an insured person. The insured must have at least 50 paid contributions.

Sickness and Maternity Benefits

Sickness benefit: The benefit is equal to 60% of average weekly insurable earnings and is payable after a 3-day waiting period for up to 26 weeks (may be extended to 40 weeks in certain circumstances).

The minimum benefit is B$53.07 a week.

Sickness allowance (means-tested): B$46.15 a week is payable for an insured person who does not meet the qualifying conditions for sickness benefit.

Maternity benefit: The benefit is equal to 60% of average weekly insurable earnings. The benefit is payable for 13 weeks (may be extended to 15 weeks) beginning not earlier than 6 weeks before the expected date of childbirth.

The minimum benefit is B$43.85 a week.

Maternity grant: A lump sum of B$400 for each live birth.

Funeral benefit: A lump sum of B$1,500.

Workers' Medical Benefits

No statutory benefits are provided.

Public and private medical care is available at public hospitals and clinics. Government subsidizes the cost for public patients, children, the elderly, and indigent persons.

Dependents' Medical Benefits

No statutory benefits are provided.

Public and private medical care is available at public hospitals and clinics. Government subsidizes the cost for public patients, children, the elderly, and indigent persons.

Administrative Organization

Prime Minister's Office provides general supervision.

National Insurance Board (http://www.nib-bahamas.com) administers the program.

Work Injury

Regulatory Framework

First law: 1943 (workmen's compensation).

Current law: 1972 (national insurance).

Type of program: Social insurance system.

Coverage

Employed persons and certain categories of the self-employed.

Exclusions: Family labor and certain categories of the self-employed.

Source of Funds

Insured person: None.

Self-employed person: Certain categories of the self-employed contribute 2% of the total 8.8% contribution made under Old Age, Disability, and Survivors, above.

Employer: Total cost for employees. (See source of funds under Old Age, Disability, and Survivors, above.)

Government: None.

Qualifying Conditions

Work injury benefits: There is no minimum qualifying period.

Temporary Disability Benefits

Temporary disability pension: The benefit is equal to 66.6% of average weekly covered earnings and is payable after a 3-day waiting period, for up to a maximum of 40 weeks.

The minimum benefit is B$53.07 a week.

Permanent Disability Benefits

Permanent disability pension: The pension is equal to 66.6% of average weekly covered earnings, if the assessed degree of permanent disability is 100%.

The minimum benefit is B$53.07 a week for total disability.

Partial disability: The pension is proportionately reduced for an assessed degree of disability of 25% or more.

The minimum benefit for a partial disability is B$36.92 a week.

Lump-sum grant: A lump sum of between B$100 and B$2,400 is also payable, depending on the assessed degree of disability.

Workers' Medical Benefits

Benefits include hospitalization, general and specialist care, medicines, and transportation.

Survivor Benefits

Survivor pension: The pension is equal to 50% of the insured's temporary disability pension.

Orphan's pension: Each dependent child younger than age 16 (age 21 if a full-time student) receives 10% of the insured's temporary disability pension, up to a family maximum of 100%.

Industrial death benefit: A lump sum equal to the monthly value of the survivor pension or orphan's pension.

Industrial funeral benefit: A lump sum of B$1,500.

Administrative Organization

Ministry of Housing and National Insurance provides general supervision.

National Insurance Board (http://www.nib-bahamas.com) administers the program.

Barbados

Exchange rate: US$1.00 equals
2.02 Barbadian dollars (B$).

Old Age, Disability, and Survivors

Regulatory Framework

First law: 1937 (social assistance).

Current law: 1966 (social insurance), with 2002 amendment.

Type of program: Social insurance and social assistance system.

Coverage

Social insurance: All employed persons, public-sector employees, and the self-employed aged 16 to 64.

Exclusions: Unpaid family labor.

Social assistance: Residents aged 65 or older; aged 18 or older and incapable of work because of defective eyesight or serious hearing and speech problems.

Source of Funds

Social insurance

Insured person: 7.43% to 8.25% of earnings.

The minimum earnings for contribution purposes are B$21 a week for employees paid weekly or B$91 a month for employees paid monthly.

The maximum earnings for contribution and benefit purposes are B$736 a week for employees paid weekly or B$3,190 a month for employees paid monthly.

The insured's contributions also finance sickness and maternity benefits and work injury benefits.

Self-employed person: 14.5% of quarterly earnings.

The minimum annual earnings for contribution purposes are B$1,092.

The self-employed person's contributions also finance sickness and maternity benefits and work injury benefits.

Employer: 7.43% to 9% of payroll.

The minimum earnings for contribution purposes are B$21 a week for employees paid weekly or B$91 a month for employees paid monthly.

The maximum earnings for contribution and benefit purposes are B$736 a week for employees paid weekly or B$3,190 a month for employees paid monthly.

The employer's contributions also finance sickness and maternity benefits and work injury benefits.

Government: None; contributes as an employer.

Social assistance

Insured person: None.

Self-employed person: None.

Employer: None.

Government: Total cost.

Qualifying Conditions

Social insurance

Old-age pension: Age 65.5 with 500 weeks of contributions, including at least 150 weeks of paid contributions.

Early pension: Age 62 and no longer employed or self-employed.

Deferred pension: The pension may be deferred until age 70.

Old-age grant: Age 65.5 with at least 50 but not more than 499 contributions.

Old-age benefits are payable abroad.

Disability pension: Younger than age 65, with at least 150 weeks of contributions, and incapable of any work. The degree of incapacity for work is assessed periodically by a National Insurance Office doctor.

Disability grant: Younger than age 65, with at least 50 but not more than 149 contributions, and incapable of any work. The degree of incapacity for work is assessed periodically by a National Insurance Office doctor.

Disability benefits are not payable abroad.

Survivor pension: The deceased had at least 150 weeks of paid contributions.

Eligible survivors are a widow(er) and children.

Funeral grant: The deceased had at least 50 weeks of paid contributions.

Survivor benefits are payable abroad.

Social assistance

Noncontributory old-age pension: Age 65, satisfies the residency conditions, and does not meet the qualifying conditions for a social insurance pension.

Noncontributory disability pension (income-tested): Aged 18 or older, satisfies the residency conditions, is assessed as incapable of work as the result of being certified as blind or having severe hearing and speech problems, and earns less than B$36 a week.

Old-Age Benefits

Social insurance

Old-age pension: The pension is equal to 40% of average insurable earnings, plus 1% of earnings for each 50-week period of contributions exceeding 500 weeks.

Average earnings are based on earnings in the best 5 years in the last 15 years; if the number of years worked is less than 5 years, the average is based on total earnings.

The maximum earnings for benefit calculation purposes are B$736 a week for employees paid weekly or B$3,190 a month for employees paid monthly.

The minimum weekly pension is B$110.

The maximum pension is equal to 60% of average insurable earnings.

Benefit adjustment: Benefits are adjusted annually according to changes in the cost of living.

Old-age grant: A lump sum equal to 6 weeks' earnings for each 50-week period of contributions.

Social assistance

Noncontributory old-age pension: The minimum weekly pension is B$90.

Benefit adjustment: Benefits are adjusted annually according to changes in the cost of living.

Permanent Disability Benefits

Social insurance

Disability pension: The pension is equal to 40% of average annual insurable earnings, plus 1% of earnings for each 50-week period of contributions exceeding 500 weeks.

Average earnings are based on earnings in the best 5 years in the last 15 years; if the number of years worked is less than 5 years, the average is based on total earnings.

The maximum earnings for benefit calculation purposes are B$736 a week for employees paid weekly or B$3,190 a month for employees paid monthly.

The minimum weekly pension is B$110.

Benefit adjustment: Benefits are adjusted annually according to changes in the cost of living.

Disability grant: A lump sum equal to 6 weeks' average insurable earnings for each 50-week period of paid or credited contributions.

Social assistance

Noncontributory disability pension (income-tested): The minimum weekly pension is B$90.

Benefit adjustment: Benefits are adjusted annually according to changes in the cost of living.

Survivor Benefits

Survivor pension: The pension is equal to 50% of the pension paid or payable to the deceased if the widow(er) is aged 50 or older and was married to the deceased for at least 3 years. A limited pension is paid for 12 months to a widow(er) younger than age 50. The pension is paid to a disabled widow(er) younger than age 50 for the duration of the disability.

Orphan's pension: Each child younger than age 16 (age 21 if student, no limit if disabled before age 16) receives 16.6% of the deceased's pension; 33.3% if a full orphan or disabled.

Funeral grant: B$1,400 is payable to the person who pays for the funeral of the insured or of the insured's spouse.

Benefit adjustment: Benefits are adjusted annually according to changes in the cost of living.

Administrative Organization

Ministry of Labor is responsible for policy.

Directed by a tripartite board, the National Insurance Office (http://www.nis.gov.bb) administers the program.

Sickness and Maternity

Regulatory Framework

First and current law: 1966 (social insurance).

Type of program: Social insurance system. Cash benefits only.

Coverage

All employed persons, public-sector employees, and the self-employed aged 16 to 64.

Exclusions: Unpaid family labor. Permanent government employees are not covered for cash sickness benefits.

Source of Funds

Insured person: See source of funds under Old Age, Disability, and Survivors, above.

Self-employed person: See source of funds under Old Age, Disability, and Survivors, above.

Employer: See source of funds under Old Age, Disability, and Survivors, above.

Government: See source of funds under Old Age, Disability, and Survivors, above.

Qualifying Conditions

Cash sickness benefits: Must have 13 weeks of insurance coverage, including 7 weeks of paid contributions in the last quarter but one before the quarter in which the onset of incapacity began, and be employed immediately before the onset of incapacity; at least 39 paid or credited contributions in the four consecutive quarters ending with the last quarter but one before the quarter of the onset of incapacity.

Cash maternity benefits: Employed women must have 26 weeks of insurance coverage, including 16 weeks of paid contributions in the two consecutive quarters ending with the last quarter but one before the quarter in which the benefit is paid.

Self-employed women must have at least 39 weeks of contributions in the four consecutive quarters ending with the last quarter but one before the quarter in which the benefit is paid; 16 weeks of paid contributions in the two consecutive quarters ending with the last quarter but one before the quarter in which the benefit is paid.

Maternity grant: Payable for a woman who is not insured or who fails to meet the coverage requirements for cash maternity benefits but whose spouse does meet the requirements.

Funeral grant: Payable for the death of an insured person who was receiving, or was entitled to receive, sickness benefits or maternity benefits.

Sickness and Maternity Benefits

Sickness benefit: The benefit is equal to 66.6% of average insurable weekly earnings and is payable after a 3-day waiting period for up to 26 weeks; may be extended to 52 weeks if the insured has paid 150 weeks of contributions, including 75 contributions paid or credited in the 3 years before the year of onset. The waiting period is waived if the illness lasts 21 or more days.

Maternity benefit: The benefit is equal to 100% of average insurable weekly earnings and is payable for up to 6 weeks before and 6 weeks after the expected date of childbirth.

Funeral grant: B$1,400 is payable to the person who pays for the cost of the funeral.

Maternity grant: A lump sum of B$800.

Workers' Medical Benefits

Medical benefits: No statutory benefits are provided.

Free medical care is available in public hospitals and health centers.

Dependents' Medical Benefits

Medical benefits for dependents: No statutory benefits are provided.

Free medical care is available in public hospitals and health centers.

Administrative Organization

Ministry of Labor is responsible for policy.

Directed by a tripartite board, the National Insurance Office (http://www.nis.gov.bb) administers the program.

Work Injury

Regulatory Framework

First law: 1916 (workmen's compensation).

Current law: 1966 (social insurance).

Type of program: Social insurance system.

Coverage

All employed persons, public-sector employees, and some categories of fishermen aged 16 to 64.

Exclusions: Self-employed persons and unpaid family labor.

Source of Funds

Insured person: See source of funds under Old Age, Disability, and Survivors, above.

Self-employed person: Not applicable.

Employer: See source of funds under Old Age, Disability, and Survivors, above.

Government: None; contributes as an employer.

Qualifying Conditions

Work injury benefits: There is no minimum qualifying period.

Temporary Disability Benefits

The benefit is equal to 90% of average insurable earnings and is payable after a 3-day waiting period for up to 52 weeks. The waiting period is waived if the disability lasts for 21 or more days.

Permanent Disability Benefits

Permanent disability pension: For a total disability, the pension is equal to 90% of the insured's average earnings.

The degree of disability is assessed by the insured's doctor and may be reviewed by National Insurance Office doctors.

Constant-attendance supplement: Equal to 50% of the pension.

Partial disability: A percentage of the full pension is paid according to the assessed degree of disability.

A lump sum is paid if the assessed degree of disability is less than 30%.

Workers' Medical Benefits

Benefits include reimbursement of expenses for medical, surgical, dental, and hospital treatment; nursing care; medicines; appliances; and transportation.

Survivor Benefits

Survivor pension: 50% of the deceased's temporary disability benefit is payable to a dependent spouse.

The pension ceases on remarriage or cohabitation.

Remarriage settlement: A lump sum equal to a year's pension is paid.

Orphan's pension: Each child younger than age 16 receives 16.6% of the deceased's temporary disability benefit; 33.3% if a full orphan or disabled. There is no age limit for a disabled orphan.

The maximum survivor pension is 100% of the deceased's temporary disability benefit.

Funeral grant: B$1,400 is payable to the person who pays for the insured's funeral.

Administrative Organization

Ministry of Labor is responsible for policy.

Directed by a tripartite board, the National Insurance Office (http://www.nis.gov.bb) administers the program.

Unemployment

Regulatory Framework

First and current law: 1981 (social insurance).

Type of program: Social insurance system.

Coverage

Employees aged 16 to 64.

Exclusions: Self-employed persons, family labor, and permanent government employees.

Source of Funds

Insured person: 0.75% of earnings.

The minimum earnings for contribution purposes are B$21 a week for employees paid weekly or B$91 a month for employees paid monthly.

The maximum earnings for contribution and benefit purposes are B$736 a week for employees paid weekly or B$3,190 a month for employees paid monthly.

Self-employed person: Not applicable.

Employer: 0.75% of payroll.

The minimum earnings for contribution purposes are B$21 a week for employees paid weekly or B$91 a month for employees paid monthly.

The maximum earnings for contribution and benefit purposes are B$736 a week for employees paid weekly or B$3,190 a month for employees paid monthly.

Government: None; contributes as an employer.

Qualifying Conditions

Unemployment benefit: Must be younger than age 65 with 52 weeks of insurance coverage; at least 20 weeks of paid or credited contributions in the three consecutive quarters ending with the last quarter but one before the onset of unemployment; at least 7 weeks of paid or credited contributions in the last quarter but one before the onset of unemployment.

Unemployment Benefits

The benefit is equal to 60% of the insured's average insurable weekly earnings. The benefit is payable after a 3-day waiting period for up to 26 weeks in any 52-week period. The waiting period is waived if the insured is unemployed for 21 or more days.

Administrative Organization

Ministry of Labor is responsible for policy.

Directed by a tripartite board, the National Insurance Office (http://www.nis.gov.bb) administers the program.

Belize

Exchange rate: US$1.00 equals
2.20 Belize dollars (B$).

Old Age, Disability, and Survivors

Regulatory Framework

First and current law: 1979 (social security), with amendments.

Type of program: Social insurance and social assistance system.

Coverage

Social insurance: Employed persons aged 14 to 64, including public servants and self-employed persons. (Persons aged 60 or older who have previously received an old-age benefit and who return to work are covered for work injury benefits only.)

Exclusions: Casual labor, persons employed for less than 8 hours a week, and military personnel.

Voluntary coverage for old-age and survivor benefits for workers younger than age 65 who become self-employed and who have paid at least 150 contributions as an employee.

Social assistance: Women aged 65 or older who are citizens or permanent residents of Belize.

Source of Funds

Social insurance

Insured person: Weekly contributions vary according to eight wage classes:

- B$0.83 if weekly earnings are under B$70;
- B$1.35 if B$70 to B$109.99;
- B$1.95 if B$110 to B$139.99;
- B$3.15 if B$140 to B$179.99;
- B$4.75 if B$180 to B$219.99;
- B$6.35 if B$220 to B$259.99;
- B$7.95 if B$260 to B$299.99; and
- B$9.55 if B$300 or over.

The insured's contributions also finance sickness and maternity benefits and work injury benefits.

Self-employed person: 7% of weekly income between B$55 and B$320.

The self-employed person's contributions also finance sickness and maternity benefits and work injury benefits.

Employer: Weekly contributions vary according to eight wage classes:

- B$3.57 if weekly earnings are under B$70;
- B$5.85 if B$70 to B$109.99;
- B$8.45 if B$110 to B$139.99;
- B$9.65 if B$140 to B$179.99;
- B$11.25 if B$180 to B$219.99;
- B$12.85 if B$220 to B$259.99;
- B$14.45 if B$260 to B$299.99; and
- B$16.05 if B$300 or over.

The employer's contributions also finance sickness and maternity benefits and work injury benefits; work injury benefits only for employees between ages 60 and 64 who have previously received an old-age benefit and for all employees aged 65 or older.

Government: Covers any deficit; contributes as an employer.

Social assistance

Insured person: None.

Self-employed person: None.

Employer: None.

Government: Total cost of the noncontributory old-age pension.

Qualifying Conditions

Old-age pension: Age 65 with 500 weeks of paid or credited contributions including 150 paid contributions. Retirement from employment is not necessary if aged 65 or older.

Early pension: From age 60 and retired from insured employment, with a total of at least 500 weeks of paid or credited contributions including 150 paid contributions.

Retirement grant: Paid at age 60 to an insured person who has at least 26 weeks of paid contributions but does not meet the qualifying conditions for an old-age pension.

Noncontributory old-age pension: Women aged 65 or older who have inadequate or no income.

Disability pension: Younger than age 60 and incapable of work with at least 150 weeks of paid contributions since 1981, with at least 110 paid contributions in the 5 consecutive contribution years before the year of the onset of disability, and 5 paid or credited contributions in the 13 weeks immediately before the week in which the incapacity leading to the onset of disability began.

The degree of disability is assessed by the medical board.

Disability grant: Paid to an insured person younger than age 60 who has at least 26 weeks of paid contributions but does not meet the qualifying conditions for a disability pension.

The degree of disability is assessed by the medical board.

Survivor pension: The deceased was eligible to receive or was receiving an old-age or disability pension at the time of death.

Eligible survivors are a widow who is pregnant or caring for the deceased's children or is aged 50 or older (or disabled) and was married to the insured for at least 3 years; a widower who was dependent on the deceased for at least 3 years; each child younger than age 16 (age 21 if a full-time student); and, in the absence of other survivors, parents aged 55 or older.

Survivor grant: The deceased was not eligible to receive an old-age or disability pension but had at least 26 paid contributions.

Eligible survivors are a widow who is pregnant or caring for the deceased's children or is aged 50 or older (or disabled) and was married to the insured for at least 3 years; a widower who was dependent on the deceased for at least 3 years; each child younger than age 16 (age 21 if a full-time student); and, in the absence of other survivors, parents aged 55 or older.

Funeral grant: The deceased insured had 50 weeks of paid contributions; 150 weeks of paid contributions for the funeral of a spouse or dependent child younger than age 16 (age 21 if a full-time student).

Old-Age Benefits

Old-age pension: The pension is equal to 30% of the insured's average weekly insurable earnings, plus 2% of earnings for each 50-week period of contributions beyond 500 weeks up to 750 weeks, plus 1% of earnings for every 50-week period of contributions over 750 weeks.

Average weekly insurable earnings are based on the best 3 years of earnings.

Early pension: Calculated in the same way as the old-age pension. The pension is suspended if the insured returns to work before age 65.

The minimum weekly pension is B$47. The pension is paid monthly.

The maximum pension is equal to 60% of average weekly insurable earnings, up to a weekly maximum of B$192.

Retirement grant: The grant is equal to six times the sum of average weekly insurable earnings in the best 3 years of earnings, divided by 150, and multiplied by the number of 50-week contribution periods; or twice the sum of weekly insurable earnings, divided by the number of contributions, and multiplied by the number of 50-week contribution periods. The higher amount is paid.

The minimum grant is B$800.

Noncontributory old-age pension: B$75 a month.

Permanent Disability Benefits

Disability pension: With at least 500 weeks of contributions, the pension is equal to 30% of the insured's average weekly insurable earnings. With less than 500 weeks of contributions, the pension is equal to 25% of average weekly insurable earnings.

Average weekly insurable earnings are based on the best 3 years of earnings.

The minimum weekly pension is B$47. The pension is paid monthly.

The maximum pension is equal to 60% of average weekly insurable earnings.

Disability grant: The grant is equal to six times the sum of average weekly insurable earnings in the best 3 years of earnings, divided by 150, and multiplied by the number of 50-week contribution periods; or twice the sum of weekly insurable earnings, divided by the number of contributions, and multiplied by the number of 50-week contribution periods. The higher amount is paid.

The minimum grant is B$800.

Survivor Benefits

Survivor pension: 66.6% of the old-age or disability pension paid or payable to the deceased is payable to an eligible widow(er).

Orphan's pension: 25% of the old-age or disability pension paid or payable to the deceased is payable to each child younger than age 16 (age 21 if a full-time student); 40% if disabled.

Dependent parent's pension (in the absence of other eligible survivors): 40% of the old-age or disability pension paid or payable to the deceased is payable to a parent aged 55 or older.

The minimum weekly survivor pension is B$47 and is split among eligible survivors. Survivor pensions are paid monthly.

The total maximum survivor pension is 100% of the pension paid or payable to the deceased. If the maximum pension exceeds the limit, each pension is reduced accordingly.

Survivor grant: The grant is equal to six times the sum of average weekly insurable earnings in the best 3 years of earnings, divided by 150, and multiplied by the number of 50-week contribution periods; or twice the sum of weekly insurable earnings, divided by the number of contributions, and multiplied by the number of 50-week contribution periods. The higher amount is paid.

The minimum grant is B$800.

Funeral grant: B$1,500 is payable for the insured's death; B$1,000 to the insured on the death of a spouse; and B$500 to the insured on the death of a dependent child.

Administrative Organization

Ministry of Finance, National Development, and the Public Service provides general supervision.

Social Security Board (http://www.socialsecurity.org.bz) administers the program.

Sickness and Maternity

Regulatory Framework

First and current law: 1979 (social security), with amendments.

Type of program: Social insurance system. Cash benefits only.

Coverage

Employed persons aged 14 to 64, including public servants and self-employed persons.

Exclusions: Casual labor, persons employed for less than 8 hours a week, and military personnel.

Source of Funds

Insured person: See source of funds under Old Age, Disability, and Survivors, above.

Self-employed person: See source of funds under Old Age, Disability, and Survivors, above.

Employer: See source of funds under Old Age, Disability, and Survivors, above.

Government: Covers any deficit; contributes as an employer.

Qualifying Conditions

Cash sickness benefits: Currently employed with 50 weeks of contributions, including 5 of the 13 weeks before the onset of incapacity.

Cash maternity benefits: Must have 50 weeks of contributions, including 25 weeks of the 39 weeks ending 6 weeks before the expected date of childbirth or the day on which the benefit was claimed.

Maternity grant: Must have 50 weeks of contributions, including 25 weeks of the 50 weeks before the expected date of childbirth. The grant is payable to an insured woman or to an insured man whose wife or common-law spouse has given birth and is not entitled to the benefit.

Sickness and Maternity Benefits

Sickness benefit: The weekly benefit is equal to 80% of average weekly insurable earnings and is payable for up to a maximum of 26 weeks; thereafter, the benefit may be payable for a further 13 weeks at 60% of average weekly insurable earnings. After 39 weeks, a disability pension may be payable.

Maternity benefit: The benefit is equal to 80% of average weekly insurable earnings and is payable for up to 14 weeks, beginning 7 weeks before the expected date of childbirth or the day on which the benefit was claimed. The benefit is paid every 2 weeks.

Maternity grant: B$300 is paid for each child.

Workers' Medical Benefits

No statutory benefits are provided.

Dependents' Medical Benefits

No statutory benefits are provided.

Administrative Organization

Ministry of Finance, National Development, and the Public Service provides general supervision.

Social Security Board (http://www.socialsecurity.org.bz) administers the program.

Work Injury

Regulatory Framework

First and current law: 1979 (social security), with amendments.

Type of program: Social insurance system.

Coverage

Employed persons aged 14 to 64, including public servants, self-employed persons, and persons aged 60 or older who have previously received an old-age benefit and who return to work.

Exclusions: Casual labor, persons employed for less than 8 hours a week, and military personnel.

Source of Funds

Insured person: See source of funds under Old Age, Disability, and Survivors, above.

Self-employed person: See source of funds under Old Age, Disability, and Survivors, above.

Employer: See source of funds under Old Age, Disability, and Survivors, above.

Government: Covers any deficit; contributes as an employer.

Qualifying Conditions

Work injury benefits: There is no minimum qualifying period and no contribution requirement.

Temporary Disability Benefits

The weekly benefit is equal to 80% of average weekly insurable earnings in the 4 weeks before the onset of disability and is payable from the first day of incapacity for up to 182 days; thereafter, the benefit may be extended and paid at 60% of average weekly insurable earnings.

Permanent Disability Benefits

Permanent disability pension: The pension is equal to 60% of average weekly insurable earnings in the 4 weeks before the onset of the disability times the assessed degree of disability.

The minimum weekly pension is B$47. The pension is paid monthly.

Constant-attendance allowance: Equal to 25% of the disability pension, if the disability is assessed at 100%.

The degree of disability is assessed and reviewed periodically by the medical board.

Disablement grant: If the assessed degree of disability is less than 25%, a lump sum is paid. The grant is equal to average insurable earnings in the 4 weeks before the onset of disability times the assessed degree of disability times 260.

The degree of disability is assessed by the medical board.

Workers' Medical Benefits

Benefits include full medical care, including treatment abroad if deemed necessary.

Survivor Benefits

Survivor pension: A widow(er) receives 66.6% of the permanent disability pension paid or payable to the deceased.

Eligible widows are a dependent widow who is pregnant or caring for the deceased's children or is aged 50 or older and was married to the deceased for at least 3 years. A limited pension may be paid to a widow for 52 weeks if the qualifying conditions are not met. A pension is also payable to a disabled widower who was fully dependent on the deceased for at least 3 years.

The widow(er) pension ceases on remarriage.

Orphan's pension: 25% of the permanent disability pension paid or payable to the deceased is paid to each child up to age 16 (age 21 if a full-time student); 40% if disabled.

Dependent parent's pension (in the absence of other eligible survivors): 40% of the pension paid or payable to the deceased is payable to parents aged 55 or older.

The minimum weekly pension is B$47 and is split among the eligible survivors. Survivor pensions are paid monthly.

The total maximum pension for all survivors is 60% of the deceased's average insurable earnings in the 4 weeks before the employment injury resulting in the insured's death. If the maximum pension exceeds the limit, each pension is reduced accordingly.

Funeral grant: B$1,500 is payable for the death of the insured.

Administrative Organization

Ministry of Finance, National Development, and the Public Service provides general supervision.

Social Security Board (http://www.socialsecurity.org.bz) administers the program.

Bermuda

Exchange rate: US$1.00 equals
1 Bermuda dollar (B$).

Old Age, Disability, and Survivors

Regulatory Framework

First law: 1967 (old-age and survivors).

Current laws: 1970 (old-age and survivors), with amendments; 1980 (disability); and 1998 (occupational pensions), implemented in 2000, with amendment.

Type of program: Social insurance, mandatory occupational pension, and social assistance system.

Coverage

Social insurance

Employed and self-employed persons older than age 16, except full-time students who work weekends or during school vacations.

Voluntary insurance for persons who were previously covered.

Exclusions: Those who are not ordinarily resident, unless gainfully employed for more than 26 consecutive weeks.

Mandatory occupational pension

Employees aged 23 or older who are Bermudian or the spouse of a Bermudian and who have worked 720 hours or more for their current employer in any calendar year; self-employed persons aged 23 or older who are Bermudian or the spouse of a Bermudian and who have annual earnings greater than B$2,000.

Social assistance

Bermudian residents.

Source of Funds

Social insurance

Insured person: B$24.19 a week; if older than age 65, none.

Self-employed person: B$48.38 a week; if older than age 65, B$24.19 a week.

Employer: B$24.19 a week for employees of any age.

Government: None; contributes as an employer.

Mandatory occupational pension

Insured person: 5% of earnings.

The maximum annual earnings for contribution purposes are B$200,000.

Self-employed person: 10% of declared earnings.

The maximum mandatory contribution on declared earnings is B$5,000 a year. Additional voluntary contributions are possible.

Employer: 5% of earnings.

The maximum annual earnings for contribution purposes are B$200,000.

Government: None.

Social assistance

Insured person: None.

Self-employed person: None.

Employer: None.

Government: Total cost.

Qualifying Conditions

Social insurance

Old-age pension: Age 65 with 484 weeks of contributions, including 50 weeks of contributions for each year of insurance. Retirement is not necessary.

Partial pension: A reduced pension is paid with between 25 and 49 weeks of contributions for each year of insurance.

The old-age pension is payable abroad.

Old-age settlement: The insured does not meet the qualifying conditions for a pension.

Disability pension: Aged 18 to 64, employed immediately before the onset of disability, and unable to work during a full year. The insured must have 150 weeks of contributions with 50 weeks of contributions for each year of insurance.

Partial pension: A reduced pension is paid with between 25 and 49 weeks of contributions for each year of insurance.

The disability pension is payable abroad.

Survivor pension: The deceased was a pensioner or met the qualifying conditions for a pension. The spouse was married to the deceased for at least 3 years. A widow is credited for contribution purposes for every week she receives a survivor pension and may substitute a year of her husband's contribution record for her own.

Partial pension: A reduced pension is paid with between 25 and 49 weeks of contributions for each year of insurance.

Eligible survivors are the widow(er) and orphans.

The survivor pension is payable abroad.

Survivor settlement: The deceased did not meet the qualifying conditions for a pension.

Eligible survivors are the widow(er) and orphans.

Mandatory occupational pension

Old-age pension: The normal retirement age is 65.

Disability pension: Assessed as incapable of work as the result of a physical or mental condition.

Survivor pension: On the insured's death, the pension is paid to a beneficiary named by the deceased.

Social assistance

Noncontributory old-age pension: Age 65 and Bermudian with at least 10 years of continuous residency in the 20 years immediately before the application and does not meet the qualifying conditions for the old-age pension.

Noncontributory disability pension: Aged 18 to 64 with 10 years of residency immediately before the application and permanently incapable of employment.

Appointed medical doctors assess the degree of disability.

Noncontributory survivor pension: No benefits are provided.

Old-Age Benefits

Social insurance

Old-age pension: B$177.10 a week (B$767.43 a month), plus B$1.04 for every 26-week period of contributions over 484 weeks.

Partial pension: The minimum monthly partial pension is B$419.80 if the yearly average number of weeks of contributions is between 25 and 29; B$522.70 with 30 to 34 weeks; B$631.91 with 35 to 39 weeks, B$747.44 with 40 to 44 weeks; or B$869.28 with 45 to 49 weeks.

Old-age settlement: The total employer and employee contributions are refunded as a lump sum.

Mandatory occupational pension

Old-age pension: Pension calculations are based on average earnings or the amount of the insured's accumulated capital.

Social assistance

Noncontributory old-age pension: B$352.21 a month.

If annual income is less than B$4,000, the minimum monthly pension is B$362.44.

Permanent Disability Benefits

Social insurance

Disability pension: B$511.55 a month.

Partial pension: If the number of average annual weeks of contributions is at least 25 but less than 50, the pension is reduced in proportion to the number of average annual weeks of contributions.

Mandatory occupational pension

Disability pension: The value of the benefit depends on the specific rules that apply to the occupational scheme.

Social assistance

Noncontributory disability pension: B$352.21 a month.

Survivor Benefits

Social insurance

Survivor pension: B$767.43 a month.

Partial pension: B$383.72 a month if the deceased's yearly average number of weeks of contributions was between 25 and 29; B$460.46 for 30 to 34 weeks; B$537.20 for 35 to 39 weeks; B$613.94 for 40 to 44 weeks; or B$690.96 for 45 to 49 weeks.

The survivor pension is payable for 26 weeks or until dependent children reach age 16; for life if the surviving spouse is older than age 50 or disabled.

The survivor pension ceases if the spouse remarries or cohabits.

Orphan's pension: B$76.57 a month until old enough to leave school.

Survivor settlement: The total employer and employee contributions are refunded as a lump sum.

Mandatory occupational pension

Survivor pension: Benefits are based on the value of the deceased's contributions, accumulated capital, or accrued benefits. The benefit is paid as a lump sum.

The pension does not cease on remarriage.

A lump sum is also paid to the survivor if the deceased had less than 2 years of membership in an occupational scheme at the time of death.

Social assistance

Noncontributory survivor pension: No benefits are provided.

Administrative Organization

Social insurance and social assistance

Ministry of Finance provides general supervision.

Department of Social Insurance (http://www.socialinsurance.gov.bm) administers the program.

Mandatory occupational pension

Pension Commission supervises and regulates the program.

Sickness and Maternity

Regulatory Framework

First and current law: 1970 (hospital insurance), with amendments.

Type of program: Compulsory insurance with a public or private carrier or an approved employer-operated plan (employed persons). Individual or voluntary insurance (nonemployed persons). Medical benefits only.

Note: Under the 2000 Employment Act, employers are required to provide paid sick leave and paid and unpaid maternity leave.

Coverage

All residents.

Employers are liable for carrying insurance for employees and employees' nonemployed spouses.

Source of Funds

Insured person: B$72.45 a month each for an employee and his or her nonemployed spouse. (Other insured persons contribute B$144.90 a month.)

Self-employed person: B$144.90 a month on an individual or voluntary basis.

Employer: B$72.45 a month each for an employee and his or her nonemployed spouse.

Government: A government grant finances 80% of the cost of medical care for residents aged 65 to 74, 90% for residents aged 75 or older, and 100% for resident children and indigent persons.

Qualifying Conditions

Cash sickness and maternity benefits: No statutory benefits are provided.

Under the 2000 Employment Act, employers are required to provide paid sick leave and paid and unpaid maternity leave.

Medical benefits: There is no minimum qualifying period, except for a 10-month waiting period for maternity care benefits.

Sickness and Maternity Benefits

Sickness benefit: No statutory benefits are provided.

The 2000 Employment Act provides for 8 days of paid sick leave a year to employees who have worked for the same employer for at least a year.

Maternity benefit: No statutory benefits are provided.

The 2000 Employment Act provides for 8 weeks of paid maternity leave and 4 weeks of unpaid maternity leave to employees who have worked for the same employer for at least a year; 8 weeks unpaid maternity leave for employees with less than a year.

Workers' Medical Benefits

The Hospital Insurance Commission, a private insurance company, or an employer plan reimburses the hospital for services provided. Benefits include inpatient and outpatient services, including room and board; nursing, laboratory, ambulance, and resident doctor services; drugs; appliances; surgery; maternity care; and physical therapy.

There is no limit to duration.

Dependents' Medical Benefits

The Hospital Insurance Commission, a private insurance company, or an employer plan reimburses the hospital for services provided. Benefits include inpatient and outpatient services, including room and board; nursing, laboratory, ambulance, and resident doctor services; drugs; appliances; surgery; maternity care; and physical therapy.

There is no limit to duration.

Administrative Organization

Ministry of Finance, through the Department of Social Insurance (http://www.socialinsurance.gov.bm), provides general supervision.

Hospital Insurance Commission administers the program.

Work Injury

Regulatory Framework

First and current law: 1965 (workmen's compensation).

Type of program: Employer-liability system. (The government may require employers to carry insurance.)

Coverage

Employed persons and apprentices aged 16 or older.

Exclusions: Casual labor, part-time workers, temporary employees, students, and voluntary workers.

Source of Funds

Insured person: None.

Self-employed person: Not applicable.

Employer: Total cost, met through the direct provision of benefits or the purchase of insurance premiums.

Government: None.

Qualifying Conditions

Work injury benefits: There is no minimum qualifying period, but the work injury must last more than 3 days.

Temporary Disability Benefits

The benefit is equal to 50% of lost earnings (up to a maximum of B$170 a week) or a lump sum. The total benefit paid must not exceed the permanent disability benefit for which the insured would be eligible.

Permanent Disability Benefits

If totally disabled, the total benefit is equal to 4 years' earnings.

The minimum benefit is B$5,000.

The maximum benefit is B$53,000.

Constant-attendance supplement: Equal to 25% of the permanent disability benefit.

Partial disability: A percentage of the full disability benefit according to the loss of earning capacity.

Appointed medical doctors assess the degree of disability.

Workers' Medical Benefits

Benefits include the cost of necessary medical care, including hospitalization (up to a maximum based on the prevailing public ward charge for 56 days); emergency outpatient treatment; surgery, according to a fee schedule; medical expenses, including the cost of nursing, ambulances, and medicines, up to B$1,000; the cost of prostheses up to B$2,000; and the cost of transportation up to B$250.

Survivor Benefits

Survivor benefit: A lump sum equal to 3 years' earnings or B$42,000 (whichever is less), minus any permanent disability benefit payments.

Eligible survivors are dependents who were totally dependent on the deceased's earnings.

Partial survivor grant: A grant is paid to those who were partially dependent on the deceased's earnings.

Funeral grant and medical expenses: Up to B$2,000 is provided if there are no dependents.

Administrative Organization

Ministry of Labor, Home Affairs, and Public Safety provides general supervision.

Supreme Court administers lump sums.

Courts supervise the agreement between an employer and the insured on the amounts payable.

Bolivia

Exchange rate: US$1.00 equals
8.07 bolivianos (Bs).

Old Age, Disability, and Survivors

Regulatory Framework

First laws: 1949 (social insurance); and 1956 (social security), implemented in 1959.

Current laws: 1996 (mandatory individual account), implemented in 1997; and 2002 (Bonosol pension), implemented in 2003.

Type of program: Mandatory individual account, private insurance, and universal pension (Bonosol) system.

Note: In 1997, all active members of the social insurance system transferred to a system of mandatory individual accounts. Until September 2005, only active members who were already eligible for a social insurance pension in 1997 were able to retire under the old system.

Coverage

Mandatory individual account: Salaried workers, including armed forces personnel, and apprentices.

Voluntary coverage for the self-employed.

Universal pension (Bonosol): All resident citizens who were born before January 1, 1974.

Source of Funds

Mandatory individual account

Insured person: 10% of gross earnings for old-age benefits, plus a fixed 1.71% of gross earnings for disability and survivor insurance and a fixed 0.5% of gross earnings for administrative fees.

The minimum earnings for contribution purposes are equal to the legal monthly minimum wage.

The maximum earnings for contribution purposes are equal to 60 times the legal monthly minimum wage.

The legal monthly minimum wage is Bs440. (The legal monthly minimum wage is adjusted for changes in the cost of living, depending on the financial resources of the state budget. The last adjustment was made in May 2003.)

Self-employed person: A voluntary contribution of 10% of declared gross earnings, plus a fixed 1.71% of declared gross earnings for disability and survivor insurance and a fixed 0.5% of declared gross earnings for administrative fees.

The minimum declared earnings for contribution purposes are equal to the legal monthly minimum wage (Bs440 a month).

The maximum declared earnings for contribution purposes are equal to 60 times the legal monthly minimum wage.

Employer: None.

Government: Finances pensions payable under the previous social insurance system and the funeral grant; contributes as an employer.

Universal pension (Bonosol)

Insured person: None.

Self-employed person: None.

Employer: None.

Government: Financed from the privatization of state-owned enterprises.

Qualifying Conditions

Old-age pension: Age 65; any age if the accumulated capital in the individual account, plus accrued interest, is sufficient to finance a monthly pension equal to 70% of the insured's average covered earnings in the last 5 years.

The sole qualifying condition for armed forces personnel is 35 years of continuous service.

The old-age pension is payable abroad temporarily in specific cases.

Universal pension (Bonosol): Resident citizens aged 65 or older who were born before January 1, 1974.

The universal pension is payable abroad temporarily in specific cases.

Disability pension: The insured must be younger than age 65 with an assessed degree of disability of at least 60%.

Must have made 60 months of contributions to the old or new scheme or have made contributions during half the period between the date of the first contribution to the new scheme and the onset of disability and must be currently contributing or have ceased contributing no longer than 12 months before the onset of disability. If the disability is due to an illness, the insured must also have 18 months of contributions in the last 36 months before the onset of disability.

The Assessment Body (EEC) assesses the degree of disability through a Medical Assessment Panel consisting of three medical professionals. The insured or his or her dependents are entitled to require the Superintendent of Pensions, Values, and Insurance to review the assessed degree of disability once only.

The disability pension is payable abroad temporarily in specific cases.

Survivor pension: The deceased was a pensioner or had made 60 months of contributions to the old or new scheme or had made contributions during half the period between the date of the first contribution to the new scheme and the date of death or was still contributing or had ceased contributing no longer than 12 months before the date of death. If the death was due to illness, the deceased must also have had 18 months of contributions in the last 36 months before the date of death.

Eligible survivors include the spouse or cohabiting partner and children younger than age 18 (age 25 if a student, no limit if disabled).

In the absence of a spouse or cohabiting partner and eligible children, eligible survivors include the insured's father and mother, the insured's brothers and sisters younger than age 18, or other survivors named by the insured.

The survivor pension is payable abroad temporarily in specific cases.

Funeral grant: Paid for the death of an insured worker or a citizen aged 65 or older who was born before January 1, 1974.

Old-Age Benefits

Old-age pension: The insured's accumulated capital (contributions plus accrued interest) is used to purchase a fixed or variable life annuity, depending on the total amount of the accumulated capital. (The value of accrued rights under the old system is combined with the individual account balance.)

The first monthly amount payable under a variable life annuity must not be less than 70% of the insured's average covered earnings in the last 5 years.

For armed forces personnel, the pension is equal to 100% of the insured's average covered earnings in the last 5 years.

Schedule of payments: Thirteen payments a year.

Benefit adjustment: Pensions are adjusted annually according to the UFV (Unidad de Fomento de Vivienda), calculated by the Central Bank for changes in the cost of living.

Universal pension (Bonosol): The annual benefit payable for life is Bs1,800.

Schedule of payments: One annual payment.

Benefit adjustment: The benefit is adjusted every 5 years according to an actuarial evaluation by the Superintendent of Pensions, Values, and Insurance. (The current value is fixed until December 31, 2007.)

Permanent Disability Benefits

Disability pension: The monthly pension is equal to 70% of the insured's average earnings in the last 5 years or in the last 18 months if the insured has less than 60 months of contributions. (Disability insurance tops up the accumulated capital in the individual account if the balance is less than the required minimum to finance the permanent disability pension.)

The minimum earnings for pension calculation purposes are equal to the legal monthly minimum wage.

The maximum earnings for pension calculation purposes are equal to 60 times the legal monthly minimum wage.

The legal monthly minimum wage is Bs440. (The legal monthly minimum wage is adjusted by decree for changes in the cost of living, depending on the financial resources of the state budget. The last adjustment was made in May 2003.)

Schedule of payments: Thirteen payments a year.

The pension ceases at age 65 when the insured becomes entitled to the old-age pension.

The insurance company also pays a monthly contribution equal to 10% of the insured's last monthly earnings before the onset of disability to the disabled insured's old-age pension account.

If a disabled insured person is not eligible for a pension, the insured may use the accumulated capital in his or her individual account to purchase a temporary annuity. The monthly amount of the annuity must not be less than 70% of the legal monthly minimum wage.

Benefit adjustment: Pensions are adjusted annually according to the UFV (Unidad de Fomento de Vivienda), calculated by the Central Bank for changes in the cost of living.

Survivor Benefits

Survivor pension: The monthly pension payable to a widow(er) or cohabiting partner with no eligible children is equal to 80% of the monthly base survivor pension; 60% if there is one eligible child; and 50% if there are two or more eligible children. (Life insurance tops up the accumulated capital in the deceased's individual account if the balance plus the compensation pension is less than the required minimum to finance the survivor pension.)

The monthly base survivor pension is equal to 70% of the deceased's average monthly earnings in the last 5 years (in the last 18 months if the deceased had less than 60 months of contributions) or 70% of the deceased's old-age or disability monthly pension.

The minimum earnings for pension calculation purposes are equal to the legal monthly minimum wage.

The maximum earnings for pension calculation purposes are equal to 60 times the legal monthly minimum wage.

The legal monthly minimum wage is Bs440. (The legal minimum wage is adjusted by decree for changes in the cost of living, depending on the financial resources of the state budget. The last adjustment was made in May 2003.)

Schedule of payments: Thirteen payments a year.

The widow(er)'s or partner's pension ceases on remarriage or if cohabiting with a new partner.

Orphan's pension: The monthly pension is equal to 20% of the monthly base survivor pension for a single orphan; 50% is split equally if there are two or more orphans; and 100% is split equally between full orphans. (Life insurance tops up the accumulated capital in the deceased's individual account if the balance plus the compensation pension is less than the required minimum to finance the survivor pension.)

The monthly base survivor pension is equal to 70% of the deceased's average monthly earnings in the last 5 years (in the last 18 months if the deceased had less than 60 months of contributions) or 70% of the deceased's old-age or disability monthly pension.

Schedule of payments: Thirteen payments a year.

When an orphan ceases to be eligible, the widow(er)'s or partner's pension is recalculated.

The total survivor pension payable to the widow(er) or cohabiting partner and to children must not exceed 100% of the base survivor pension.

Other eligible survivors (in the absence of the above): The monthly pension is equal to 20% of the monthly base survivor pension for each parent and 10% for each brother or sister younger than age 18. Other persons named by the insured may also be eligible.

The monthly base survivor pension is equal to 70% of the deceased's average monthly earnings in the last 5 years (in the last 18 months if the deceased had less than 60 months of contributions) or 70% of the deceased's old-age or disability monthly pension.

Schedule of payments: Thirteen payments a year.

The total pension for other survivors must not exceed 60% of the base survivor pension.

If the deceased was not eligible to receive a pension, the accumulated capital plus interest of the deceased's individual account may be used to finance temporary payments to the eligible survivors according to pension allocation rules. The monthly payments are based on a hypothetical base survivor pension equal to at least 70% of the legal monthly minimum wage.

If the deceased died before age 65, contributions made to the social insurance system are recognized as a compensation pension, which is paid to survivors on the date of the deceased's 65th birthday. The compensation pension is

split among survivors in the same way as the survivor pension.

Benefit adjustment: Pensions are adjusted annually according to the UFV (Unidad de Fomento de Vivienda), calculated by the Central Bank for changes in the cost of living.

Funeral grant: A lump sum of Bs900.

Administrative Organization

Superintendent of Pensions, Values, and Insurance (http://www.spvs.gov.bo) supervises the Pension Fund Administrators (AFPs) and defines the investment limits for each financial instrument.

Pension Fund Administrators (AFPs) administer the old-age benefits (including Bonosol benefits and funeral grants) and contract with insurance companies for disability and survivor insurance.

Insurance companies administer the disability pension and survivor pension program.

Assessment Body (EEC), established by the AFPs and the insurance companies, determine the origin, cause, degree, and date of the disability for disability benefit calculation purposes as well as the origin and cause of death.

Sickness and Maternity

Regulatory Framework

First law: 1949.

Current laws: 1987 (social security), 1988, 1998 (health), and 2002 (maternity).

Type of program: Social insurance system.

Coverage

Cash and medical benefits: All workers.

Voluntary coverage for the self-employed.

Medical benefits only: Persons older than age 60.

Source of Funds

Insured person: None; pensioners contribute 5% of the pension.

Self-employed person: Voluntary contributions. (Self-employed miners contribute 10% of 1.3 times the minimum wage.)

The self-employed person's contributions also finance temporary disability benefits and medical benefits under Work Injury, below.

Employer: 10% of payroll.

The employer contributions also finance temporary disability benefits and medical benefits under Work Injury, below.

Government: None.

Qualifying Conditions

Cash sickness benefits: Must have at least two contributions before the onset of incapacity.

Cash maternity and medical benefits: Must have at least 4 months of contributions before the start of pregnancy for cash and medical benefits. The benefit is payable to an insured woman or to the spouse of an insured man.

Medical benefits: Must have at least 1 month of contributions in the previous 2 months.

Sickness and Maternity Benefits

Sickness benefit: The benefit is equal to 75% of the insured's last earnings and is payable after a 3-day waiting period for up to 26 weeks; may be extended to 52 weeks if continuing medical care will prevent permanent disability.

Maternity benefit: The benefit is equal to 95% of the insured's earnings and is payable for up to 45 days before and 45 days after the expected date of childbirth.

Nursing and prenatal allowances: See Family Allowances, below.

Workers' Medical Benefits

Medical benefits include general, specialist, and preventive care; diagnostic services; surgery; hospitalization; and medicines.

Dependents' Medical Benefits

Medical benefits include general, specialist, and preventive care; diagnostic services; surgery; hospitalization; and medicines.

Administrative Organization

Minister of Health (http://www.sns.gov.bo) provides supervision.

National Health Fund administers the program.

Work Injury

Regulatory Framework

First law: 1924.

Current laws: 1987 (social security); and 1996 (mandatory individual account), implemented in 1997.

Type of program: Social insurance and mandatory individual account system.

Coverage

Salaried workers and apprentices.

Voluntary coverage for the self-employed.

Source of Funds

Insured person: None.

Self-employed person: Voluntary contributions of 1.71% of declared gross earnings for permanent disability and survivor pensions. For temporary disability benefits and medical benefits, see source of funds under Sickness and Maternity, above.

Employer: 1.71% of payroll for permanent disability and survivor pensions. For temporary disability benefits and medical benefits, see source of funds under Sickness and Maternity, above.

Government: None; contributes as an employer.

Qualifying Conditions

Work injury benefits: There is no minimum qualifying period. Accidents that occur while commuting to and from work are covered if the employer provides the transportation.

Voluntarily insured self-employed workers must have 6 months of contributions in the 12 months before the onset of disability or death. Coverage is extended for up to 6 months after the last contribution.

Temporary Disability Benefits

The benefit is the same as the cash sickness benefit payable under Sickness and Maternity, above. The benefit is equal to 75% of the insured's last earnings and is payable after a 3-day waiting period for up to 26 weeks; may be extended to 52 weeks if continuing medical care will prevent permanent disability.

Permanent Disability Benefits

Permanent disability pension: If the assessed degree of disability is at least 60%, the monthly pension is equal to 100% of the insured's average earnings in the last 5 years.

The minimum earnings for pension calculation purposes are equal to the legal monthly minimum wage.

The maximum earnings for pension calculation purposes are equal to 60 times the legal monthly minimum wage.

The legal monthly minimum wage is Bs440. (The legal monthly minimum wage is adjusted by decree for changes in the cost of living, depending on the financial resources of the state budget. The last adjustment was made in May 2003.)

Partial disability: If the assessed degree of disability is between 25% and 60%, the pension is equal to a percentage of the total disability pension according to the assessed degree of disability.

The disability pension is replaced by the old-age pension at age 65.

Disability grant: If the assessed degree of disability is between 10% and 25%, a lump sum equal to 4 years' partial disability pension is paid according to the assessed degree of disability.

The insurance company also pays a monthly contribution equal to 10% of the insured's last monthly earnings before the onset of disability to the disabled person's old-age pension mandatory individual account.

The Assessment Body (EEC) assesses the degree of disability through a Medical Assessment Panel consisting of three medical professionals. The insured or his or her dependents are entitled to require the Superintendent of Pensions, Values, and Insurance to review the assessed degree of disability once only.

Benefit adjustment: Pensions are adjusted annually according to the UFV (Unidad de Fomento de Vivienda), calculated by the Central Bank for changes in the cost of living.

Workers' Medical Benefits

Benefits include necessary medical and surgical care, hospitalization, and medicines.

Survivor Benefits

Survivor pension: The monthly pension payable to a widow(er) or cohabiting partner with no eligible children is equal to 80% of the monthly base survivor pension; 60% if there is one eligible child; and 50% if there are two or more eligible children.

The monthly base survivor pension is equal to 100% of the deceased's average monthly earnings in the last 5 years (in the last 18 months if the deceased had less than 60 months of contributions) or 100% of the deceased's old-age pension or disability pension.

The minimum earnings for pension calculation purposes are equal to the legal monthly minimum wage.

The maximum earnings for pension calculation purposes are equal to 60 times the legal monthly minimum wage.

The legal monthly minimum wage is Bs440. (The legal monthly minimum wage is adjusted by decree for changes in the cost of living, depending on the financial resources of the state budget. The last adjustment was made in May 2003.)

Schedule of payments: Thirteen payments a year.

The widow(er)'s or partner's pension ceases on remarriage or if cohabiting with a new partner.

Orphan's pension: The monthly pension is equal to 20% of the monthly base survivor pension for a single orphan; 50% is split equally if there are two or more orphans; 100% is split equally between full orphans.

The monthly base survivor pension is equal to 100% of the deceased's average monthly earnings in the last 5 years (in the last 18 months if the deceased had less than 60 months of contributions) or 100% of the deceased's old-age or disability monthly pension.

Schedule of payments: Thirteen payments a year.

When an orphan ceases to be eligible, the widow(er)'s or partner's pension is recalculated.

The total survivor pension payable to the widow(er) or cohabiting partner and to orphans must not exceed 100% of the base survivor pension.

Other eligible survivors (in the absence of the above): The monthly pension is equal to 20% of the monthly base survivor pension for each parent and 10% for each brother or sister younger than age 18. Other persons named by the insured may also be eligible.

The monthly base survivor pension is equal to 100% of the deceased's average monthly earnings in the last 5 years (in the last 18 months if the deceased had less than 60 months of contributions) or 100% of the deceased's old-age or disability monthly pension.

Schedule of payments: Thirteen payments a year.

The total pension for other survivors must not exceed 60% of the base survivor pension.

If the deceased was not eligible for a pension, the accumulated capital, plus interest, of the deceased's mandatory individual account may be used to finance temporary payments to the eligible survivors according to pension allocation rules. The monthly payments must be based on a hypothetical base survivor pension equal to at least 70% of the legal monthly minimum wage.

Benefit adjustment: Pensions are adjusted annually according to the UFV (Unidad de Fomento de Vivienda), calculated by the Central Bank for changes in the cost of living.

Funeral grant: A lump sum of Bs900.

Administrative Organization

Superintendent of Pensions, Values, and Insurance (http://www.spvs.gov.bo) supervises the Pension Fund Administrators (AFPs) and defines the investment limits for each financial instrument.

The authorized Pension Fund Administrators (AFPs) collect contributions and contract insurance companies for work injury disability and survivor insurance.

Insurance companies administer work injury disability and survivor programs.

Assessment Body (EEC), established by the AFPs and the insurance companies under the legal form of a civil association, determines the origin, cause, degree, and date of the disability for disability benefit purposes as well as the origin and cause of death for survivor benefit purposes.

National Health Fund administers temporary disability benefits and medical benefits.

Unemployment

Regulatory Framework

No statutory unemployment benefits are provided.

Labor law requires employers to grant severance pay to dismissed employees. Dismissed workers are covered for medical and maternity benefits for 2 months after employment ceases.

Family Allowances

Regulatory Framework

First law: 1953.

Current laws: 1956 (social security), implemented in 1959; and 1987 (social security).

Type of program: Employment-related system.

Coverage

All workers.

Special systems for bank employees, military personnel, drivers, miners, railroad employees, petroleum workers, and other groups of workers.

Source of Funds

Insured person: None.

Self-employed person: Not applicable.

Employer: Total cost.

Government: None.

Qualifying Conditions

Family allowances: The child must be between age 1 (when the nursing allowance ceases) and age 19; no limit if disabled. The family head must be currently working more than 15 days a month.

Housing allowance: Provided to single and married workers.

Prenatal grant: Provided from the 5th month of pregnancy.

Birth grant: Payable for the birth of a child.

Nursing allowance: Provided for each child for the 12-month period following birth (paid in kind).

Burial allowance: Paid for the funeral of a child younger than age 19.

Family Allowance Benefits

Family allowances: A monthly allowance is paid for each child.

Housing allowance: An allowance is provided to single and married workers.

Prenatal grant: Milk and a cash benefit is provided from the fifth month of pregnancy.

Birth grant: A grant equal to the national monthly minimum wage is paid for each birth.

Nursing allowance: A monthly milk allowance is provided for each child for the 12-month period following birth (paid in kind).

Burial allowance: An allowance equal to the national monthly minimum wage is paid.

Administrative Organization

Ministry of Housing and Economic Development (http://www.desarrollo.gov.bo) provides general supervision.

National Secretariat of Pensions, through the National Institute of Pensions, administers the program.

Employers pay allowances for single and married adults to employees.

Brazil

Exchange rate: US$1.00 equals 2.41 reais.

Old Age, Disability, and Survivors

Regulatory Framework

First laws: 1923 (railroads), 1934 (commerce), and 1936 (industry).

Current laws: 1991 (social security), with 1999 amendment; 1991 (social insurance); 1993 (social assistance); and 1999 (social insurance regulations).

Type of program: Social insurance and social assistance system.

Coverage

Social insurance: Employed persons in industry, commerce, and agriculture; domestic servants; some categories of casual worker; elected civil servants; and the self-employed.

Voluntary coverage for students, housewives, the unemployed, and other categories.

Special systems for public-sector employees and military personnel.

Social assistance: Needy elderly or disabled persons.

Source of Funds

Social insurance

Insured person: 7.65% of gross earnings with earnings up to 800.45 reais; 8.65% with earnings from 800.46 reais up to 900 reais; 9% with earnings from 900.01 reais up to 1,334.07 reais; or 11% with earnings from 1,334.08 reais up to 2,668.15 reais. Voluntary contributors and members of cooperatives contribute 20% of declared earnings.

The minimum monthly earnings for contribution purposes are equal to the minimum monthly wage (300 reais).

The maximum monthly earnings for contribution purposes are 2,668.15 reais.

The above contributions also finance sickness and maternity benefits and family allowances.

Self-employed person: 20% of declared earnings.

The minimum monthly earnings for contribution purposes are equal to the minimum monthly wage (300 reais).

The maximum monthly earnings for contribution purposes are 2,668.15 reais.

The above contributions also finance sickness and maternity benefits.

Employer: 20% of payroll (22.5% of payroll for employers in the financial sector); 15% of earnings for work cooperatives; 12% of payroll on behalf of domestic workers; and 2.7% of earnings for rural employers.

There are no maximum monthly earnings for contribution purposes.

Small-enterprise employers may contribute from 1.2% to 4.3% of monthly declared earnings, depending on annual earnings declared in the last year.

The above contributions also finance sickness and maternity benefits and family allowances.

Government: Earmarked taxes are used to finance administrative costs and any deficit.

Social assistance

Insured person: None.

Self-employed: None.

Employer: None.

Government: Total cost.

Qualifying Conditions

Old-age pension

Age pension (social insurance): Age 65 (men) or age 60 (women) for employees and the urban self-employed; age 60 (men) or age 55 (women) for the rural self-employed.

Persons who were first insured before July 25, 1991, must have at least 144 months of contributions; persons first insured since July 25, 1991, must have at least 180 months of contributions.

Contributory pension (social insurance): The insured must have at least 35 years of contributions (men) or 30 years of contributions (women). For arduous employment, the coverage period is between 15 years and 25 years.

Proportional pension (social insurance): Age 53 with 30 years of contributions (men) or age 45 with 25 years of contributions (women); for persons first insured before December 16, 1998, the insured must also contribute 40% of the difference between the required contribution years at age 53 (men) or age 45 (women) and the number of years actually paid as of December 16, 1998.

All contributory pensions are payable abroad under bilateral or multilateral agreement.

Old-age assistance (means-tested): Age 65, without remunerated work, and with family monthly earnings less than 25% of the minimum monthly wage for each person (75 reais). Eligibility is reviewed every 2 years.

Disability pension

Disability pension (social insurance): Assessed as permanently incapable for work with at least 12 months of contributions. The contribution period is waived if the disability is the result of an accident.

The degree of disability is assessed by the Ministry of Social Insurance.

Disability assistance (means-tested): Assessed as disabled with family monthly earnings less than 25% of the minimum monthly wage for each person (75 reais). Eligibility is reviewed every 2 years.

Survivor pension (social insurance): The deceased was a pensioner or insured.

Eligible survivors include the widow(er) or partner and children younger than age 21 (no limit if disabled); in absence of the above (in order of priority), parents and brothers and sisters younger than age 21 (no limit if disabled).

Survivor pensions are payable abroad under bilateral or multilateral agreement.

Old-Age Benefits

Old-age pension

Age pension (social insurance): The monthly benefit is equal to 70% of average earnings plus 1% of average earnings for each year of contributions, up to a maximum of 100%.

For persons first insured before November 29, 1999, average earnings for benefit calculation purposes are based on earnings in the best 4/5 of the total number of months of earnings. Monthly earnings since July 1994 are adjusted.

For persons first insured since November 29, 1999, average earnings for benefit calculation purposes are based on earnings in the best 4/5 of the total number of months of earnings.

Persons first insured since November 29, 1999, may opt for the pension to be calculated using the Fator Previdenciario method. The monthly pension is equal to the Fator Previdenciario times 70% of average earnings (based on earnings in the best 4/5 of the total number of months of earnings).

The Fator Previdenciario is based on the insured's contribution rate, contribution period, age, and life expectancy.

The minimum monthly earnings for benefit calculation purposes are equal to the minimum monthly wage (300 reais).

The maximum monthly earnings for benefit calculation purposes are 2,668.15 reais.

The minimum monthly age pension is equal to the minimum monthly wage (300 reais).

The maximum age pension is equal to 100% of average earnings.

Pensioners are not required to cease gainful activity.

Schedule of payments: Thirteen payments a year.

Benefit adjustment: Benefits are adjusted annually according to changes in the consumer price index.

Contributory pension (social insurance): The monthly benefit is equal to 100% of average earnings for persons first insured before November 29, 1999.

Average earnings for benefit calculation purposes are based on earnings in the best 4/5 of the total number of months of earnings. Monthly earnings since July 1994 are adjusted.

For persons first insured since November 29, 1999, the monthly benefit is equal to the Fator Previdenciario times 100% of average earnings (based on earnings in the best 4/5 of the total number of months of earnings).

The Fator Previdenciario is based on the insured's contribution rate, contribution period, age, and life expectancy.

The minimum monthly earnings for benefit calculation purposes are equal to the minimum monthly wage (300 reais).

The maximum monthly earnings for benefit calculation purposes are 2,668.15 reais.

Pensioners are not required to cease gainful activity.

Schedule of payments: Thirteen payments a year.

Benefit adjustment: Benefits are adjusted annually according to changes in the consumer price index.

Proportional pension (social insurance): For persons first insured before November 29, 1999, the monthly benefit is equal to 70% of average earnings plus 5% of average earnings for each additional year of contributions, up to a maximum of 100%.

Average earnings for benefit calculation purposes are based on earnings in the best 4/5 of the total number of months of earnings. Monthly earnings since July 1994 are adjusted.

For persons first insured since November 29, 1999, the monthly benefit is equal to the Fator Previdenciario times 70% of average earnings plus 5% of average earnings for each additional year of contributions. Average earnings are based on earnings in the best 4/5 of the total number of months of earnings.

The Fator Previdenciario is based on the insured's contribution rate, contribution period, age, and life expectancy.

The minimum monthly earnings for benefit calculation purposes are equal to the minimum monthly wage (300 reais).

The maximum monthly earnings for benefit calculation purposes are 2,668.15 reais.

Pensioners are not required to cease gainful activity.

Schedule of payments: Thirteen payments a year.

Benefit adjustment: Benefits are adjusted annually according to changes in the consumer price index.

Old-age assistance (means-tested): The monthly benefit is equal to the minimum monthly wage (300 reais).

Benefit adjustment: Benefits are adjusted annually according to changes in the minimum wage.

Permanent Disability Benefits

Disability pension

Disability pension (social insurance): The monthly benefit is equal to 100% of average earnings; 100% of the minimum wage for rural workers.

For persons first insured before November 29, 1999, average earnings for benefit calculation purposes are based on earnings in the best 4/5 of the total number of months of earnings. Monthly earnings since July 1994 are adjusted.

For persons first insured since November 29, 1999, average earnings for benefit calculation purposes are based on earnings in the best 4/5 of the total months of earnings.

The minimum monthly earnings for benefit calculation purposes are equal to the minimum monthly wage (300 reais).

The maximum monthly earnings for benefit calculation purposes are 2,668.15 reais.

Constant-attendance allowance: Equal to 25% of the disability pension.

Schedule of payments: Thirteen payments a year.

Benefit adjustment: Benefits are adjusted annually according to changes in the consumer price index.

Disability assistance (means-tested): The monthly benefit is equal to the minimum monthly wage (300 reais).

Benefit adjustment: Benefits are adjusted annually according to changes in the minimum wage.

Survivor Benefits

Survivor pension (social insurance): The monthly pension is equal to 100% of the pension paid or payable to the deceased; 100% of the minimum wage for rural workers. The pension is split equally among eligible survivors. If one survivor ceases to be eligible, the pensions for the remaining survivors are recalculated.

The minimum monthly pension is equal to the minimum monthly wage (300 reais).

The maximum monthly pension is 2,668.15 reais.

Schedule of payments: Thirteen payments a year.

Benefit adjustment: Benefits are adjusted annually according to changes in the consumer price index; the minimum wage for rural workers' benefits.

Administrative Organization

Ministry of Social Insurance (http://www.previdencia.gov.br) provides general supervision.

National Social Security Institute (http://www.inss.gov.br) administers benefits.

Sickness and Maternity

Regulatory Framework

First laws: 1923 (railroads), 1934 (commerce), and 1936 (industry).

Current laws: 1990 (health); 1991 (social security), with 1999 amendment; and 1991 (social insurance).

Type of program: Social insurance system.

Coverage

Employed persons in industry, commerce, and agriculture; domestic servants; some categories of casual worker; elected civil servants; and the self-employed.

Voluntary coverage for students, housewives, the unemployed, and other categories.

Special systems for public-sector employees and military personnel.

Source of Funds

Insured person: See source of funds under Old Age, Disability, and Survivors, above.

Self-employed person: See source of funds under Old Age, Disability, and Survivors, above.

Employer: See source of funds under Old Age, Disability, and Survivors, above.

Government: The cost of medical benefits.

Qualifying Conditions

Cash sickness and medical benefits: Must have contributed in the last 12 months. There is no qualifying period in case of an accident or serious illness.

Cash maternity benefits: There is no minimum qualifying period; 10 months of contributions for self-employed persons and rural workers.

Sickness and Maternity Benefits

Sickness benefit: The monthly benefit is equal to 91% of average earnings; 100% of the minimum wage for rural workers. The benefit is payable after a 15-day waiting period (during which the employer is required to pay 100% of the wage); there is no waiting period for self-employed persons and voluntarily covered persons.

There is no limit to duration.

Average earnings are based on earnings in the best 4/5 of the total number of months of earnings. Monthly earnings since July 1994 are adjusted.

The minimum monthly earnings for benefit calculation purposes are equal to the minimum monthly wage (300 reais).

The maximum monthly earnings for benefit calculation purposes are 2,668.15 reais.

Schedule of payments: Thirteen payments a year.

Benefit adjustment: Benefits are adjusted annually according to changes in the consumer price index; the minimum wage for rural workers' benefits.

Maternity benefit: The monthly benefit is equal to 100% of the last wage; 100% of average earnings in the last 12 months for self-employed and voluntarily covered women; 100% of the minimum wage for rural workers. The benefit is payable for a total of 120 days, from 28 days before until 91 days after the expected date of childbirth.

The benefit is payable for 2 weeks in the case of a miscarriage.

The benefit is also payable for 120 days to the adopting mother of a child younger than age 1; 60 days if the child is aged 1 to 4; or 30 days if the child is aged 5 to 8.

The minimum monthly earnings for benefit calculation purposes are equal to the minimum monthly wage (300 reais).

The maximum monthly earnings for benefit calculation purposes are 2,668.15 reais.

Workers' Medical Benefits

Medical services are provided directly to patients in rural and urban areas through the Unified Health System. Benefits include general, specialist, maternity, and dental care; hospitalization; medicines (some cost sharing is required); and necessary transportation.

There is no limit to duration.

Dependents' Medical Benefits

Medical services are provided directly to patients in rural and urban areas through the Unified Health System. Benefits include general, specialist, maternity, and dental care; hospitalization; medicines (some cost sharing is required); and necessary transportation.

There is no limit to duration.

Administrative Organization

Ministry of Health (http://www.saude.gov.br) provides general supervision of the Unified Health System.

National Social Security Institute (http://www.inss.gov.br) administers cash benefits.

Federal, state, and municipal institutions are part of the Unified Health System and administer medical benefits.

Work Injury

Regulatory Framework

First laws: 1919, 1944, and 1967.

Current laws: 1991; and 1991, with 1999 amendment.

Type of program: Social insurance system.

Coverage

Employed persons.

Exclusions: The self-employed.

Special systems for rural workers, public-sector employees, and military personnel.

Source of Funds

Insured person: None.

Self-employed person: Not applicable.

Employer: 1% to 3% of payroll according to the assessed degree of risk; 1% of payroll for employers of rural workers.

There are no minimum or maximum earnings for contribution purposes.

Government: None.

Qualifying Conditions

Work injury benefits: There is no minimum qualifying period. Accidents that occur while commuting to and from work are covered.

Temporary Disability Benefits

The monthly benefit is equal to 91% of average earnings. The benefit is payable after a 15-day waiting period (during which the employer is required to pay 100% of the wage).

There is no limit to duration.

Average earnings are based on earnings in the best 4/5 of the total number of months of earnings. Monthly earnings since July 1994 are adjusted.

The minimum monthly earnings for benefit calculation purposes are equal to the minimum monthly wage (300 reais).

The maximum monthly earnings for benefit calculation purposes are 2,668.15 reais.

Schedule of payments: Thirteen payments a year.

Benefit adjustment: Benefits are adjusted annually according to changes in the consumer price index.

Permanent Disability Benefits

Permanent disability pension: The monthly pension is equal to 100% of average earnings and is payable if incapable of any work.

Average earnings for benefit calculation purposes are based on earnings in the best 4/5 of the total number of months of earnings. Monthly earnings since July 1994 are adjusted.

The minimum monthly earnings for benefit calculation purposes are equal to the minimum monthly wage (300 reais).

The maximum monthly earnings for benefit calculation purposes are 2,668.15 reais.

Constant-attendance supplement: Equal to 25% of the pension.

Schedule of payments: Thirteen payments a year.

The degree of disability is assessed by National Social Security Institute doctors. The degree of disability is reassessed every 2 years.

Accident benefit (partial disability): The monthly benefit is equal to 50% of average earnings and is payable to disabled workers who are capable of some kind of work.

Average earnings for benefit calculation purposes are based on earnings in the best 4/5 of the total number of months of earnings. Monthly earnings since July 1994 are adjusted.

Schedule of payments: Thirteen payments a year.

Benefit adjustment: Benefits are adjusted annually according to changes in the consumer price index.

Workers' Medical Benefits

Medical and dental treatment, hospital treatment, medicines, rehabilitation, and transportation.

Survivor Benefits

Survivor pension: The monthly benefit is equal to 100% of the pension paid or payable to the deceased; 100% of the minimum wage for rural workers. The pension is split equally among eligible survivors. If one survivor ceases to be eligible, the pensions for the remaining survivors are recalculated.

Eligible survivors include the widow(er) or partner and children younger than age 21 (no limit if disabled); in absence of the above (in order of priority), parents and brothers and sisters younger than age 21 (no limit if disabled).

The minimum monthly pension is equal to the minimum monthly wage (300 reais).

The maximum monthly pension is 2,668.15 reais.

Schedule of payments: Thirteen payments a year.

Benefit adjustment: Benefits are adjusted annually according to changes in the consumer price index; the minimum wage for rural workers' benefits.

Administrative Organization

Ministry of Health (http://www.saude.gov.br) provides general supervision of the Unified Health System.

National Social Security Institute (http://www.inss.gov.br) administers cash benefits.

Federal, state, and municipal institutions are part of the Unified Health System and administer medical benefits.

Unemployment

Regulatory Framework

First laws: 1965 (severance pay fund) and 1986 (unemployment insurance).

Current law: 1990 (unemployment insurance), with 1994 and 2002 amendments.

Type of program: Social assistance system.

Note: Employers contribute 8% of earnings to the Guarantee Fund for Severance Pay (FGTS), which has individual savings accounts to which the insured has access in the event of unemployment, marriage, retirement, and other contingencies.

Coverage

Employed persons.

Exclusions: The self-employed.

Special system for craft fishermen, domestic workers, and workers formerly engaged in forced or bonded labor.

Source of Funds

Insured person: None.

Self-employed person: Not applicable.

Employer: None.

Government: Total cost is financed by earmarked taxes.

Qualifying Conditions

Unemployment benefit: The benefit varies according to whether the insured had 6 months to 11 months of coverage, 12 months to 23 months of coverage, or 24 or more months of coverage in the last 36 months. Unemployment must not be due to misconduct. The insured must lack other resources to support self or family and must not receive other social insurance benefits.

Unemployment Benefits

Unemployment benefit (means-tested): The monthly benefit varies according to average earnings in the last 3 months of employment: 80% of average earnings is paid with average earnings up to 495.23 reais; 396.18 reais, plus 50% of earnings exceeding 495.23 reais, is paid with average earnings between 495.23 reais and 825.47 reais; and 561.30 reais is paid with average earnings of 825.47 reais or more.

The benefit is payable for 3 to 5 months, depending on the insured's duration of coverage in any 16-month period.

The minimum monthly benefit is equal to the minimum monthly wage (300 reais).

Benefit adjustment: Benefits are adjusted annually according to changes in the minimum wage.

Administrative Organization

Ministry of Labor and Employment (http://www.mte.gob.br) provides general supervision.

Worker Assistance Fund Advisory Council administers the program.

Family Allowances

Regulatory Framework

First law: 1941 (large families).

Current laws: 1991 (social insurance) and 1998 (family allowances).

Type of program: Employment-related system.

Coverage

Low-income employees with one or more children.

Exclusions: Domestic workers, casual workers, elected civil servants, and the self-employed.

Special system for public-sector employees.

Source of Funds

Insured person: See source of funds under Old Age, Disability, and Survivors, above.

Self-employed person: Not applicable.

Employer: See source of funds under Old Age, Disability, and Survivors, above.

Government: See source of funds under Old Age, Disability, and Survivors, above.

Qualifying Conditions

Family allowances (income-tested): Employees with monthly income up to 623.44 reais. The child must be younger than age 14 (no limit if disabled) and attending school. The parent must be currently in insured employment or receiving a sickness benefit. The allowance is payable to both parents if both are insured.

Family Allowance Benefits

Family allowances (income-tested): 21.27 reais is paid monthly for each child if the insured's earnings do not exceed 414.77 reais; 14.99 reais a month if earnings are between 414.77 reais and 623.45 reais.

Employers pay allowances, and the total cost is reimbursed by government.

Benefit adjustment: Benefits are adjusted annually according to changes in the consumer price index.

Administrative Organization

Ministry of Social Insurance (http://www.previdencia.gov.br) provides general supervision.

National Social Security Institute (http://www.inss.gov.br) administers benefits.

Employers pay benefits to employees.

British Virgin Islands
Exchange rate: Uses the US dollar (US$).

Old Age, Disability, and Survivors

Regulatory Framework

First law: 1979 (social security).

Current law: 1980 (social security).

Type of program: Social insurance system.

Coverage

All employed and self-employed persons aged 16 to 65.

There are no special systems for any specified groups of employees.

Source of Funds

Insured person: 3.25% of monthly insured earnings.

The maximum annual earnings for contribution and benefit purposes are US$23,400 (US$30,420 from January 2006).

Self-employed person: 8.5% of declared monthly earnings.

The maximum annual earnings for contribution and benefit purposes are US$23,400 (US$30,420 from January 2006).

Employer: 3.25% of monthly covered wages.

The maximum annual earnings for contribution and benefit purposes are US$23,400 (US$30,420 from January 2006).

Government: None; contributes as an employer.

Qualifying Conditions

Old-age pension: Age 65 with 500 weeks of contributions.

Partial pension: A reduced pension is payable with between 51 and 499 weeks of contributions.

Early pension: There is no early pension.

Old-age grant: Age 65 with at least 50 weeks of contributions and ineligible for any periodic benefit.

All old-age benefits are payable abroad.

Disability pension: Younger than age 65 with 500 weeks of contributions and permanently incapable of any work.

The degree of disability is assessed every 6 months by any medical doctor.

Disability grant: Younger than age 65 with at least 50 weeks of contributions, ineligible for any periodic benefit, and permanently incapable of any work.

All disability benefits are payable abroad.

Survivor pension: The deceased was a pensioner or was eligible for a pension at the time of death.

Eligible survivors are widow(er)s (including an unmarried spouse) aged 40 or older or caring for a dependent child younger than age 15 (age 21 if a student) and orphans younger than age 15 (age 21 if a student).

All survivor benefits are payable abroad.

Survivor grant: Payable if the deceased was not eligible for a pension but had at least 50 weeks of contributions.

Funeral grant: Payable for the death of an insured person or his or her dependents. The insured must have at least 26 weeks of paid contributions.

Old-Age Benefits

Old-age pension: The pension is equal to 30% of average covered earnings, plus 1% of average covered earnings for every 50-week period of contributions above 500 weeks.

Average covered earnings are based on the sum of earnings in the best 3 years in the last 15 years, divided by three.

The maximum annual earnings for benefit calculation purposes are US$23,400.

Partial pension: The full pension is reduced in proportion to the number of weeks of contributions.

Early pension: There is no early pension.

The minimum old-age pension is US$208 (January 2005).

The maximum old-age pension is equal to 60% of the insured's average annual covered earnings.

Retirement from gainful employment is not necessary.

Old-age grant: The grant is equal to six times average weekly earnings for every 50-week period of contributions above 50 weeks and below 500 weeks.

Retirement from gainful employment is not necessary.

Permanent Disability Benefits

Disability pension: The pension is equal to 30% of average covered earnings, plus 1% of average covered earnings for every 50-week period of contributions above 500 weeks.

Average covered earnings are based on the sum of earnings in the best 3 years in the last 15 years (or in the total number of covered years where less) before the year of the onset of disability, divided by three.

The maximum annual earnings for benefit calculation purposes are US$23,400.

The minimum disability pension is US$208 (January 2005).

The maximum disability pension is equal to 60% of the insured's average annual covered earnings.

The disability pension is replaced by the old-age pension at age 65.

Disability grant: The grant is equal to six times average weekly earnings for every 50-week period of contributions above 50 weeks and below 500 weeks.

Survivor Benefits

Survivor pension: The widow(er)'s pension is equal to 2/3 of the old-age pension paid or payable to the deceased.

Orphan's pension: The pension is equal to 1/3 of the widow(er)'s pension; 2/3 if a full orphan.

Survivor grant: The widow(er)'s grant is equal to 2/3 of the old-age grant paid or payable to the deceased.

Orphan's grant: The grant is equal to 1/3 of the widow(er)'s grant; 2/3 if a full orphan.

Funeral grant: The grant depends on the age of the person at death. For a child younger than age 1, US$300; for a child aged 1 to 15, US$1,300; for persons aged 16 or older, US$2,000. The grant is paid to the person who meets the cost of the funeral.

Administrative Organization

Chief Minister's Office provides general supervision.

Social Security Board (http://www.bvissb.vg) administers the program.

Sickness and Maternity

Regulatory Framework

First law: 1979 (social security).

Current law: 1980 (social security).

Type of program: Social insurance system. Cash benefits only.

Coverage

All employed and self-employed persons aged 16 to 65.

There are no special systems for any specified groups of employees.

Source of Funds

Insured person: 0.75% of monthly insured earnings.

The maximum weekly and monthly earnings for contribution and benefit purposes are US$450 and US$1,950, respectively.

Self-employed person: 1.5% of declared monthly earnings.

The maximum weekly and monthly earnings for contribution and benefit purposes are US$450 and US$1,950, respectively.

Employer: 0.75% of covered monthly wages.

The maximum weekly and monthly earnings for contribution and benefit purposes are US$450 and US$1,950, respectively.

Government: None; contributes as an employer.

Qualifying Conditions

Cash sickness benefits: Must have 26 weeks of contributions, including 8 weeks of contributions in the 13 weeks before the onset of illness.

Cash maternity benefits: Must have 26 weeks of contributions, including 20 weeks of contributions in the 39 weeks before the expected date of childbirth.

Maternity grant: The insured must have 26 weeks of contributions. The insured can be a woman or her husband or cohabiting partner. A cohabiting partner must have lived with the woman for at least 2 years. If both parents are eligible, 100% of the grant is payable to each.

Sickness and Maternity Benefits

Sickness benefit: The benefit is equal to 2/3 of average weekly insured earnings and is payable for up to 26 weeks. The benefit is payable after a 3-day waiting period.

Average weekly insured earnings are based on insured earnings in the 13 weeks before the onset of the incapacity.

There is no minimum weekly sickness benefit.

The maximum weekly sickness benefit is US$300.

Maternity benefit: The benefit is equal to 2/3 of average weekly insured earnings in the 39 weeks before the expected date of childbirth. The benefit is payable for up to 13 weeks, beginning no earlier than 6 weeks before the expected date of childbirth.

Average weekly insured earnings are based on insured earnings in the 39 weeks before the expected date of childbirth.

There is no minimum weekly maternity benefit.

The maximum weekly maternity benefit is US$300.

Maternity grant: A lump sum of US$200 for each eligible insured parent per child.

Workers' Medical Benefits

No statutory benefits are provided.

Dependents' Medical Benefits

No statutory benefits are provided.

Administrative Organization

Chief Minister's Office provides general supervision.

Social Security Board (http://www.bvissb.vg) administers the program.

Work Injury

Regulatory Framework

First and current law: 1994 (employment injury).

Type of program: Social insurance system.

Coverage

All employed and self-employed persons from age 16.

There are no special systems for any specified groups of employees.

Source of Funds

Insured person: None.

Self-employed person: 0.5% of declared monthly earnings.

The maximum earnings for contribution purposes are US$23,400 (US$30,420 from January 2006).

Employer: 0.5% of covered monthly wages (including on behalf of employees aged 65 or older).

The maximum annual earnings for contribution and benefit purposes are US$23,400 (US$30,420 from January 2006).

Government: None; contributes as an employer.

Qualifying Conditions

Work injury benefits: There is no minimum qualifying period for a work injury or an occupational disease.

Temporary Disability Benefits

The benefit is equal to 75% of average weekly covered earnings and is payable for up to 26 weeks.

The maximum temporary disability benefit is US$975.

Permanent Disability Benefits

For a total disability (100%), the benefit is equal to 75% of average weekly covered earnings and is payable for up to 26 weeks.

The maximum permanent disability benefit is US$975.

Partial disability: For an assessed degree of disability of 30% to 99%, a percentage of the full pension is paid according to the assessed degree of disability.

The degree of disability is assessed every 6 months by any medical doctor.

A lump sum is paid for an assessed degree of disability of less than 30%.

Workers' Medical Benefits

Benefits include medical, surgical, dental, and hospital treatment; skilled nursing services; the supply of medicines; the supply, fitting, maintenance, repair, and renewal of artificial limbs; and the cost of transportation for the purpose of obtaining medical services.

Survivor Benefits

Survivor pension: The maximum survivor pension is 3/4 of the pension paid or payable to the deceased. The surviving spouse receives 1/2 of this amount.

Eligible survivors are married or unmarried spouses who lived with the deceased for at least 3 years.

The pension ceases if the surviving spouse remarries or cohabits.

Orphan's pension: Each orphan younger than age 15 (age 21 if a student, no limit if disabled) receives 1/6 of the maximum survivor pension.

Other eligible survivors: Up to 1/2 of the maximum survivor pension is split equally among other dependent survivors.

Funeral grant: A lump sum of US$2,000 is payable to the person who meets the cost of the funeral.

Administrative Organization

Chief Minister's Office provides general supervision.

Social Security Board (http://www.bvissb.vg) administers the program.

Canada

Exchange rate: US$1.00 equals
1.25 Canadian dollars (C$).

Old Age, Disability, and Survivors

Regulatory Framework

First laws: 1927 (old-age assistance), 1937 (blind assistance), and 1955 (disability assistance).

Current laws: 1952 (universal pension), 1965 (earnings-related pension), and 1967 (income-tested supplement).

Type of program: Universal pension and social insurance system.

Coverage

Universal pension (old-age security): All residents.

Earnings-related pension (Canada Pension Plan/Quebec Pension Plan): All employees and all self-employed persons working in Canada.

Exclusions: Those in casual employment (annual earnings less than C$3,500) or in seasonal agricultural employment.

A province may opt out of the federal earnings-related Canada Pension Plan if it establishes a comparable program. This is the case with the Quebec Pension Plan; benefits are portable between the two plans.

Source of Funds

Universal pension

Insured person: None.

Self-employed person: None.

Employer: None.

Government: Total cost, including the total cost of income-tested benefits.

Earnings-related pension

Insured person: 4.95% of earnings.

The minimum annual earnings for benefit and contribution purposes are C$3,500.

The maximum annual earnings for benefit and contribution purposes are C$41,100.

Earnings limit adjustment: Adjusted annually according to increases in the average industrial wage.

Self-employed person: 9.9% of earnings.

The minimum annual earnings for benefit and contribution purposes are C$3,500.

The maximum annual earnings for benefit and contribution purposes are C$41,100.

Earnings limit adjustment: Adjusted annually according to increases in the average industrial wage.

Employer: 4.95% of the employee's earnings.

The minimum annual earnings for benefit and contribution purposes are C$3,500.

The maximum annual earnings for benefit and contribution purposes are C$41,100.

Earnings limit adjustment: Adjusted annually according to increases in the average industrial wage.

Government: None; contributes as an employer.

Qualifying Conditions

Old-age pension

Universal pension: Age 65 with 10 years of residence in Canada after age 18. Retirement is not necessary.

The pension is payable abroad if the beneficiary resided in Canada for at least 20 years after age 18.

Low-income supplement (income-tested): Age 65, receiving the old-age pension, and low annual income. Income is based on individual income or family income if the pensioner has a spouse or common-law (same sex or opposite sex) partner.

Low-income allowance (income-tested): Aged 60 to 64, with 10 years of residence in Canada after age 18, and the claimant's spouse or common-law partner (same sex or opposite sex) is entitled to the old-age pension and the low-income supplement. At age 65, the allowance is replaced by the universal old-age pension and, depending on income, the low-income supplement.

Earnings-related retirement pension (Canada Pension Plan/Quebec Pension Plan): Age 60 with at least 1 valid contribution. If the pension is awarded before age 65, the insured must have fully or substantially ceased employment. If the pension is awarded at age 65 or older, retirement is not necessary.

Early pension: A reduced pension is payable from age 60.

Deferred pension: The deferred pension is possible.

The pension is payable abroad.

Earnings-related disability pension (Canada Pension Plan/Quebec Pension Plan): Severe and prolonged incapacity for any gainful activity with contributions in 4 of the last 6 years. (The Quebec Pension Plan normally requires contributions in half the years in which contributions could have been made; the minimum contribution period is 2 of the last 3 years.)

The pension is payable abroad.

Survivor pension

Universal pension (survivor allowance, income-tested): Payable to widow(er)s aged 60 to 64. The survivor must be a resident of Canada and have resided in Canada for

10 years after age 18. The pension is replaced by the universal old-age pension at age 65.

Earnings-related pension (Canada Pension Plan/Quebec Pension Plan): The deceased had made contributions during the lesser of 10 years or one-third of the years in which contributions could have been made; the minimum contribution period is 3 years.

The pension is payable abroad.

Spouse and widow(er) include legally married persons and common-law partners (including same-sex partners).

Old-Age Benefits

Old-age pension

Universal pension: The maximum monthly pension is C$476.97. The pension is calculated as 1/40th of the maximum pension for each year of residence in Canada after age 18, up to a maximum of 40 years. The pension of high-income earners is subject to recovery (the pension is reduced by 15% of annual income, minus allowable income tax deductions and expenses, over C$60,806).

Low-income supplement (income-tested): The supplement increases the maximum monthly universal pension to C$1,043.84 for a single person or C$1,692.42 for a couple.

Benefit adjustment: Automatic quarterly adjustments of the universal pension for changes in the consumer price index.

Low-income allowance (income-tested): Up to a maximum of C$846.21 a month for a pensioner's spouse between ages 60 and 64.

Earnings-related retirement pension (Canada Pension Plan/Quebec Pension Plan): The pension is equal to 25% of average adjusted yearly covered earnings. 15% of the years with the lowest income are disregarded; years in which the insured was caring for a child younger than age 7 may also be disregarded if it is in the insured's favor; months when the insured was receiving a disability benefit are also disregarded.

Early pension: The pension is reduced by 0.5% a month if awarded at any age after 60 but before age 65.

Deferred pension: The pension is increased by 0.5% a month if awarded after age 65 but before age 70.

The maximum monthly pension is C$828.75.

Pension credits accumulated by spouses or common-law partners (including same-sex partners) during marriage or cohabitation may be divided equally in case of divorce or separation.

Recorded earnings are adjusted for changes in national average wages.

Benefit adjustment: Automatic annual adjustments of the earnings-related pension for changes in the consumer price index.

Permanent Disability Benefits

Earnings-related disability pension (Canada Pension Plan/Quebec Pension Plan): A basic monthly pension of C$388.67 is paid, plus 75% of the earnings-related retirement pension.

The maximum monthly pension is C$1,010.23.

The disability pension is replaced by a retirement pension at age 65.

Recorded earnings are adjusted for changes in national average wages.

Child's supplement: C$195.96 a month for each child younger than age 18; age 25 if a student. (Quebec Pension Plan: C$62.22 for each child younger than age 18 only.)

Benefit adjustment: Automatic annual adjustment of all benefits for changes in the consumer price index.

Survivor Benefits

Survivor pension

Universal pension (survivor allowance, income-tested): For a widow(er) aged 60 to 64.

The allowance ceases on remarriage or if the person enters into a common-law relationship that lasts for at least a year.

The maximum monthly allowance is C$934.24.

The survivor allowance is replaced by the universal old-age pension at age 65.

Earnings-related survivor pension (Canada Pension Plan/ Quebec Pension Plan): A surviving spouse aged 65 or older receives 60% of the deceased's earnings-related retirement pension, up to a maximum of C$497.25 a month. (Quebec Pension Plan: The provision is the same for a surviving spouse aged 65 or older.)

A surviving spouse younger than age 65 receives 37.5% of the deceased's earnings-related retirement pension plus C$151.64, up to a maximum of C$462.42 a month. (Quebec Pension Plan: A surviving spouse aged 55 to 64 receives up to a maximum of C$710.37 a month; aged 45 to 54, up to a maximum of C$699.42 a month. For a surviving spouse younger than age 45 and disabled, the maximum pension is C$699.42 a month; if not disabled but caring for a dependent child, up to a maximum of C$671.62; if not disabled and with no dependent children, up to a maximum of C$410.31.)

Orphan's pension (Canada Pension Plan/Quebec Pension Plan): C$195.96 a month for each child younger than age 18; age 25 if a student. (Quebec Pension Plan: C$62.22 for each child below age 18 only.)

Death benefit: Equal to 6 months' earnings-related retirement pension, up to a maximum of C$2,500.

Benefit adjustment: Automatic annual adjustment of earnings-related pensions for changes in the consumer price index.

Administrative Organization

Department of Social Development (http://www.sdg.ca), through district and local offices, administers the universal and earnings-related pensions and income-tested supplements.

Canada Revenue Agency (http://cra.gc.ca) collects contributions for the earnings-related pensions.

Quebec Department of Revenue (http://revenue.gouv.qc.ca) and Quebec Pension Board (http://www.rrq.gouv.qc.ca) administer the earnings-related Quebec Pension Plan.

Sickness and Maternity

Regulatory Framework

Cash benefits

First and current law: 1996 (employment insurance).

Physician and hospital services

First laws: 1957 (hospital services) and 1968 (physician services).

Current law: 1984 (health).

Type of program: Social insurance (cash benefits) and universal system (physician and hospital services).

Coverage

Cash benefits: All salaried workers, including federal government employees; self-employed fishermen.

Provincial government employees may be covered with the consent of provincial government.

Exclusions: Self-employed persons other than fishermen.

Physician and hospital services: All residents satisfying federal and provincial criteria for eligibility and insured status. (Virtually the total population is covered.) Coverage is portable from province to province and for emergency care anywhere in the world. In the latter case, payment is limited to the rate payable in the person's home province.

Special provisions for certain groups, including members of the armed forces.

Source of Funds

Insured person

Cash benefits: See source of funds under Unemployment, below.

Physician and hospital benefits: Through general taxation. Premiums are paid in Alberta and British Columbia. Ontario has a health premium that is based on taxable income above a certain threshold. None in the other provinces.

Self-employed person

Cash benefits: See source of funds under Unemployment, below.

Physician and hospital benefits: Through general taxation. Premiums are paid in Alberta and British Columbia. Ontario has a health premium that is based on taxable income above a certain threshold. None in the other provinces.

Employer

Cash benefits: See source of funds under Unemployment, below.

Physician and hospital benefits: Contributions vary by province from 1% to 4.5%.

Government

Cash Benefits: None.

Physician and hospital benefits: Most of the cost is met from federal, provincial, and territorial general revenues. Federal government makes contributions to provinces and territories through block transfers, part of which are conditional on provinces and territories meeting federal program requirements as set out in the Canada Health Act.

Qualifying Conditions

Cash sickness and maternity benefits: Must have a minimum of 600 hours of insurable employment in the previous 52 weeks.

Compassionate care benefits: Must have a minimum of 600 hours of insurable employment in the previous 52 weeks. Payable to insured persons who leave work temporarily to provide care or support to a family member with a grave illness.

Medical and hospitalization benefits: Generally, 3 months' residence in the province is required to be insured. When the insured moves from one province to another, the former province continues to provide insurance coverage during the waiting period.

In Alberta, British Columbia, and Ontario, the payment of premiums is an additional condition, but such payment is not linked to entitlement to services.

Sickness and Maternity Benefits

Sickness benefit: The benefit is equal to 55% of average weekly insurable earnings in the last 26 weeks, plus a family supplement for low-income and modest-income earners with dependent children. The supplement is awarded if annual net family income (after application of allowable deductions under the Income Tax Act) is less than C$25,921. The benefit is paid after a 2-week waiting period, for up to 15 weeks.

Maternity benefit: The benefit is equal to 55% of average weekly insurable earnings in the last 26 weeks, plus a family supplement for low-income and modest-income earners with dependent children. The supplement is awarded if annual net family income (after application of allowable deductions under the Income Tax Act) is less than C$25,921. The benefit is paid for up to 15 weeks, plus up to 35 additional weeks for parental care (the mother, father, or both) on the birth or adoption of a child.

Compassionate care benefit: The benefit is equal to 55% of average weekly insurable earnings in the last 26 weeks, plus a family supplement for low-income and modest-income earners with dependent children. A supplement is awarded if annual net family income (after application of allowable deductions under the Income Tax Act) is less than C$25,921. The benefit is paid after a 2-week waiting period for up to 6 weeks.

The maximum weekly benefit is C$413.

Workers' Medical Benefits

Medical benefits: Benefits include general medical and maternity care; and surgical, specialist, and laboratory services. Benefits are paid directly by provincial authorities according to predetermined formulas and agreed-upon fee schedules.

Hospital benefits: Benefits include standard ward care, necessary nursing, pharmaceuticals provided in hospital, and diagnostic and therapeutic services. Benefits are paid directly by provincial authorities according to predetermined formulas and agreed-upon fee schedules.

Other benefits include oral surgery if required and performed in an approved hospital and, in some provinces, services of osteopaths, chiropractors, and optometrists; dental care for children; prosthetics; and prescribed drugs. Some cost sharing may be required in such cases.

In some provinces, welfare recipients and persons older than age 65 are eligible for free drugs, eyeglasses, and subsidized nursing home care.

Dependents' Medical Benefits

Medical benefits: Benefits include surgical, specialist, and laboratory services and general medical and maternity care. Benefits are paid directly by provincial authorities according to predetermined formulas and agreed-upon fee schedules.

Hospital benefits: Benefits include standard ward care, necessary nursing, pharmaceuticals provided in hospital, and diagnostic and therapeutic services. Benefits are paid directly by provincial authorities according to predetermined formulas and agreed-upon fee schedules.

Other benefits include oral surgery if required and performed in an approved hospital and, in some provinces, services of osteopaths, chiropractors, and optometrists;

free dental care for children; prosthetics; and prescribed drugs. Some cost sharing may be required in such cases.

Administrative Organization

Health Canada (http://www.hc-sc.gc.ca/index_e.html) administers programs for groups not covered under provincial plans; monitors provincial compliance with conditions of national legislation; and provides provinces with technical, consultative, and coordinating services.

Provincial authorities administer their health insurance plans, establish resident eligibility status, assess hospital and medical claims, pay providers, and monitor all aspects of programs.

Providers are usually public, not-for-profit hospitals and other specialized institutions; doctors and allied practitioners in entrepreneurial practice.

Human Resources and Skills Development Canada, through Service Canada (http://www.canadabenefits.gc.ca), is responsible for cash sickness, maternity, parental and compassionate care benefits provided under the Employment Insurance program.

Work Injury

Regulatory Framework

First and current laws: 1908 and 1994 (Newfoundland), 1915 and 1996 (Nova Scotia), 1915 and 1996 (Ontario), 1916 and 1993 (British Columbia), 1916 and 1993 (Manitoba), 1918 and 1994 (New Brunswick), 1918 and 1995 (Alberta), 1928 and 1994 (Quebec), 1930 and 1994 (Saskatchewan), 1949 and 1995 (Prince Edward Island), 1974 and 1992 (Northwest Territories/Nunavut), and 1993 (Yukon).

Type of program: Social insurance system.

Coverage

Employees in industry and commerce (some differences exist among provinces).

Exclusions: Domestic workers, professional athletes, and members of sports clubs (some differences exist among provinces).

Special systems for merchant seamen and federal civil servants.

Source of Funds

Insured person: None.

Self-employed person: Not applicable.

Employer: Total cost, met through contributions varying by industry and according to the assessed degree of risk (large firms in some provinces may self-insure).

Government: None.

Qualifying Conditions

Work injury benefits: There is no minimum qualifying period.

Temporary Disability Benefits

The benefit varies from 75% to 90% of gross earnings, according to province.

There is no nationally enforced minimum benefit. The minimum benefit varies according to province.

Permanent Disability Benefits

Permanent disability pension: In most provinces, the pension is either 75% or 90% of the insured's earnings for full disability.

There is no nationally enforced maximum benefit. The maximum benefit varies according to province.

Partial disability: The pension is equal to a percentage of the full benefit according to the assessed degree of loss of earning capacity; in some provinces, the pension is converted to a lump sum if the assessed degree of loss is 10% or less.

Workers' Medical Benefits

Benefits in all provinces include medical, surgical, nursing, and hospital services; medicines; and appliances.

Survivor Benefits

Survivor pension: The pension varies according to province. The pension is payable to a widow(er).

Orphan's pension: Either a monthly flat-rate pension set slightly higher than that for children residing with a parent or a percentage of the deceased's wages, according to province.

Other dependents (in the absence of a spouse or orphan): A reasonable sum in proportion to the loss of income.

Funeral grant: The grant varies according to province.

Administrative Organization

Workers' Compensation Board, or a Work Safety Commission, in each province and territory administers the program.

Unemployment

Regulatory Framework

First law: 1940.

Current law: 1996 (employment insurance), with amendments.

Type of program: Social insurance system.

Coverage

All salaried workers, including federal government employees; self-employed fishermen.

Exclusions: Self-employed persons other than fishermen.

Source of Funds

Insured person: 1.95% of insurable earnings.

The maximum annual earnings for contribution and benefit purposes are C$39,000.

Self-employed person: Not applicable.

Employer: 2.73% of the insured's earnings.

The maximum annual earnings for contribution and benefit purposes are C$39,000.

Government: None.

Qualifying Conditions

Unemployment benefit: The qualifying conditions vary from 420 hours to 700 hours of covered employment during the last year, depending on the regional unemployment rate, or 910 hours for a new entrant or reentrant to the labor force.

The insured must be registered, able, willing, and available to work and unable to obtain suitable employment; unable to work because of sickness, maternity, or providing parental care or compassionate care to a gravely ill family member with a potentially fatal condition.

If unemployment is due either to voluntary leaving without just cause or to misconduct, the disqualification is indefinite and applies until the insured requalifies for the benefit.

Unemployment Benefits

The benefit is equal to 55% of average insurable earnings in the last 26 weeks, plus a family supplement for low-income and modest-income earners with dependent children. The supplement is awarded if annual net family income (after application of allowable deductions and expenses under the Income Tax Act) is less than C$25,921. The benefit is payable after a 2-week waiting period for between 14 and 45 weeks, depending on the claimant's employment history and regional unemployment rates.

The maximum weekly benefit is C$413.

Administrative Organization

Human Resources and Skills Development Canada, through Service Canada (http://www.canadabenefits.gc.ca) regional and local offices, administers the program.

Canada Revenue Agency (http://www.cra-arc.gc.ca/menu-e.html) collects contributions.

Family Allowances

Regulatory Framework

First law: 1944.

Current law: 1998.

Type of program: Refundable tax credit system.

Coverage

All residents.

Source of Funds

Insured person: None.

Self-employed person: None.

Employer: None.

Government: Total cost.

Qualifying Conditions

A child must be younger than age 18 and live with the primary caregiver who has Canadian citizenship or who has permanent resident, refugee, or visitor status, and who must file an annual income tax return to be eligible.

Family Allowance Benefits

Canada child tax benefit (income-tested): The benefit is delivered through the income tax system.

The maximum annual benefit is C$2,950 for the first child, C$2,730 for the second child, and C$2,734 for the third and subsequent children.

The benefit has two components: the base tax benefit, which is paid to low- and middle-income families with children, and the national child benefit supplement, which is paid to low-income families with children. For the period July 2005 to June 2006, families with net income up to C$96,995 receive the base tax benefit. Families with net income up to C$35,595 also receive the benefit supplement.

The Canada child tax benefit contains an additional benefit of up to C$243 a year for children younger than age 7.

Benefits are paid monthly and are based on total family income during the previous year.

Administrative Organization

Canada Revenue Agency (http://www.cra-arc.gc.ca/menu-e.html) administers the program.

Quebec Pension Board administers the program in Quebec.

Chile

Exchange rate: US$1.00 equals 582.60 pesos.

Old Age, Disability, and Survivors

Regulatory Framework

First law: 1924.

Current laws: 1952 (wage earners and salaried employees); 1980 and 1981 (new system).

Type of program: Mandatory individual account, social insurance, and social assistance system.

Note: A system of mandatory private individual accounts was introduced in May 1981. Workers entering the labor force after December 31, 1982, must join the new system. The social insurance system is being phased out.

Coverage

Mandatory individual account

All private-sector employees.

Voluntary coverage for the self-employed and workers who paid social insurance contributions before January 1, 1983.

Social insurance

Wage earners' program: Wage earners and the self-employed with earnings lower than three times the minimum monthly wage.

The minimum monthly wage is 127,500 pesos.

Salaried employees' program: Salaried employees in private-sector employment.

Special systems for railroad employees, seamen and port workers, public-sector employees, the armed forces, the police, and over 30 other occupations.

Source of Funds

Mandatory individual account

Insured person: 10% of gross earnings for the old-age pension, plus an average 0.75% of gross earnings for disability and survivor insurance and an average 1.55% of gross earnings for administrative fees. (Persons working under arduous conditions contribute an additional 1% or 2% of gross earnings.)

The minimum monthly earnings for contribution purposes are equal to the minimum monthly wage of 127,500 pesos; 95,927 pesos for insured persons younger than age 18 or older than age 65.

The maximum monthly earnings for contribution purposes are equal to 60 UFs (unidad de fomento). The UF is equal to 17,491 pesos and is adjusted monthly according to changes in the consumer price index.

Self-employed person: 10% of declared earnings for the old-age pension, plus an average 0.75% of declared earnings for disability and survivor insurance and an average 1.55% of declared earnings for administrative fees.

The minimum monthly declared earnings for contribution purposes are 82,889 pesos.

The maximum monthly declared earnings for contribution purposes are 60 UFs. The UF is equal to 17,491 pesos and is adjusted monthly according to changes in the consumer price index.

Employer: None, except 1% or 2% of gross earnings for employees working under arduous conditions.

The maximum monthly earnings for contribution purposes are 60 UFs. The UF is equal to 17,491 pesos and is adjusted monthly according to changes in the consumer price index.

Government: The cost of the guaranteed minimum pension.

Social insurance

Insured person: Wage earners contribute 18.84% of wages; salaried employees contribute from 20% to 30% of gross earnings depending on the nature of the job. (A reduction of 7.75% is granted to some workers with 40 years of contributions.)

The minimum monthly earnings for contribution purposes are equal to the minimum monthly wage of 127,500 pesos; 95,927 pesos for insured persons younger than age 18 or older than age 65.

The maximum monthly earnings for contribution purposes are 60 UFs. The UF is equal to 17,491 pesos and is adjusted monthly according to changes in the consumer price index.

Self-employed person: 18.84% of declared income.

The minimum monthly declared earnings for contribution purposes are 82,889 pesos.

The maximum monthly declared earnings for contribution purposes are 60 UFs. The UF is equal to 17,491 pesos and is adjusted monthly according to changes in the consumer price index.

Employer: None.

Government: Special subsidies as needed to finance the program and the cost of the guaranteed minimum pension.

Qualifying Conditions

Mandatory individual account

Old-age pension: Age 65 (men) or age 60 (women).

If aged 55 or older (men) or aged 50 or older (women) on August 19, 2004, retirement before the normal retirement age is possible for insured persons with a pension equal to at least 50% of the insured's average wage in the last 10 years and at least equal to 110% of the minimum old-age pension.

If younger than age 55 (men) or age 50 (women) on August 19, 2004, retirement before the normal retirement age is possible for insured persons with a pension equal to 55% of the insured's average wage in the last 10 years (rising to 70% by August 19, 2010) and at least equal to a 130% of the minimum old-age pension (rising to 150% by August 19, 2007).

The normal retirement age for insured persons with 20 years of contributions is reduced by 2 years or 1 year for each 5 years of work under arduous conditions, depending on the activity. The maximum reduction of the normal retirement age is 10 years.

Guaranteed minimum pension: Age 65 (men) or age 60 (women) with 20 years of contributions if the sum of the insured's pensions, income, and taxable earnings is less than the minimum pension.

Disability pension: Payable for at least a 66% loss in earning capacity. The loss of earning capacity must not be caused by a work-related accident. Coverage is extended for up to 12 months after employment ceases if the insured has 6 months of contributions in the last year of employment.

Partial disability: Payable for the loss of between 50% and 65% of earning capacity. The loss of earning capacity must not be caused by a work-related accident. Coverage is extended for up to 12 months after employment ceases if the insured has 6 months of contributions in the last year of employment.

District medical commissions assess the degree of disability.

Guaranteed minimum pension: Payable with at least 10 years of contributions; at least 2 years of contributions in the 5 years before the onset of disability; at least 16 months of contributions if the insured has less than 2 years of employment; or employed at the onset of disability. The guarantee is paid if the insured's pension is less than the minimum pension.

Survivor pension: The insured was in covered employment (coverage is extended for up to 12 months after employment ceases if the insured had 6 months of contributions in the last year of employment) or was a pensioner at the time of death.

Eligible survivors are a widow or disabled widower who was married to the insured person for at least 6 months (at least 3 years if the insured was a pensioner); the mother of the deceased's children; children younger than age 18 (age 24 if a student, no age limit if disabled); and parents in the absence of other eligible survivors.

Guaranteed minimum pension: Payable if the deceased had at least 10 years of contributions; at least 2 years of contributions in the 5 years before death; at least 16 months of contributions if the deceased had less than 2 years of employment; or employed or a pensioner at the time of death.

Social insurance

Old-age pension: Wage earners must be age 65 with 1,040 weeks of contributions (men); 800 weeks of contributions including 50% of the weeks since coverage began (men); or age 60 with 520 weeks of contributions (women).

Wage earners are not required to cease gainful activity, depending on the nature of the job.

Salaried employees must be age 65 with at least 10 years of contributions (men) or age 60 with at least 10 years of contributions (women).

Salaried employees must cease all gainful activity.

The normal retirement age for insured persons with 1,020 weeks of contributions is reduced by 1 year for each 5 years of work under arduous conditions. The maximum reduction of the normal retirement age is 10 years.

Deferred pension: The pension for a salaried employee is increased for each year of economic activity during which the claim for an old-age pension is deferred.

Disability pension: Wage earners must be assessed as totally or partially disabled and be younger than age 65 (men) or younger than age 60 (women) at the onset of disability. Must have a minimum of 50 weeks of contributions, including at least 40% of the weeks in the last 5 years and 50% of the weeks since coverage began (women are exempt from this last condition, as are men with a total of at least 400 weeks of coverage).

Wage earners are assessed as totally disabled with a loss in earning capacity of at least 70%; partial disability is assessed as a loss in earning capacity of between 30% and 69%.

Preventive and disability medical commissions assess the degree of disability for wage earners.

Salaried employees must be assessed as 2/3 disabled with 3 years of contributions.

Health services assess the degree of disability for salaried employees.

Survivor pension: The pensioner was previously a wage earner; had at least 400 weeks of paid coverage; or at least 50 weeks of paid coverage, including at least 40% of the weeks in the last 5 years and 50% of the weeks since coverage began (women are exempt from this last condition).

The pensioner was previously a salaried employee or had at least 3 years of contributions.

Eligible survivors are a widow(er) who was married for at least 6 months to an insured person who was an active contributor (at least 3 years if the insured was a pensioner); the mother of the deceased's children; and children younger than age 18 (age 24 if students, no limit if disabled).

Funeral grant: The grant is paid to the widow(er), children, or parents.

Social assistance

Old-age assistance pension: Age 65 with 300 weeks of contributions (men) or age 60 with 200 weeks of contributions (women). The insured must have been registered before 1937 and have no entitlement to a pension.

Old-age pension for a low-income person (income-tested): Age 65 (men and women) with 3 years of residence and no entitlement to a pension. Family income must be lower than 50% of the minimum monthly old-age pension (38,538 pesos).

Disability assistance pension: Age 65 (men) or age 60 (women) with 75 weeks of contributions and declared disabled. The insured must have been registered before 1937 and have no entitlement to a pension.

Disability pension for low-income persons (income-tested): Physically or mentally disabled with 3 years of residence and no entitlement to a pension. Individual income must be lower than 50% of the minimum disability pension.

Survivor assistance pension: The pension is paid to a widow older than age 45 and children younger than age 18 (age 24 if a student, no limit if disabled) if the deceased was registered before 1937 and had no entitlement to a pension.

Old-Age Benefits

Mandatory individual account

Old-age pension: The value of the pension is dependent on the insured's contributions plus accrued interest, minus administrative fees. At retirement, the accumulated capital can be used to provide an immediate life annuity, temporary income with a deferred life annuity, programmed withdrawals, or an immediate life annuity with programmed withdrawals. (The value of accrued rights under the social insurance system is combined with the individual account balance.)

Guaranteed minimum pension: The monthly pension is 77,076.54 pesos for a pensioner younger than age 70; 84,277.26 pesos from age 70 up to age 75; or 88,213.76 pesos if older than age 75.

Benefit adjustment: Automatic annual adjustment according to variations in the value of the UF. The UF is equal to 17,491 pesos and is adjusted monthly according to changes in the consumer price index.

Social insurance

Old-age pension: Wage earners receive a monthly pension equal to 50% of the base wage, plus 1% of wages for each 50-week period of contributions beyond 500 weeks.

The base wage is equal to the average monthly wage in the last 5 years, with the first 2 years adjusted for wage changes.

The minimum monthly pension is 77,076.54 pesos for a pensioner younger than age 70; 84,277.26 pesos from age 70 up to age 75; or 88,213.76 pesos if older than age 75.

The maximum monthly pension is 70% of the base wage or 791,578 pesos, whichever is lower.

Salaried employees receive a monthly pension equal to 1/35 of the base salary times the number of years of contributions.

The base salary is equal to the average monthly salary in the last 5 years, with the first 2 years adjusted for salary changes.

Salaried woman's child supplement: A supplement of 1/35 of the base salary is paid for each dependent child to a woman with over 20 years of contributions; 2/35 of the base salary if a widow.

The minimum monthly pension is 77,076.54 pesos for a pensioner younger than age 70; 84,277.26 pesos from age 70 up to age 75; or 88,213.76 pesos if older than age 75.

The maximum monthly pension is 100% of the base salary or 791,578 pesos, whichever is lower.

Deferred pension: For each year of economic activity during which the claim is deferred, the pension is increased by 5% of the base salary, up to a maximum of 25%.

Winter voucher: A lump sum of 31,982 pesos is paid in May.

Benefit adjustment: Automatic annual adjustment of pensions for changes in the consumer price index; may be earlier if the variation of the consumer price index within the year is at least 15%.

Social assistance

Old-age assistance pension: The monthly pension is 43,252.91 pesos for a pensioner younger than age 70; 84,277.26 pesos from age 70 up to age 75; or 88,213.76 pesos if older than age 75.

Old-age pension for a low-income person (income-tested): The minimum monthly pension is 38,572.20 pesos for a pensioner younger than age 70; 40,238.14 pesos from age 70 up to age 75; or 42,195.84 pesos if older than age 75.

Benefit adjustment: Automatic annual adjustment of pensions for changes in the consumer price index; may be earlier if the variation of the consumer price index within the year is at least 15%.

Permanent Disability Benefits

Mandatory individual account

Disability pension: Following an assessment and certification by the medical commission, the AFP (individual pension fund management company) finances a benefit for up to 3 years. The monthly benefit is equal to 70% of the base salary for a total disability; 50% for a partial disability.

The base salary is equal to the average monthly wage in the last 10 years.

Long-term pension: Following a second level of assessment and certification, the pension is financed through the individual account. (Disability insurance tops up the accumulated capital in the individual account if the balance is less than the required minimum to finance the permanent disability pension.)

Guaranteed minimum pension: The monthly pension is 77,076.54 pesos for a pensioner younger than age 70; 84,277.26 pesos from age 70 up to age 75; or 88,213.76 pesos if older than age 75.

Benefit adjustment: Automatic annual adjustment according to variations in the value of the UF. The UF is equal to 17,491 pesos and is adjusted monthly according to changes in the consumer price index.

Social insurance

Disability pension: For a total disability, wage earners receive a monthly pension equal to 50% of the base wage, plus 1% of wages for every 50-week period of contributions beyond 500 weeks.

The base wage is equal to the average monthly wage in the last 5 years, with the first 2 years adjusted for wage changes.

The minimum monthly disability pension is 77,076.54 pesos for a pensioner younger than age 70; 84,277.26 pesos from age 70 up to age 75; or 88,213.76 pesos if older than age 75.

The maximum monthly disability pension is 70% of the base wage or 791,578 pesos, whichever is lower.

Partial disability: 50% of the total disability pension.

Salaried employees receive a monthly pension equal to 70% of the base salary, plus 2% of the salary for every year of contributions beyond 20 years.

The base salary is equal to the average monthly salary in the last 5 years, with the first 2 years adjusted for salary changes.

The minimum monthly disability pension is 77,076.54 pesos for a pensioner younger than age 70; 84,277.26 pesos from age 70 up to age 75; or 88,213.76 pesos if older than age 75.

The maximum monthly disability pension is 100% of the base salary or 791,578 pesos, whichever is lower.

Salaried woman's child supplement: A supplement of 1/35 of the base salary is paid for each dependent child to a woman with over 20 years of contributions; 2/35 of the base salary if a widow.

Benefit adjustment: Automatic annual adjustment of pensions for changes in the consumer price index; may be earlier if the variation of the consumer price index within the year is at least 15%.

Social assistance

Disability assistance pension: The monthly pension is 43,252.91 pesos for a pensioner younger than age 70; 84,277.26 pesos from age 70 up to age 75; or 88,213.76 pesos if older than age 75.

Disability pension for a low-income person (income-tested): The minimum monthly pension is 38,572.20 pesos for a pensioner younger than age 70; 40,238.14 pesos from age 70 up to age 75; or 42,195.84 pesos if older than age 75.

Benefit adjustment: Automatic annual adjustment of pensions for changes in the consumer price index; may be earlier if the variation of the consumer price index within the year is at least 15%.

Survivor Benefits

Mandatory individual account

Survivor pension: A widow or a disabled widower without eligible children receives a monthly pension equal to 60% of the deceased's pension (43% for a partially disabled widower); 50% if a pension is also paid to children (36% for a partially disabled widower). The mother of the insured's extramarital children receives 36% of the deceased's pension; 30% if the children are younger than age 18 (age 24 if a student, no limit if disabled). Each orphan younger than age 18 (age 24 if a student, no limit if disabled) receives 15% of the deceased's pension; 11% for each partially disabled orphan older than age 24.

Other eligible survivors (in the absence of the above): A parent receives 50% of the deceased's monthly pension.

If the deceased was actively contributing to an individual account, survivor pensions are calculated according to a reference pension equal to 70% of the average monthly wage in the last 10 years.

The pension paid as the result of the death of an insured person or a temporary disability beneficiary is financed with the deceased's individual account balance; if the deceased was a pensioner, the type of benefit depends on the type of pension that the deceased chose. (Life insurance tops up the accumulated capital in the deceased's individual account if the balance is less than the required minimum to finance the survivor pension.)

The minimum monthly widow(er) pension varies from 39,309.05 pesos to 88,213.76 pesos, depending on the survivor's age and the number of children.

The minimum monthly orphan's pension varies from 8,855.59 pesos to 13,232.66 pesos.

There is no maximum survivor pension.

Benefit adjustment: Automatic annual adjustment according to variations in the value of the UF. The UF is equal to 17,491 pesos and is adjusted monthly according to changes in the consumer price index.

Funeral grant: A withdrawal of 15 UFs (262,365 pesos) form the deceased's individual account is granted to the relative who paid for the funeral expenses. The UF is equal to 17,491 pesos and is adjusted monthly according to changes in the consumer price index.

Social insurance

Survivor pension (wage earner): The monthly pension paid to a wage earner's widow of any age or a disabled widower is equal to 50% of the base wage (50% of the disability pension payable to the deceased) or 100% of the deceased's pension. Each orphan receives 20% of the base wage or average monthly pension in the preceding year. The mother of the deceased's extramarital children receives 60% of the widow pension.

The pension is suspended if the widow(er) remarries.

A widow younger than age 55 receives a lump sum equal to 2 years' pension.

The minimum monthly widow(er) pension is 50,017.65 pesos for a survivor younger than age 70 without children; 62,409.54 pesos from age 70. The minimum monthly widow(er) pension is 41,838.53 pesos for a survivor younger than age 70 with children; 53,892.19 pesos from age 70.

The minimum monthly orphan's pension is 11,561.48 pesos.

The minimum monthly survivor pension is 30,010.58 pesos for the deceased's extramarital partner younger than age 70 without children; 41,590.72 pesos from age 70. The minimum monthly survivor pension is 25,103.12 pesos for the deceased's extramarital partner younger than age 70 with children; 36,480.38 pesos from age 70.

The maximum monthly survivor pension is 791,578 pesos.

Benefit adjustment: Automatic annual adjustment of pensions for changes in the consumer price index; may be earlier if the variation of the consumer price index within the year is at least 15%.

Funeral grant: For the funeral of a wage earner or pensioner, the grant is equal to three times the monthly minimum income used for funeral grant calculation purposes (234,150 pesos).

Survivor pension (salaried employee): For a salaried employee's widow or dependent widower, the monthly pension is equal to 50% of the deceased's base salary (the average monthly wage in the last 5 years) or the deceased's pension. Each orphan and dependent parent receives 15% of the base salary or deceased's pension. The mother of the deceased's extramarital children receives 60% of the widow pension.

The pension ceases if the widow(er) remarries, and the pension is paid to eligible children.

The minimum monthly widow(er) pension is 50,017.65 pesos for a survivor younger than age 70 without children; 62,409.54 pesos from age 70. The minimum monthly

widow(er) pension is 41,838.53 pesos for a survivor younger than age 70 with children; 53,892.19 pesos from age 70.

The minimum monthly orphan's pension is 11,561.48 pesos.

The minimum monthly survivor pension is 30,010.58 pesos for the deceased's extramarital partner younger than age 70 without children; 41,590.72 pesos from age 70. The minimum monthly survivor pension is 25,103.12 pesos for the deceased's extramarital partner younger than age 70 with children; 36,480.38 pesos from age 70.

The maximum survivor pension is 100% of the deceased's base salary or pension, or 791,578 pesos, whichever is lower.

Benefit adjustment: Automatic annual adjustment of pensions for changes in the consumer price index; may be earlier if the variation of the consumer price index within the year is at least 15%.

Funeral grant: For the funeral of a salaried employee or pensioner, the grant is equal to three times the monthly minimum income used for funeral grant calculation purposes (234,150 pesos).

Social assistance

Survivor assistance pension: For a widow(er) without children, the monthly pension is 25,008.83 pesos; 20,919.26 pesos with children.

The monthly orphan's pension is 5,780.74 pesos.

Benefit adjustment: Automatic annual adjustment of pensions for changes in the consumer price index; may be earlier if the variation of the consumer price index within the year is at least 15%.

Administrative Organization

Mandatory individual account

Superintendent of Pension Fund Management Companies (http://www.safjp.cl) provides general supervision.

Individual pension fund management companies (AFPs) administer individual capitalization accounts.

Social insurance

Ministry of Labor and Social Welfare, through the Superintendent of Social Security (http://www.suseso.cl), provides general supervision.

Institute of Social Security Normalization (http://www.inp.cl) administers the program and pays social security and social assistance benefits.

Sickness and Maternity

Regulatory Framework

First law: 1924.

Current laws: 1979 (national health system), with 2004 amendment; 1985 (public health system), implemented in 1986; 1990 (private health system); and 2004 (health guarantees), implemented in 2005.

Type of program: Social insurance and private insurance system.

Note: Insured persons choose to be covered by the public national health system or by private social security health institutes.

Coverage

Public and private systems: All public- and private-sector workers; the self-employed; contract workers; pensioners; persons receiving work injury, unemployment, or social assistance benefits; persons entitled to family allowances; and pregnant women. (Persons without earnings, beneficiaries of social assistance pensions, and pregnant women and mothers up to 6 months after child-birth are covered by the public system.)

Those who opt out of the public system must sign a contract with a private health institution.

Voluntary coverage for all other persons.

Source of Funds

Public system

Insured person: 7% of gross earnings; pensioners, 7% of the pension; voluntary contributors, 7% of declared earnings.

The minimum monthly earnings for contribution purposes are equal to the minimum monthly wage (127,500 pesos); 95,927 pesos for insured persons younger than age 18 or older than age 65; 82,889 pesos for voluntary contributors.

The maximum monthly earnings for contribution purposes are equal to 60 UFs (unidad de fomento). The UF is equal to 17,491 pesos and is adjusted monthly according to changes in the consumer price index.

Self-employed person: 7% of declared earnings.

The minimum monthly declared earnings for contribution purposes are 82,889 pesos.

The maximum monthly earnings for contribution purposes are equal to 60 UFs. The UF is equal to 17,491 pesos and is adjusted monthly according to changes in the consumer price index.

Employer: None.

Government: Subsidizes maternity benefits and meets any deficit.

Private system

Insured person: 7% of gross earnings; pensioners, 7% of the pension.

Voluntary contributors must pay the total cost of the plan.

The minimum monthly earnings for contribution purposes are equal to the minimum monthly salary (127,500 pesos); 95,927 pesos for insured persons younger than age 18 or older than age 65.

The maximum monthly earnings for contribution purposes are equal to 60 UFs. The UF is equal to 17,491 pesos and is adjusted monthly according to changes in the consumer price index.

Self-employed person: 7% of declared earnings.

The minimum monthly declared earnings for contribution purposes are 82,889 pesos.

The maximum monthly earnings for contribution purposes are equal to 60 UFs. The UF is equal to 17,491 pesos and is adjusted monthly according to changes in the consumer price index.

Employer: None.

Government: Subsidizes maternity benefits.

Qualifying Conditions

Cash sickness and maternity benefits: Workers with a total of 6 months of contributions including 3 months of contributions in the last 6 months; contract workers with a total of 6 months of contributions including 30 days of contributions in the last 12 months; and self-employed persons with 12 months of enrollment and 6 months of contributions in the last 12 months.

Medical benefits: Currently covered.

The qualifying conditions for the public and private systems are the same.

Sickness and Maternity Benefits

Public system

Sickness benefit: For public-sector employees, the benefit is equal to 100% of net earnings before the onset of incapacity. For private-sector employees, the benefit is equal to average monthly net earnings in the last 3 months. For self-employed persons, the benefit is equal to average monthly declared earnings in the last 6 months.

Sickness benefits are paid from the first day if sick leave is longer than 9 days; from the fourth day if sick leave is shorter than 10 days. The employer is not required to pay benefits for the first 3 days, unless established under a collective agreement.

The duration of benefit is the same as the period of sick leave.

The minimum daily sickness benefit is 1,381.48 pesos.

Maternity benefit: For employees, the monthly benefit is equal to average monthly net earnings in the 3 months before the expected date of childbirth. For self-employed persons, the monthly benefit is equal to average monthly declared earnings in the last 6 months. Benefit is payable for 6 weeks before and 12 weeks after the expected date of childbirth.

The minimum daily maternity benefit is 1,381.48 pesos.

Maternity benefit is paid for 12 months for the adoption of a child younger than 6 months.

Private system

Sickness benefit: No benefits are provided.

Maternity benefit: No benefits are provided.

Workers' Medical Benefits

Public system

Medical benefits: Benefits are provided to patients through public or private health institutions and professionals registered with the Ministry of Health. Benefits include general and specialist care, periodic medical examinations, hospitalization, medicines, dental care, and maternity care.

There is no limit to duration.

General Scheme of Health Guarantees establishes the minimum benefits to be provided by the public system.

Cost sharing: 0%, 20%, or 30% depending on the insured's income and dependents; from 30% to 80% for dental treatment.

There is no cost-sharing for primary assistance and for low-income persons, beneficiaries of assistance pensions or family allowances, and persons older than age 65.

Private system

Medical benefits: The insured signs a minimum 12-month contract with a private health institute. The insured may choose among open or closed plans or preferred doctor plans. Benefits, as well as cost sharing, vary by contract but must not be less than those provided by the public system.

Dependents' Medical Benefits

Public system

Medical benefits: Benefits include general and specialist care, periodic medical examinations, hospitalization, medicines, dental care, and maternity care.

There is no limit to duration.

General Scheme of Health Guarantees establishes the minimum benefits to be provided by the public system.

Cost sharing: 0%, 20%, or 30% depending on the insured's income and dependents; from 30% to 80% for dental treatment.

There is no cost sharing for primary assistance and for low-income persons, beneficiaries of assistance pensions or family allowances, and persons older than age 65.

Private system

Medical benefits: Benefits, as well as cost sharing, vary by contract but must not be less than those provided by the public system.

The widow(er) and children are covered for a year after the insured's death.

Administrative Organization

Ministry of Health (http://www.minsal.cl) provides general supervision of the system.

Superintendent of Health (http://www.superintendenciadesalud.cl) oversees the public and private schemes and public and private health providers.

National Health Fund (http://www.fonasa.gov.cl) administers cash benefits and the public system.

Health Institutions (http://www.isapre.cl) administer the private system.

Work Injury

Regulatory Framework

First law: 1916.

Current law: 1968 (work injury and professional diseases).

Type of program: Social insurance system.

Coverage

All public- and private-sector workers, domestic workers, contract and temporary workers, students, some self-employed persons, apprentices, and trade union representatives.

Exclusions: Some self-employed persons.

Source of Funds

Insured person: None.

Self-employed person: 0.95% of declared income, plus up to 3.4% of declared earnings, depending on the activity.

The minimum monthly declared earnings for contribution purposes are 82,889 pesos.

The maximum monthly earnings for contribution purposes are equal to 60 UFs (unidad de fomento). The UF is equal to 17,491 pesos and is adjusted monthly according to changes in the consumer price index.

Employer: 0.95% of payroll, plus up to 3.4% of payroll according to the industry and the assessed degree of risk.

The minimum monthly earnings for contribution purposes are equal to the minimum monthly wage (127,500 pesos); 95,927 pesos for insured persons younger than age 18 or older than age 65; and 95,625 pesos for domestic workers.

The maximum monthly earnings for contribution purposes are equal to 60 UFs. The UF is equal to 17,491 pesos and is adjusted monthly according to changes in the consumer price index.

Government: None; contributes as an employer.

Qualifying Conditions

Work injury benefits: There is no minimum qualifying period. Accidents that occur while commuting to and from work are covered.

Self-employed persons must have paid all due contributions.

Temporary Disability Benefits

For public-sector employees, the monthly benefit is equal to 100% of net earnings. For private-sector employees, the monthly benefit is equal to average monthly net earnings in the 3 months before the onset of disability. The benefit is payable from the day of injury for up to 12 months (may be extended up to 24 months).

The maximum monthly pension is 791,578 pesos.

Benefit adjustment: Benefits are adjusted according to wage increases.

Permanent Disability Benefits

Permanent disability pension: With an assessed degree of disability of at least 70% (total disability), the monthly pension is equal to 70% of the base salary; 22.3% of the minimum monthly wage for students with earnings lower than 44.5% of the minimum monthly wage (127,500 pesos).

The base salary is equal to average monthly net earnings in the 6 months before the onset of disability.

The maximum monthly pension is 791,578 pesos.

In most cases, Preventive and Disability Medical Commissions assess the degree of disability. The degree of disability is reassessed once every 2 years in the 8 years after the pension is awarded.

Constant-attendance allowance: The pension is increased by 30% of the base salary.

Child supplement: The pension is increased by 5% for the third and each subsequent child entitled to family allowances.

Partial disability: With an assessed degree of disability of between 40% and 70%, the monthly pension is equal to 35% of the base salary. A lump sum of up to 15 months' base salary is paid for an assessed degree of disability of 15% to 40%.

Students with an assessed degree of disability of between 15% and 70% and with earnings lower than the minimum monthly wage (127,500 pesos) receive a monthly benefit equal to 22.3% of the monthly minimum wage.

Benefit adjustment: Automatic annual adjustment of pensions for changes in the consumer price index; may be earlier if the variation of the consumer price index within the year is at least 15%.

Workers' Medical Benefits

Benefits include necessary medical, surgical, dental, and pharmaceutical services; hospitalization; prosthesis; rehabilitation; transfer costs, and occupational retraining. Benefits are provided from the first day after the onset of disability or diagnosis of the occupational disease. Occupational diseases are defined according to a schedule in law.

There is no limit to duration.

There is no cost sharing.

Survivor Benefits

Survivor pension: A monthly benefit equal to 50% of the deceased's pension is payable to a widow older than age 44 (at any age if disabled or caring for a child) or a disabled widower.

A widow younger than age 45 receives a limited pension for a year. If a widow caring for a child reaches age 45 during the eligible period, the benefit becomes payable for life.

The minimum monthly pension is 50,017.65 pesos for a widow(er) younger than age 70 without children; 62,409.54 pesos from age 70. The minimum monthly pension is 41,838.53 pesos for a widow(er) younger than age 70 with children; 53,892.19 pesos from age 70.

The pension ceases if the widow(er) remarries, and a lump sum equal to 2 years' pension is paid.

Orphan's pension: A monthly pension equal to 20% of the deceased's pension is paid for each orphan younger than age 18 (age 24 if a student, no limit if disabled); 50% for each full orphan.

The minimum monthly orphan's pension is 11,561.48 pesos.

The maximum survivor pension is 100% of the deceased's pension.

Benefit adjustment: Automatic annual adjustment of pensions for changes in the consumer price index; may be earlier if the variation of the consumer price index within the year is at least 15%.

Funeral grant: For the funeral of a wage earner, a salaried employee, or a pensioner, the grant is equal to three times the monthly minimum income used for funeral grant calculation purposes (234,150 pesos); 44.5% of the minimum monthly wage (127,500 pesos) for a student.

Administrative Organization

Ministry of Labor and Social Welfare, through the Superintendent of Social Security (http://www.suseso.cl), provides general supervision.

Institute of Social Security Normalization (http://www.inp.cl) and three employers' mutual societies administer the program.

Unemployment

Regulatory Framework

First law: 1937.

Current laws: 1981 (unemployment), implemented in 1982; and 2001 (severance account system), implemented in 2002.

Type of program: Employment-related and mandatory individual severance account system.

Coverage

Employment-related system: Employed persons.

Individual severance account: Employed persons; new entrants aged 18 or older and workers who sign a new work agreement after October 1, 2002.

Voluntary coverage for other persons.

Exclusions: Persons younger than age 18, domestic workers, apprentices, pensioners (unless partially disabled), the self-employed, and armed forces personnel.

Source of Funds

Employment-related system

Insured person: None.

Self-employed person: None.

Employer: None.

Government: Total cost met through the Unified Family Allowances and Unemployment Fund.

Individual severance account

Insured person: 0.6% of gross monthly earnings (plus an administrative fee) for up to 11 years for each job; voluntary contributors, 0.6% of gross monthly earnings (plus an administrative fee). Workers employed under a fixed-term contract do not contribute.

The maximum monthly earnings for contribution purposes are equal to 90 UFs (unidad de fomento). The UF is equal to 17,491 pesos and is adjusted monthly according to changes in the consumer price index.

Self-employed person: Not applicable.

Employer: 2.4% of payroll a month for up to 11 years (1.6% to the insured's individual account and 0.8% to the Solidarity Severance Fund). If an employee has more than one employment contract, each employer must contribute (3% of earnings for workers employed under a fixed-term contract).

The maximum monthly earnings for contribution purposes are equal to 90 UFs. The UF is equal to 17,491 pesos and is adjusted monthly according to changes in the consumer price index.

Government: Annual contribution to the Solidarity Severance Fund.

Qualifying Conditions

Unemployment benefits

Employment-related system: Must be involuntarily unemployed with 12 months of contributions in the previous 2 years, registered for employment, and able and willing to work. The receipt of benefit with an individual severance account benefit is not possible.

Individual severance account: Must be voluntarily or involuntarily unemployed with at least 12 months of contributions; insured persons with fixed-term contracts must have 6 months of contributions since they first joined the system or since the individual account was last fully drawn down. The benefit is suspended if the insured starts a new job.

If the balance in the individual account is insufficient to pay a benefit, the insured is eligible for a benefit under the Solidarity Severance Fund provided that unemployment was involuntary and the insured had contributed 12 months before unemployment began, was not employed on a fixed-term contract, and had not refused a suitable job offer. Benefit under the Solidarity Severance Fund is available only twice in any 5-year period.

Unemployment Benefits

Unemployment benefit

Employment-related system: For the first 90 days, the benefit is equal to 17,338 pesos a month; between 91 days and 180 days, 11,560 pesos a month; between 181 days and 360 days, 8,669 pesos a month.

Persons who are eligible for benefits may also continue to receive family allowances, maternity benefits, and medical benefits.

If benefit ceases because the insured has started a new job before 360 days of benefits have been paid, but the insured subsequently becomes unemployed again, the insured may continue receiving the benefit for the remaining period, up to the maximum of 360 days.

Individual severance account: The benefit paid depends on the individual account balance, plus accrued interest. The benefit decreases each month and lasts from 1 to

5 months depending on the length of the contribution period: with at least 12 months and up to 17 months of contributions, 1 month of benefit is paid; with 18 to 29 months, 2 months; with 30 to 41 months, 3 months; with 42 to 53 months, 4 months; and with 54 months, 5 months.

The first monthly benefit is calculated as a percentage of total contributions, and the amounts of the second and following payments are 90%, 80%, and 70% of the first monthly amount, respectively. The fifth payment is equal to the remaining balance in the individual account.

If the insured is eligible to a benefit from the Solidarity Severance Fund, the fund may top up the individual account benefit. The first monthly benefit is equal to 50% of average earnings in the last 12 months; 45% for the second; 40% for the third; 35% for the fourth; and 30% for the fifth month.

Insured persons leaving employment under a fixed-term contract or who retire (not under temporary disability benefit) are entitled to a single lump-sum payment equal to the total accumulated capital in the individual account, plus interest. If the insured dies before retirement, the accumulated capital is transferred to a named survivor.

The insured can opt to stop receiving benefits in order to safeguard the accumulated capital for a future period of unemployment. Persons who are eligible for benefits may also continue to receive family allowances, maternity benefits, and medical benefits.

The minimum monthly benefit is equal to the minimum wage (127,500 pesos).

The minimum monthly benefit for insured workers entitled to a Solidarity Severance Fund benefit is 67,292 pesos for the first payment, decreasing gradually to 31,058 pesos for the fifth payment.

The maximum monthly benefit for insured workers entitled to a Solidarity Severance Fund benefit is 129,408 pesos for the first payment, decreasing gradually to 77,645 pesos for the fifth payment.

Benefits are paid 10 days after the claim is accepted.

Benefit adjustment: The minimum and maximum benefits provided under the Solidarity Severance Fund are adjusted annually in February according to the consumer price index.

Administrative Organization

Employment-related system: Ministry of Labor and Social Welfare, through the Superintendent of Social Security (http://www.suseso.cl), provides general supervision.

Institute of Social Security Normalization (http://www.inp.cl) and Family Allowance Compensation Funds administers the program.

Individual severance account: Superintendent of Pension Fund Management Companies (http://www.safjp.cl) provides general supervision.

Society of Severance Fund Managers (http://afcchile.cl), instituted by the six pension fund management companies, administers the program.

Family Allowances

Regulatory Framework

First laws: 1937 (salaried employees) and 1953 (wage earners).

Current laws: 1981 (low-income persons), with 1996 amendment; and 1981 (wage earners and salaried employees), implemented in 1982, with 1999 amendment.

Type of program: Employment-related (unified program for wage and salaried workers) system.

Note: A social assistance program provides cash benefits to persons assessed as needy.

Coverage

All public- and private-sector workers; some self-employed persons; persons receiving work injury, temporary disability, or unemployment benefits; and pensioners.

Exclusions: Some self-employed persons.

Source of Funds

Insured person: None.

Self-employed: None.

Employer: None.

Government: Total cost met through the Unified Family Allowances and Severance-pay Fund.

Qualifying Conditions

Family allowances (income-tested): The child must be younger than age 18 (age 24 if a student; no limit if disabled); benefit is also payable from the fifth month of pregnancy.

Allowances are also paid for a wife, a disabled husband, a widowed mother, stepchildren, orphaned or abandoned grandchildren and great-grandchildren, orphans, and disabled or aged parents older than age 65 (no limit if disabled). All beneficiaries must be the insured's dependent and have monthly earnings lower than 63,750 pesos.

Maternity allowance (income-tested): Paid from childbirth for up to 9 months.

Family Allowance Benefits

Family allowances (income-tested): A monthly allowance is paid for each dependent, depending on the insured's income: 3,930 pesos with monthly earnings up to 122,329 pesos; 3,823 pesos with earnings between 122,329 and 239,606 pesos; and 1,245 pesos with earnings between 239,605 and 373,703 pesos.

All monthly allowances are doubled for disabled dependents.

Income test: No allowance is paid with monthly earnings of 373,702 pesos or more.

Maternity allowance (income-tested): An allowance is paid for 9 months, depending on the insured's income: 3,930 pesos with monthly earnings up to 122,329 pesos; 3,823 pesos with earnings between 122,329 and 239,606 pesos; and 1,245 pesos with earnings between 239,605 and 373,703 pesos.

All monthly allowances are doubled for disabled dependents.

Income test: No allowance is paid with monthly earnings of 373,702 pesos or more.

Benefit adjustment: Benefits are adjusted periodically.

Administrative Organization

Ministry of Labor and Social Welfare, through the Superintendent of Social Security (http://www.suseso.cl), provides general supervision.

Institute of Social Security Normalization (http://www.inp.cl) and Family Allowance Compensation Funds administer the program.

Colombia

Exchange rate: US$1.00 equals 2,338.14 pesos.

Old Age, Disability, and Survivors

Regulatory Framework

First law: 1946, implemented in 1965.

Current law: 1993 (social insurance), implemented in 1994, with 2003 amendments.

Type of program: Social insurance and mandatory individual account system.

Note: The insured may choose either the social insurance system or the system of mandatory individual accounts and may switch membership every 3 years.

The labor code requires larger employers to provide generally similar benefits to employees in regions where either program has not yet been applied.

Coverage

All employees, including public-sector employees, domestic workers, and new employees joining the state oil company (Ecopetrol) after January 29, 2003; and the self-employed. (The program is being gradually extended to all regions.)

Exclusions: Agricultural employees in some regions.

Voluntary coverage is possible.

Special systems for employees of the state oil company (Ecopetrol) who joined before January 30, 2003; teachers; armed forces personnel; and national police personnel.

Source of Funds

Insured person: 3.75% of earnings (3.875% of earnings from January 2006), plus 1% of earnings for income greater than four times the minimum wage and between 0.2% and 1% of earnings for income greater than 16 times the minimum wage to finance the solidarity fund, which subsidizes low earners. (Insured persons who opt for the individual account also contribute up to a maximum of 1.39% of earnings for disability and survivor insurance and up to a maximum of 1.61% of earnings for administrative fees.)

The minimum earnings for contribution purposes are equal to the legal monthly minimum wage (381,500 pesos); half the legal monthly minimum wage for domestic workers.

The maximum earnings for contribution purposes are equal to 25 times the legal monthly minimum wage (381,500 pesos).

Self-employed person: 15% of declared earnings (15.5% of declared earnings from January 2006.) (Self-employed persons who opt for the individual account also contribute up to a maximum of 1.39% of declared earnings for disability and survivor insurance and up to a maximum of 1.61% of declared earnings for administrative fees.)

The minimum earnings for contribution purposes are equal to the legal monthly minimum wage (381,500 pesos).

Employer: 11.25% of payroll (11.625% of payroll from January 2006.)

The minimum earnings for contribution purposes are equal to the legal monthly minimum wage (381,500 pesos).

The maximum earnings for contribution purposes are equal to 25 times the legal monthly minimum wage (381,500 pesos).

Government: A partial subsidy to the solidarity fund; contributes as an employer.

Qualifying Conditions

Old-age pension

Note: Insured persons who were aged 40 (men) or aged 35 (women) and workers with 15 years of contributions when the mandatory individual account system was implemented receive social insurance benefits.

Social insurance old-age pension: Age 60 (men) or age 55 (women) with 1,050 weeks of contributions.

Beginning January 2006, the required number of weeks of contributions is to increase by 25 weeks each year, up to a maximum of 1,300 weeks by 2015.

Special pension: Aged 50 to 55 with 1,050 weeks of contributions for certain hazardous forms of employment, according to specified qualifying conditions.

Social insurance old-age settlement: Payable if the insured does not meet the full qualifying conditions for a social insurance old-age pension.

Mandatory individual account: Payable if the accumulated capital in the individual account is sufficient to purchase an annuity greater than 110% of the minimum wage.

Guaranteed minimum pension: Age 62 (men) or age 57 (women) with 1,150 weeks of contributions and the pension (based on the value of the accumulated capital plus accrued interest) is less than the minimum pension set by law.

Disability pension: If younger than age 20, the insured must be assessed with at least a 50% loss in normal earning capacity and have 26 weeks of contributions in the year before the onset of disability. If aged 20 or older, the insured must have 50 weeks of contributions in the last 3 years and contributions for at least 20% of the period between age 20 and the onset of disability.

The assessed degree of disability is reviewed every 3 years.

Disability settlement: Payable if the insured does not meet the qualifying conditions for a disability pension.

Survivor pension: If the deceased was younger than age 20, must have had 50 weeks of contributions at the time of death. If the deceased was aged 20 or older, must have had 50 weeks of contributions in the last 3 years and contributions for 25% of the period between age 20 and the date of death if the death was the result of an illness; 20% of the period if the death was the result of an accident.

Survivor settlement: Payable if the deceased did not meet the qualifying conditions for a pension.

Old-Age Benefits

Old-age pension

Social insurance old-age pension: The pension is equal to between 55% and 65% of the basic monthly wage, plus 1.5% for each 50-week period of contributions, up to a maximum of 80% of the basic monthly wage.

The basic monthly wage is based on the insured's average earnings in the last 10 years before receiving the pension.

The minimum earnings for benefit calculation purposes are equal to the legal monthly minimum wage (381,500 pesos).

The maximum earnings for benefit calculation purposes are equal to 25 times the legal monthly minimum wage (381,500 pesos).

The minimum social insurance pension is equal to the legal monthly minimum wage (381,500 pesos).

Schedule of payments: Thirteen or fourteen payments a year, according to the value of the pension.

Benefit adjustment: Pensions are adjusted annually for changes in the consumer price index.

Social insurance old-age settlement: If the insured does not meet the contributions requirement at the normal retirement age, a pension is provided.

Mandatory individual account: The pension is based on the value of the insured's contributions plus accrued interest. At retirement, the insured may make periodic withdrawals from the individual account to guarantee income for the expected lifespan, buy an annuity from a private insurance company, or a combination of the two. (The value of accrued rights under the social insurance system is combined with the individual account balance.)

Guaranteed minimum pension: If the pension is less than the minimum pension set by law, the government makes up the difference.

Permanent Disability Benefits

Disability pension: For an assessed degree of disability greater than 66%, the pension is equal to 54% of the basic monthly wage, plus 2% of earnings for each 50-week period of contributions exceeding 800 weeks. For an assessed degree of disability of between 50% and 66%, the pension is equal to 45% of the basic monthly wage, plus 1.5% of

earnings for each 50-week period of contributions exceeding 500 weeks. (Disability insurance tops up the accumulated capital in the individual account if the balance is less than the required minimum to finance the permanent disability pension.)

The basic monthly wage is based on the insured's average earnings in the last 10 years before receiving the pension.

The minimum earnings for benefit calculation purposes are equal to the legal monthly minimum wage (381,500 pesos).

The maximum earnings for benefit calculation purposes are equal to 25 times the legal monthly minimum wage (381,500 pesos).

The minimum pension is equal to the legal monthly minimum wage (381,500 pesos).

The maximum pension is equal to 75% of the basic monthly wage.

Schedule of payments: Thirteen or fourteen payments a year, according to the value of the pension.

Benefit adjustment: Pensions are adjusted annually for changes in the consumer price index.

Disability settlement: If the insured does not meet the contributions requirements for a disability pension, a pension is provided.

Survivor Benefits

Survivor pension: The pension is equal to 45% of the basic monthly wage, plus 2% for each 50-week period of contributions exceeding 500 weeks, up to a maximum of 75% of the basic monthly wage. (Life insurance tops up the accumulated capital in the deceased's individual account if the balance is less than the required minimum to finance the survivor pension.)

The basic monthly wage is based on the deceased's average earnings in the last 10 years.

Orphan's pension: Each orphan younger than age 18 (age 25 if a student, no limit if disabled) receives 20% of the deceased's pension; 30% for a full orphan. (Life insurance tops up the accumulated capital in the deceased's individual account if the balance is less than the required minimum to finance the survivor pension.)

The minimum earnings for benefit calculation purposes are equal to the legal monthly minimum wage (381,500 pesos).

The maximum earnings for benefit calculation purposes are equal to 25 times the legal monthly minimum wage (381,500 pesos).

The minimum survivor pension is equal to the legal monthly minimum wage (381,500 pesos).

The maximum survivor pension is equal to 100% of the deceased's pension.

Schedule of payments: Thirteen or fourteen payments a year, according to the value of the pension.

Survivor settlement: A pension is provided to dependents.

Funeral grant: The cost of the funeral up to the value of the monthly old-age pension or the last wage, but not less than five times and not greater than 10 times the legal monthly minimum wage (381,500 pesos).

Administrative Organization

Social insurance: Ministry of Labor and Social Security (http://www.minproteccionsocial.gov.co) provides general supervision.

Social Security Institute (http://www.iss.gov.co) administers the program nationally.

Regional funds and local offices, established and supervised by the Social Security Institute, administer contributions and benefits locally.

Mandatory individual account: National Banking Superintendent (http://www.superbancaria.gov.co) provides general supervision.

Individual pension fund management companies (SAFPs) administer individual accounts.

Sickness and Maternity

Regulatory Framework

First law: 1938.

Current laws: 1993 (social insurance), implemented in 1994, with 2003 amendments; and 2002 (parental leave).

Type of program: Social insurance system. Cash and medical benefits.

Coverage

All resident employees, including pensioners, students, and apprentices; self-employed workers and residents with earnings greater than twice the legal minimum monthly wage (381,500 pesos).

Coverage is to be extended gradually to all, regardless of their ability to contribute.

Special systems for armed forces personnel and national police personnel.

Source of Funds

Insured person: 4% of earnings.

The minimum earnings for contribution purposes are equal to the legal minimum monthly wage (381,500 pesos); half the legal minimum monthly wage for domestic workers.

Self-employed person: 12% of declared earnings.

Declared earnings for contribution purposes are equal to 1.5 or 2 times the legal minimum monthly wage (381,500 pesos), depending on trade union affiliation.

Employer: 8% of payroll; 12% for students and apprentices.

The minimum earnings for contribution purposes are equal to the legal minimum monthly wage (381,500 pesos).

Government: Finances the program for low earners through the solidarity fund and through additional government contributions; contributes as an employer.

Qualifying Conditions

Cash sickness and medical benefits: Must have 4 weeks of contributions immediately before the claim, except in emergency cases.

Cash maternity benefits: Must have 9 months of contributions before the expected date of childbirth. (Benefits are also payable to parents of adopted children.)

Paternity leave: Fathers must have 100 weeks of contributions.

Sickness and Maternity Benefits

Sickness benefit: The benefit is equal to 66.6% of the insured's earnings in the month before the onset of incapacity and is payable after a 4-day waiting period for up to 180 days.

Maternity benefit: The benefit is equal to 100% of the insured's earnings and is payable for 12 weeks. The spouse may take one of the 12 weeks as paternity leave, with the benefit period for the mother reduced to 11 weeks.

Paternity leave: Up to 4 days of paid leave; 8 days if both parents are insured.

Workers' Medical Benefits

The insured may choose either public or private health care. Benefits and facilities vary depending on the health plan. Benefits include medical, surgical, hospital, pharmaceutical, maternity, and dental care and related services. Preexisting conditions must be covered, although they may be subject to a waiting period; no waiting period for pregnant women.

Dependents' Medical Benefits

The insured may choose either public or private health care. Benefits and facilities vary depending on the health plan. Benefits include medical, surgical, hospital, pharmaceutical, maternity, and dental care and related services. Preexisting conditions must be covered, although they may be subject to a waiting period; no waiting period for pregnant women and babies younger than 1 year.

Administrative Organization

Superintendent of Health (http://www.supersalud.gov.co) provides general supervision.

Ministry of Labor and Social Security (http://www.minproteccionsocial.gov.co) and the National Social Security Council on Health administer the program.

State Social Enterprises (ESSs) and private health institutions (IPSs) provide health services.

Work Injury

Regulatory Framework

First law: 1915.

Current laws: 1993 (social insurance), implemented in 1994, with 2003 amendments; and 1994 (work injury), with 2003 amendment.

Type of program: Social insurance system.

Coverage

All employees, including new employees joining the state oil company (Ecopetrol) after January 29, 2003; student placements; and casual workers.

Voluntary coverage for the self-employed.

Special systems for employees of the state oil company (Ecopetrol), teachers, armed forces personnel, and national police personnel.

Source of Funds

Insured person: None.

Self-employed person: 0.348% to 8.7% of declared earnings, according to the assessed degree of risk.

The minimum earnings for contribution purposes are equal to the legal monthly minimum wage (381,500 pesos).

The maximum earnings for contribution purposes are equal to 25 times the legal monthly minimum wage (381,500 pesos).

Employer: 0.348% to 8.7% of payroll, according to the assessed degree of risk. (1% of the employer's contribution finances the work injury fund, which promotes health and safety for workers.)

The minimum earnings for contribution purposes are equal to the legal monthly minimum wage (381,500 pesos).

The maximum earnings for contribution purposes are equal to 25 times the legal monthly minimum wage (381,500 pesos).

Government: Contributes to the work injury fund from general revenue; contributes as an employer.

Qualifying Conditions

Work injury benefits: There is no minimum qualifying period. If the employer delays the payment of contributions for 2 consecutive months, the employer is automatically disqualified from the program.

Temporary Disability Benefits

The benefit is equal to 100% of earnings in the month before the onset of disability and is payable for up to 180 days; may be extended to 360 days.

Permanent Disability Benefits

Permanent disability pension: For an assessed degree of disability of more than 66%, the pension is equal to 75% of base earnings; for an assessed degree of disability of between 50% and 66%, the pension is equal to 60% of base earnings.

Base earnings are equal to average earnings in the last 6 months for work accidents or in the last 12 months for occupational diseases.

Constant-attendance allowance: Equal to 15% of the pension.

Partial disability: For an assessed degree of disability between 5% and 49%, the pension is from a minimum of one times base earnings up to a maximum of 24 times base earnings.

The minimum earnings for benefit calculation purposes are equal to the legal monthly minimum wage (381,500 pesos).

The maximum earnings for benefit calculation purposes are equal to 25 times the legal monthly minimum wage (381,500 pesos).

The minimum pension is equal to the legal minimum wage (381,500 pesos).

The maximum pension is equal to 20 times the legal minimum wage (381,500 pesos).

Benefit adjustment: Pensions are adjusted annually for changes in the consumer price index.

Workers' Medical Benefits

Benefits include medical, surgical, and hospital care; medicines; appliances; rehabilitation; and transportation.

Survivor Benefits

Survivor pension: The survivor pension is equal to 75% of the insured's earnings or 100% of the insured's disability pension.

Eligible survivors are a widow or partner who lived with the deceased for at least 5 years or who had children with the deceased, a dependent disabled widower, children younger than age 18 (age 25 if a student, no limit if disabled), dependent parents, or a disabled brother or sister.

Administrative Organization

Ministry of Labor and Social Security, Ministry of Health, National Banking Superintendent, and the National Council of Professional Risks provide general supervision.

Social Security Institute (http://www.iss.gov.co) and life insurance companies authorized by the National Banking Superintendent administer the program nationally.

Unemployment

Regulatory Framework

First and current law: 1990 (severance).

Type of program: Mandatory individual severance account system.

Note: Beginning January 1, 1991, acquired rights under the previous public system were transferred to the new private severance pay program.

Coverage

All private-sector employees.

Voluntary coverage for public-sector employees and self-employed workers.

Source of Funds

Insured person: None.

Self-employed person: 8.3% of annual declared earnings.

Employer: 8.3% of the insured's annual salary.

Government: None; contributes as an employer.

Qualifying Conditions

Unemployment benefits: The insured must be unemployed or retired.

Unemployment Benefits

The benefit is equal to 1 monthly wage for each year of employment; a reduced benefit is paid for less than a year of employment. (The insured may make authorized partial withdrawals from the individual account to meet specified contingencies.)

Administrative Organization

Mandatory individual accounts are administered by Severance Pay Funds (SAFCs).

National Banking Superintendent (http://www.superbancaria.gov.co) supervises the SAFCs.

Juntas Directives, involving employer and employee representatives, monitor the SAFCs.

Family Allowances

Regulatory Framework

First law: 1957.

Current law: 1982 (family allowances), with 2002 amendment.

Type of program: Employment-related system.

Coverage

All employees.

Voluntary coverage for pensioners, self-employed workers, and the unemployed.

Exclusions: Occasional workers.

Special systems for armed forces personnel and national police personnel.

Source of Funds

Insured person: None. Voluntary contributors pay 2% of the legal monthly minimum wage or the pension; 0.6% of the legal monthly minimum wage for reduced allowances.

The legal monthly minimum wage is 381,500 pesos.

Self-employed person: 2% of declared earnings; 0.6% of the legal monthly minimum wage for reduced allowances.

The legal monthly minimum wage is 381,500 pesos.

Employer: 4% of payroll.

Government: None; contributes as an employer.

Qualifying Conditions

Family allowances (income-tested): The child must be younger than age 18 (age 23 if a student, no limit if disabled). The parent must be older than age 60 or assessed as 60% disabled; must have completed 60 days of continuous employment with the same employer of which not less than 96 hours were credited during the last 25 working days.

Income test: Monthly income must not exceed four times the legal monthly minimum wage (381,500 pesos).

Family Allowance Benefits

Family allowances: Benefit amounts vary among funds and may be paid in cash or in kind. A child assessed as at least 60% disabled receives a double allowance.

Surviving spouse allowance: Twelve months' payment to a widow or the guardian of dependent children. If the dependent dies, the family receives a lump sum equal to 12 monthly payments.

Administrative Organization

Superintendent for Family Subsidies (http://www.ssf.gov.co) supervises family allowance funds.

Costa Rica

Exchange rate: US$1.00 equals 474.35 colones.

Old Age, Disability, and Survivors

Regulatory Framework

First law: 1941 (social insurance fund).

Current laws: 1993 (pensions), 1995 (self-employed), 1995 (mandatory individual accounts), and 2000 (workers' protection).

Type of program: Social insurance and mandatory individual account system.

Note: In 2000, a system of mandatory private individual accounts was introduced to complement the social insurance old-age pension program.

Coverage

Social insurance: Employees in public- and private-sector employment and the self-employed.

There are no special systems for any specified groups of employees.

Mandatory individual account: Employees in public- and private-sector employment.

Exclusions: The self-employed.

Source of Funds

Social insurance

Insured person: 2.5% of gross earnings.

The minimum monthly earnings for contribution purposes are 88,847 colones.

There are no maximum earnings for contribution purposes.

Self-employed person: Between 4.75% and 7.25% of gross declared earnings.

The minimum monthly earnings for contribution purposes are 88,847 colones.

There are no maximum earnings for contribution purposes.

Employer: 4.5% of payroll.

The minimum monthly earnings for contribution purposes are 88,847 colones.

There are no maximum earnings for contribution purposes.

Government: 0.25% of total covered earnings.

Mandatory individual account

Insured person: 1% of gross earnings, plus up to a maximum of 0.19% of gross earnings for administrative fees.

The minimum monthly earnings for contribution purposes are 88,847 colones.

There are no maximum earnings for contribution purposes.

Self-employed person: Not applicable.

Employer: 3.25% of payroll (1.5% of which is for the mandatory severance pay scheme).

The minimum monthly earnings for contribution purposes are 88,847 colones.

There are no maximum earnings for contribution purposes.

Government: None.

Qualifying Conditions

Old-age pension

Old-age pension (social insurance): Age 61 and 11 months with 462 months of contributions (men) or age 59 and 11 months (women) with 450 months of contributions.

Age 62 with 456 monthly contributions (men) or age 60 with 450 monthly contributions (women) for insured persons younger than age 44 on November 1, 2005.

Deferred pension: A deferred pension is possible. The total number of required contributions decreases the longer the pension is deferred, down to 300 monthly contributions at age 65 for insured persons younger than age 44 on November 1, 2005.

The maximum pension is 700,000 colones (November 2005).

Retirement from covered employment is not necessary.

The old-age pension is payable abroad.

Old-age pension (mandatory individual account): Age 61 and 11 months (men) or age 59 and 11 months (women). The insured must also submit proof of eligibility for benefits under the social insurance program.

Age 62 (men) or age 60 (women) for insured persons younger than age 44 on November 1, 2005.

Retirement from covered employment is necessary; the pensioner may resume employment 6 months after retirement, in which case social insurance contributions must be paid.

Deferred pension: A deferred pension is possible.

Old-age benefit (noncontributory): See Family Allowances, below.

Disability pension (social insurance): A loss of 2/3 of normal earning capacity. The total number of required contributions varies by age.

The minimum number of required contributions for an insured person up to age 24 is 12.

The maximum number of required contributions for an insured person between ages 52 and 65 is 120.

The disability pension is payable abroad.

Disability grant (social insurance): A loss of 2/3 of normal earning capacity and with at least 60 contributions.

Disability benefit (noncontributory): See Family Allowances, below.

Survivor pension (social insurance): The deceased was eligible for the old-age pension or disability pension or had made 12 contributions in the last 24 months or had a total of 180 contributions.

Survivor settlement: The deceased had paid at least 12 contributions but the other requirements for the survivor pension were not met.

Survivor benefit (noncontributory): See Family Allowances, below.

Old-Age Benefits

Old-age pension

Old-age pension (social insurance): The pension is based on the length of the total contribution period and average earnings in the last 240 months.

Earnings adjustment: Earnings are adjusted in line with inflation, according to changes in the consumer price index.

The basic benefit is increased by 0.0835% of average earnings for each month of contributions above 240, plus an increment of 1.6% of the pension for each year above 20 years.

The minimum monthly pension is 46,523 colones; if the calculated pension amount is smaller, a lump sum is paid. (Beginning January 2006, the minimum monthly pension is 50,000 colones.)

The maximum monthly pension is 700,000 colones. (Beginning January 2006, the maximum monthly pension is 742,000 colones.)

Deferred pension: The pension is increased by 0.133% of average earnings for each month of deferred retirement beyond the normal pensionable age.

The maximum deferred pension is 1 million colones (November 2005).

Schedule of payments: Thirteen payments a year.

Benefit adjustment: Benefits are adjusted twice a year, in January and July, according to changes in the cost of living.

Old-age pension (mandatory individual account): The value of the pension is dependent on the insured's contributions plus accrued interest. The insured can choose to draw down the accumulated capital in programmed periodic withdrawals or to purchase an annuity at retirement. In most cases, the withdrawal of funds before retirement is not permitted.

Deferred pension: The value of the pension is dependent on the insured's contributions plus accrued interest.

Old-age benefit (noncontributory): See Family Allowances, below.

Permanent Disability Benefits

Disability pension (social insurance): The pension is equal to 60% of average earnings based on the highest 48 monthly earnings in the last 5 years of coverage.

The basic benefit is increased by 0.0835% of average earnings for each month of contributions above 240.

The minimum monthly pension is 46,523 colones; if the computed pension amount is smaller, a lump sum is paid. (Beginning January 2006, the minimum monthly pension is 50,000 colones.)

The maximum monthly pension is 700,000 colones. (Beginning January 2006, the maximum monthly pension is 742,000 colones.)

Schedule of payments: Thirteen payments a year.

Disability grant (social insurance): A lump sum equal to 7 months' average earnings.

Benefit adjustment: Benefits are adjusted twice a year, in January and July, according to changes in the cost of living.

Disability benefit (noncontributory): See Family Allowances, below.

Survivor Benefits

Survivor pension (social insurance): A widow(er) or partner younger than age 50 receives 50% of the deceased's pension; 60% if aged 50 or older but younger than age 60; 70% if older than age 60 or disabled.

Orphan's pension (social insurance): Each orphan younger than age 18 (age 25 if a student) or disabled receives 30% of the deceased's pension; 60% for a full orphan.

In cases when 12 contributions were paid by the deceased but the other requirements were not met, the survivors have a right to receive a compensation equal to 1/12 of the average monthly salary for every covered month and no less than the minimum pension.

Other eligible survivors (social insurance): Dependent parents and dependent brothers and sisters receive 20% of the deceased's pension each; dependents older than age 55 receive 60% of the deceased's pension each.

The total maximum survivor pension is 100% of the deceased's pension.

Benefit adjustment: Benefits are adjusted twice a year, in January and July, according to changes in the cost of living.

Survivor settlement: A lump sum equal to 1/12 of the average monthly salary for each month of insurance coverage. The settlement must be no less than the minimum monthly old-age pension.

Survivor benefit (noncontributory): See Family Allowances, below.

Administrative Organization

Social insurance: Directed by an executive president and a nine-member board, the Costa Rican Social Insurance Fund (http://www.ccss.sa.cr) administers the program.

State auditor supervises the financial operations of the fund.

Mandatory individual account: Superintendent of Pensions (http://www.supen.fi.cr) regulates and supervises pension operators and service providers.

National Council for the Supervision of the Financial System provides regulatory oversight.

Sickness and Maternity

Regulatory Framework

First laws: 1941 and 1943.

Current laws: 1961, 1973 (health), and 1993 (social insurance).

Type of program: Social insurance system. Cash and medical benefits.

Coverage

Cash sickness and maternity benefits: Employed persons, including the self-employed, indigent persons, prisoners, and pensioners.

Medical benefits: All residents; international agreements provide emergency medical care for visitors to the country.

Source of Funds

Insured person: 5.5% of gross earnings; pensioners make a contribution equal to 5% of the pension, which is complemented by an 8.75% contribution made by the Social Insurance Fund on the pensioner's behalf.

The minimum earnings for contribution purposes are 88,847 colones.

Self-employed person: The self-employed contribute between 4.75% and 7.75% of declared earnings.

The minimum earnings for contribution purposes are 88,847 colones.

Employer: 9.25% of payroll. (The employer pays 50% of the cost of maternity benefits, and the Social Insurance Fund pays the remaining 50% of the cost.)

Government: 0.25% of total covered earnings.

Qualifying Conditions

Cash sickness benefits: Must have contributed in the month before the onset of incapacity and be currently registered.

Cash maternity benefits and maternity care: Must have 26 weeks of contributions in the last 52 weeks; the wife of an insured man is eligible for maternity care if the insured contributed in the month before the date of childbirth.

Medical benefits: Coverage begins in the month in which the insured first registers.

Sickness and Maternity Benefits

Sickness benefit: The benefit is equal to 60% of earnings in the last 3 months and is payable after a 3-day waiting period. Benefits are payable for up to 52 weeks; may be extended in special cases.

Maternity benefit: The benefit is equal to 50% of earnings and is payable for 30 days before and 90 days after the expected date of childbirth.

Funeral grant: 80,000 colones is payable for the funeral of the insured or his or her spouse or partner.

Workers' Medical Benefits

Medical services are normally provided directly to patients through the medical facilities of the Social Insurance Fund. Benefits include general, specialist, and maternity care; hospitalization; medicines; dental, auditory, and limited optometry services; and appliances (at a reduced cost).

Dependents' Medical Benefits

Medical services are normally provided directly to patients through the medical facilities of the Social Insurance Fund. Benefits include general, specialist, and maternity care; hospitalization; medicines; dental, auditory, and limited optometry services; and appliances (at a reduced cost).

Administrative Organization

Costa Rican Social Insurance Fund (http://www.ccss.sa.cr) administers the program.

Costa Rican Social Insurance Fund owns and operates 29 hospitals and 152 clinics and is gradually extending jurisdiction over other hospitals and clinics.

Work Injury

Regulatory Framework

First law: 1925.

Current law: 1982 (labor code).

Type of program: Employer-liability system, involving compulsory and voluntary insurance with a public carrier.

Coverage

Employed persons.

Source of Funds

Insured person: None.

Self-employed person: Not applicable.

Employer: Total cost, met through insurance premiums varying according to the assessed degree of risk.

Government: None.

Qualifying Conditions

Work injury benefits: There is no minimum qualifying period.

Temporary Disability Benefits

The benefit is equal to 75% of the insured's daily earnings for the first 45 days; thereafter, 100% of the minimum salary plus 75% of the insured's earnings over this amount. The benefit is payable from the onset of disability for up to 2 years.

The minimum benefit is equal to the legal minimum wage at the time of the onset of disability.

Permanent Disability Benefits

Permanent disability pension: For an assessed degree of disability of more than 67% (total disability), the monthly pension is equal to 100% of the minimum wage plus 90% of the insured's earnings that exceed the minimum wage.

Constant-attendance allowance: 78,275 colones for a total permanent disability; an additional 44,547 colones is paid for a severe disability.

Grants may be awarded to disabled insured persons in order to purchase, rent, or modify a house.

Partial disability: If the assessed degree of disability is between 50% and 67%, the benefit is equal to 67% of earnings and is payable for up to 10 years. If the assessed degree of disability is between 0.5% and 50%, the benefit is equal to the assessed degree of disability times annual earnings and is payable for up to 5 years. The benefit may be extended for additional 5-year periods on a means-tested basis.

Workers' Medical Benefits

Benefits include medical and surgical care, hospitalization, medicines, appliances, and rehabilitation.

Survivor Benefits

Survivor pension: 40% of the deceased's earnings is payable to a widow or to a disabled widower. The pension is payable for 10 years; may be extended for additional 5-year periods in special cases.

The maximum widow(er) pension is equal to 40% of the deceased's earnings; 30% if there are other eligible dependents.

Orphan's pension: 15% to 40% of the deceased's earnings is payable for up to three orphans younger than age 18 (age 25 if a student, no limit if disabled).

Other eligible survivors: 20% of the deceased's earnings is payable to the deceased's mother (30% if there are no dependent children) for a period of 10 years. A pension is also payable to a dependent father or other dependent adults, including those aged 60 or older and unable to work.

The maximum total survivor pension is 75% of the insured's earnings.

Funeral grant: 75,000 colones, plus transportation costs (15,000 colones if the death occurred in Cost Rica; 60,000 colones if the death occurred abroad).

Administrative Organization

Ministry of Labor and Social Security (http://www.ministrabajo.go.cr) provides general supervision.

National Insurance Institute administers the program.

Unemployment

Regulatory Framework

No statutory benefits are provided.

Labor law requires employers to contribute 1.5% of payroll to finance a mandatory severance pay scheme.

Family Allowances

Regulatory Framework

First and current law: 1974 (family allowances and social development).

Type of program: Social insurance system.

Coverage

Indigent persons who are not entitled to a contributory pension.

Source of Funds

Insured person: None.

Self-employed person: None.

Employer: 5% of payroll.

Government: 20% of proceeds from the sales tax.

Qualifying Conditions

Family allowances (means-tested): Allowances are payable to persons older than age 65, disabled persons, widows with dependents younger than age 18 or disabled, widows older than age 50 without dependents, and orphans younger than age 18.

Family Allowance Benefits

Family allowances (means-tested): 13,800 colones a month for a beneficiary, plus 10% for each dependent up to a maximum of three.

Administrative Organization

Ministry of Labor and Social Security (http://www.ministrabajo.go.cr) provides general supervision.

Social Development and Family Allowances Fund directs the program.

Costa Rican Social Insurance Fund (http://www.ccss.sa.cr) administers the program.

Cuba

Exchange rate: US$1.00 equals 1 peso.

Old Age, Disability, and Survivors

Regulatory Framework

First laws: 1963 and 1964.

Current law: 1979, implemented in 1980.

Type of program: Social insurance and social assistance system.

Coverage

All wage earners.

Special systems for armed forces personnel, interior ministry staff, the self-employed, artists, and members of agricultural cooperatives.

Source of Funds

Insured person: None.

Self-employed person: 10% of earnings; certain artists contribute 12% of earnings.

There are no minimum or maximum monthly earnings for contribution purposes.

The above contributions also finance sickness and maternity benefits and work injury benefits.

Employer: 14% of payroll.

There are no minimum or maximum monthly earnings for contribution purposes.

The above contributions also finance sickness and maternity benefits and work injury benefits.

Government: Finances the cost of burial services and any deficit and guarantees minimum pensions; contributes as an employer.

There are no minimum or maximum monthly earnings for contribution purposes.

Qualifying Conditions

Old-age pension: Age 60 (men) or age 55 (women) with 25 years of work.

Age 55 (men) or age 50 (women) if the last 12 years or 75% of employment was in dangerous or arduous work.

Partial pension: Age 65 (men) or age 60 (women) with 15 years of work.

Early pension: There is no early pension.

Deferred pension: A deferred pension is possible, subject to the insured's physical and mental health.

Retirement is not necessary, but total income must not exceed former income.

The pension is not payable abroad.

Old-age social assistance (means-tested): Cash or in-kind benefits are payable to any person of pensionable age, subject to assessed needs.

Disability pension: A pension is payable for a partial, total, or severe disability. The full pension is payable if assessed as physically or mentally incapable of work.

The Expert Medical Labor Commission assesses the degree of disability.

Partial pension: If younger than age 23, must be assessed as unable to perform usual work and be employed at the onset of disability. If aged 23 or older, the number of years of employment needed to qualify increases with age. (A partial pension at age 28 or older requires 3 years of employment.)

The disability pension is not replaced by the old-age pension at pensionable age.

The pension is not payable abroad.

Disability social assistance (means-tested): Cash or in-kind benefits are payable to any person assessed as disabled, subject to assessed needs.

Survivor pension: The deceased was a pensioner at the time of death or was employed 6 months before the date of death and for 75% of his or her adult life.

The pension is not payable abroad.

Survivor social assistance (means-tested): Cash or in-kind benefits are payable to any survivor, subject to assessed needs.

Old-Age Benefits

Old-age pension: The monthly pension is equal to 50% of average earnings (the portion of earnings exceeding 3,000 pesos a year is reduced by 50%) in the best 5 of the last 10 years, plus 1% of earnings for each year of employment exceeding 25 years (1.5% for each year of dangerous or arduous work).

Partial pension: The monthly pension is equal to 40% of average earnings, plus 1% of earnings for each year of employment exceeding 15 years.

Deferred pension: The pension is increased by 1.5% to 4% for each year of deferral between ages 60 and 65 (men) and between ages 55 and 60 (women); thereafter, by 1% a year. The maximum pension is equal to 90% of the insured's salary.

The minimum monthly pension is 164 pesos.

The maximum pension is equal to 90% of the insured's average earnings if they were higher than 300 pesos.

Old-age social assistance (means-tested): Benefits may be paid periodically or as a lump sum.

Benefit adjustment: Benefits are adjusted by government decree according to social and economic factors.

Permanent Disability Benefits

Disability pension: For an assessed total disability caused by a general disease, the monthly pension is equal to 50% of average annual earnings (the portion of earnings exceeding 3,000 pesos a year is reduced by 50%) if the insured has 25 years of work; 40% of average annual earnings with less than 15 years of work.

The minimum monthly pension is 164 pesos.

The maximum pension is equal to 90% of the insured's average earnings if they were higher than 300 pesos.

Partial disability: The pension is equal to between 30% and 50% of lost earnings, depending on the number of years of work up to a maximum of 25 years: 30% with less than 9 years; 40% with more than 9 years to 14 years; 50% with more than 14 years. The pension is increased by 1% for each year of employment exceeding 25 years. During rehabilitation, the pension is equal to 70% of the insured's former earnings.

If the insured is unemployed as the result of a common disability, a pension is paid equal to 50% of former earnings in the first year; thereafter, 25% of former earnings.

Disability social assistance (means-tested): Benefits may be paid periodically or as a lump sum.

Benefit adjustment: Benefits are adjusted by government decree according to social and economic factors.

Survivor Benefits

Survivor pension: If the deceased was employed at the time of death, the pension is equal to 100% of earnings for the first month and 50% of earnings for the next 2 months. If the deceased was a pensioner, then the pension is equal to 100% of the deceased's pension for 3 months; thereafter, 70%, 85%, or 100% of the deceased's pension for one, two, or three or more dependent survivors, respectively (80%, 90%, or 100% of the deceased's pension if the pension is less than 60 pesos a month). The pension is split equally among all eligible dependents.

Eligible survivors are a widow (or partner), a needy widower (or partner) aged 60 or older or disabled, orphans younger than age 17 or disabled, and needy parents.

The minimum monthly pension is 164 pesos.

The maximum pension for a working widow is equal to 25% of the survivor pension.

Unemployed widows aged 40 or older receive the full pension. A nonworking widow younger than age 40 with no dependents receives the full pension for a limited period of 2 years.

Free burial services are provided by the government for all residents.

Survivor social assistance (means-tested): Benefits may be paid periodically or as a lump sum.

Benefit adjustment: Benefits are adjusted by government decree according to social and economic factors.

Administrative Organization

Ministry of Labor and Social Security administers the program through the National Institute of Social Security.

Municipal social security offices and work centers process applications.

Pensions are paid through the Popular Savings Bank.

Sickness and Maternity

Regulatory Framework

First law: 1934 (maternity benefits).

Current laws: 1979 (sickness) and 2003 (maternity).

Type of program: Social insurance (cash benefits) and universal (medical care) system.

Coverage

Cash sickness and maternity benefits: Employed persons, members of agricultural cooperatives, armed forces personnel, interior ministry staff, the self-employed, and artists.

Medical benefits: All residents.

Source of Funds

Insured person: See source of funds under Old Age, Disability, and Survivors, above.

Self-employed person: See source of funds under Old Age, Disability, and Survivors, above.

Employer: See source of funds under Old Age, Disability, and Survivors, above.

Government: See source of funds under Old Age, Disability, and Survivors, above. The cost of medical benefits and services.

Qualifying Conditions

Cash sickness benefits: Must be currently employed or self-employed.

Cash maternity benefits: Must be currently employed with 75 days of employment in the 12 months before maternity leave. Maternity leave must start no later than the 34th or 32nd (for a multiple birth) week of pregnancy.

Medical benefits: Resident in Cuba.

Sickness and Maternity Benefits

Sickness benefit: The benefit is equal to 60% of average daily earnings in the last 6 months; if hospitalized, 50% of earnings. The benefit is payable after a 3-day waiting period (if hospitalized, no waiting period) until medical certification expires (new certification by a medical committee is required every 26 weeks) or a disability pension is payable.

The minimum benefit is 1.5 pesos a day (80% of earnings if the wage is less than 1.65 pesos a day).

The maximum benefit is equal to 90% of earnings.

Tuberculosis benefit: The benefit is equal to 100% of earnings until cured.

Maternity benefit: The benefit is equal to 100% of earnings and is payable for 6 weeks before and 12 weeks after the expected date of childbirth.

The minimum maternity benefit is 20 pesos a week.

Maternity social benefit: Beginning 12 weeks after the birth, the benefit is equal to 60% of earnings if the mother is unable to work as the result of having to care for the child. The benefit is payable until the child is 12 months old; earlier if the mother returns to work.

Workers' Medical Benefits

Free medical services are provided by public medical centers. Benefits include medical, dental, and maternity care; prenatal and postnatal care; hospitalization; medicines during hospitalization; and rehabilitation. Benefits are provided until recovery.

Dependents' Medical Benefits

Free medical services are provided by public medical centers. Benefits include medical, dental, and maternity care; prenatal and postnatal care; hospitalization; medicines during hospitalization; and rehabilitation. Benefits are provided until recovery.

Administrative Organization

Ministry of Labor and Social Security administers the program through the National Institute of Social Security.

Work centers assume the costs and pay short-term cash benefits.

Ministry of Public Health supervises the administration of medical services provided by public medical and hospital centers.

Work Injury

Regulatory Framework

First law: 1916.

Current law: 1979, implemented in 1980.

Type of program: Social insurance (cash benefits) and universal (medical care) system.

Coverage

Employed persons, civilian personnel of the armed forces and interior ministry, the self-employed, artists, and members of agricultural cooperatives.

Source of Funds

Insured person: See source of funds under Old Age, Disability, and Survivors, above.

Self-employed person: See source of funds under Old Age, Disability, and Survivors, above.

Employer: See source of funds under Old Age, Disability, and Survivors, above.

Government: See source of funds under Old Age, Disability, and Survivors, above.

Qualifying Conditions

Work injury benefits: There is no minimum qualifying period but must be employed at the onset of disability.

Temporary Disability Benefits

The benefit is equal to 80% of the insured's earnings; if hospitalized, 70% of earnings. The benefit is payable from the first day of disability until medical certification expires (new certification by a medical committee is required every 26 weeks) or a permanent disability pension is payable.

The minimum benefit is 1.5 pesos a day (80% of earnings if the wage is less than 1.65 pesos a day).

The maximum benefit is equal to 90% of the insured's earnings.

Benefit adjustment: Benefits are adjusted by government decree according to social and economic factors.

Permanent Disability Benefits

Permanent disability pension: The pension is equal to 50% of the insured's average earnings in the best 5 of the last 10 years, plus 1% of earnings for each year of work exceeding 25 years.

Work injury or occupational disease supplement: Equal to 10% of the pension.

Heroic act supplement: Equal to 20% of the pension.

Constant-attendance allowance: Equal to 20% of the pension.

The minimum monthly pension is 164 pesos.

The maximum pension is equal to 90% of the insured's average earnings.

Partial disability: The pension is equal to between 30% and 50% of lost earnings, depending on the number of years of work up to a maximum of 25 years: 30% with less than 9 years; 40% with 9 to 14 years; 50% with more than 14 years. The pension is increased by 1% for each year of employment exceeding 25 years.

Work injury or occupational disease supplement: Equal to 10% of the pension.

During rehabilitation, the pension is equal to 70% of the insured's former earnings.

If the insured is unemployed as a result of a work-related disability, a pension is paid equal to 70% of former earnings in the first year; thereafter, 35% of former earnings.

Benefit adjustment: Benefits are adjusted by government decree according to social and economic factors.

Workers' Medical Benefits

Free medical services are provided by public medical centers. Benefits include medical and dental care, hospitalization, medicines, appliances, and rehabilitation. Benefits are provided until recovery.

Survivor Benefits

Survivor pension: If the deceased was employed at the time of death, the pension is equal to 100% of earnings for the first month and 50% of earnings for the next 2 months. If the deceased was a pensioner, the pension is equal to 100% of the deceased's pension for 3 months; thereafter, 70%, 85%, or 100% of the deceased's pension for one, two, or three or more dependent survivors, respectively (80%, 90%, or 100% of the deceased's pension if the pension is less than 60 pesos a month). The pension is spit equally among all eligible survivors.

Eligible survivors are a widow (or partner), a needy widower (or partner) aged 60 or older or disabled, orphans younger than age 17 or disabled, and needy parents.

The maximum pension for a working widow is equal to 25% of the survivor pension.

Unemployed widows aged 40 or older receive the full pension. A nonworking widow younger than age 40 with no

dependents receives the full pension for a limited period of 2 years.

Free burial services are provided by the government.

Benefit adjustment: Benefits are adjusted by government decree according to social and economic factors.

Administrative Organization

Ministry of Labor and Social Security administers the program through the National Institute of Social Security.

Work centers assume the costs and pay short-term cash benefits.

Ministry of Public Health supervises the administration of medical services provided by public medical and hospital centers.

Family Allowances

Regulatory Framework

Dependents of young workers conscripted into military service are eligible for assistance from the Social Security Fund.

Dominica

Exchange rate: US$1.00 equals
2.70 East Caribbean dollars (EC$).

Old Age, Disability, and Survivors

Regulatory Framework

First law: 1970 (provident fund).

Current law: 1975 (social security).

Type of program: Social insurance system.

Note: Government-financed social assistance benefits are administered by the Division of Social Welfare.

Coverage

Employees, self-employed persons, voluntary contributors, and apprentices aged 16 to 60.

There are no special systems for any specified groups of employees.

Source of Funds

Insured person: 3% of gross earnings.

There are no minimum earnings for contribution purposes.

The maximum annual earnings for contribution purposes are EC$60,000.

The insured's contributions also finance sickness and maternity benefits.

Self-employed person: 7.65% of declared net earnings.

The minimum declared annual earnings for contribution purposes are EC$600.

The maximum annual earnings for contribution purposes are EC$60,000.

Employer: 6.75% of gross earnings. (Employers also contribute on their own behalf as self-employed persons.)

Government: None; contributes as an employer.

Qualifying Conditions

Old-age pension: Aged 60 or older with at least 500 weeks of paid or credited contributions, including at least 150 paid contributions.

Early pension: There is no early pension.

Deferred pension: A deferred pension is possible.

Old-age grant: Payable for an insured person aged 60 or older who does not meet the qualifying conditions for a pension but has at least 50 weeks of contributions.

Old-age benefits are payable abroad.

Disability pension: Permanently incapable of work and younger than age 60 with 150 weeks of paid or credited contributions.

Disability grant: Permanently incapable of work and younger than age 60 but does not meet the qualifying conditions for a disability pension.

Incapacity for work is assessed by a medical referee. Reviews of the assessed incapacity for work may be requested by the medical referee.

Disability benefits are payable abroad if the purpose of travel is to receive medical treatment.

Survivor pension: The deceased met the qualifying conditions for an old-age pension or disability pension or was a pensioner at the time of death.

Eligible survivors are the spouse and dependent children younger than age 16 (age 18 if a full-time student); dependent parents in the absence of other either a spouse or dependent children.

Survivor grant: The deceased did not meet the qualifying conditions for a pension but had at least 150 weeks of contributions.

Survivor benefits are payable abroad.

Funeral grant: The insured must satisfy the qualifying conditions for any benefit. The grant is payable for the death of the insured, the insured's noninsured spouse, and the insured's dependent children.

Old-Age Benefits

Old-age pension: The pension is equal to 30% of the insured's average earnings, plus 2% for every 50-week period of contributions between 500 weeks and 750 weeks and 1% for every 50-week period above 750.

Average earnings are based on the insured's 3 best years of the last 10 years.

The minimum old-age pension is EC$25.

The maximum old-age pension is equal to 70% of the insured's average earnings.

Early pension: There is no early pension.

Deferred pension: The pension is increased by 6% for every complete year of deferral.

Old-age grant: A lump sum equal to three times the insured's average weekly covered earnings for every 50-week period of paid or credited contributions.

Average weekly covered earnings are based on total insured earnings divided by the total number of weeks of contributions.

Permanent Disability Benefits

Disability pension: The pension is equal to 30% of the insured's average earnings, plus 2% for every 50-week period of contributions between 500 weeks and 750 weeks and 1% for every 50-week period above 750.

Average earnings are based on the insured's 3 best years of the last 10 years.

The maximum pension is equal to 70% of average earnings.

Disability grant: A lump sum equal to three times the insured's average weekly covered earnings for every 50-week period of paid or credited contributions.

Average weekly covered earnings are based on total insured earnings divided by the total number of weeks of contributions.

Survivor Benefits

Survivor pension: 50% of the deceased's pension is payable to a widow(er) aged 50 or older. If the surviving spouse was married to the deceased for less than 3 years or is younger than age 50, the widow(er) receives a limited survivor pension for 1 year or for as long as caring for dependent children.

The pension ceases if the surviving spouse remarries or cohabits.

Orphan's pension: The pension is equal to 25% of the deceased's pension for each of the first two orphans (33% if a full orphan or disabled). If there are more than two orphans, the total pension amount is split equally between them.

The minimum monthly orphan's pension is EC$50.

The maximum total survivor pension is equal to 100% of the deceased's pension.

Survivor grant: A lump sum equal to three times the deceased's average weekly covered earnings for every 50-week period of paid or credited contributions.

Weekly covered earnings are based on total insured earnings divided by the total number of weeks of contributions.

Funeral grant: A lump sum is payable to the person who meets the cost of the funeral. EC$1,800 is payable for the death of the insured; EC$1,500 for the death of a noninsured spouse; and EC$750 for the death of a dependent child younger than age 16 (age 18 if a full-time student).

Administrative Organization

Ministry of Health and Social Security provides general supervision.

Governed by the Social Security Board, Dominica Social Security administers the social insurance program.

Division of Social Welfare administers social assistance benefits.

Sickness and Maternity

Regulatory Framework

First and current law: 1975 (social security).

Type of program: Social insurance system. Cash benefits only.

Coverage

Employed persons and apprentices aged 16 to 60.

Exclusions: The self-employed.

There are no special systems for any specified groups of employees.

Source of Funds

Insured person: See source of funds under Old Age, Disability, and Survivors, above.

Self-employed person: Not applicable.

Employer: See source of funds under Old Age, Disability, and Survivors, above.

Government: See source of funds under Old Age, Disability, and Survivors, above.

Qualifying Conditions

Cash sickness benefits: Must have 13 weeks of insured employment immediately before the onset of the incapacity, including 8 weeks of paid contributions.

Cash maternity benefits: Must have 13 weeks of contributions, with at least 20 weeks in the 30-week period before the start of maternity leave.

Cash maternity grant: Payable to an insured woman or a noninsured spouse of an insured man with at least 26 weeks of paid contributions in the 52-week period before the expected date of childbirth.

Medical benefits: Must be the holder of a Social Security card.

Sickness and Maternity Benefits

Sickness benefit: The benefit is equal to 60% of average weekly earnings in the last 13 weeks and is payable from the first day of incapacity if the incapacity lasts beyond 4 days. The benefit is payable for up to 26 weeks.

Maternity benefit: The benefit is equal to 60% of average weekly earnings in the last 30 weeks and is payable 6 weeks before and 6 weeks after the expected date of childbirth; in certain cases, the benefit may be payable from 3 weeks before and up to 9 weeks after the date of childbirth.

Maternity grant: A lump sum of EC$500.

Workers' Medical Benefits

Benefits include a reduction on medical bills, subject to government-stipulated costs and conditions.

Dependents' Medical Benefits

No statutory benefits are provided.

Administrative Organization

Ministry of Health and Social Security provides general supervision.

Governed by the Social Security Board, Dominica Social Security administers the program.

Work Injury

Regulatory Framework

First law: 1938 (workmen's compensation).

Current law: 1985 (employment injury and occupational diseases).

Type of program: Employer-liability system.

Coverage

Employed persons and apprentices aged 16 to 60.

Source of Funds

Insured person: None.

Self-employed person: Not applicable.

Employer: Total cost. The cost of the program is equal to 1% of employees' gross earnings.

Government: None; contributes as an employer.

Qualifying Conditions

Work injury benefits: There is no minimum qualifying period. The disability must last at least 4 days.

Temporary Disability Benefits

The benefit is equal to 60% of average earnings in the last 13 weeks and is payable until the disability ends, subject to a maximum of 26 weeks. For an insured person with less than 13 weeks of insured earnings, the benefit is the average of the insured weeks, with a minimum number of 2 weeks used as the divisor.

Permanent Disability Benefits

The benefit is based on 60% of average earnings in the last 13 weeks and the assessed degree of disability. The benefit is payable until the disability ends. For an insured person with less than 13 weeks of insured earnings, the benefit is the average of the insured weeks, with a minimum number of 2 weeks used as the divisor.

Constant-attendance allowance: If assessed as 100% disabled, the allowance is equal to 50% of the benefit. The allowance is suspended if the insured is hospitalized.

A lump sum is paid if the assessed degree of disability is more than 1% but less than 30%.

Incapacity for work is assessed by a medical referee. Reviews of the assessed incapacity for work may be requested by the medical referee.

Workers' Medical Benefits

Medical expenses are reimbursed up to a maximum of EC$5,000 for local and overseas treatment.

Survivor Benefits

Survivor pension: 50% of the deceased's pension is payable to a fully or partially dependent widow(er) aged 50 or older.

The pension ceases if the surviving spouse remarries or cohabits.

Orphan's pension: The pension is equal to 25% of the deceased's pension (33% if a full orphan or disabled) for each of the fist two dependent children younger than age 16 (age 18 if a full-time student). If there are more than two orphans, the total pension amount is split equally among them.

The minimum monthly orphan's pension is EC$50.

The maximum total survivor pension is 100% of the deceased's pension.

Funeral grant: EC$1,800 is payable for the death of the insured; EC$1,500 for the death of a noninsured spouse; and EC$750 for the death of a dependent child younger than age 16 (age 18 if a full-time student).

Administrative Organization

Ministry of Health and Social Security provides general supervision.

Governed by the Social Security Board, Dominica Social Security administers the program.

Dominican Republic
Exchange rate: US$1.00 equals 28.60 pesos.

Old Age, Disability, and Survivors

Regulatory Framework

First law: 1947.

Current laws: 2001 (social security), implemented in 2003; and 2002 (pensions regulation).

Type of program: Mandatory individual account and social assistance system.

Note: The 2001 law created a three-part system that will be implemented in stages. A system of individual accounts for public- and private-sector workers began in June 2003. The scheduled introduction in August 2004 of a social assistance program for those with very low income has been delayed. Subsidized individual accounts for the self-employed are scheduled to begin in August 2006. The old social insurance system, which covers current pensioners and public-sector employees who opt not to join the new system, is being phased out.

Coverage

Mandatory individual account: All public- and private-sector workers, employers, and Dominican citizens living abroad. During the transition, mandatory coverage for all private-sector workers younger than age 45 in 2003 and voluntary coverage for workers aged 45 or older in 2003 and current public-sector employees.

Exclusions: The self-employed.

Mandatory individual account (subsidized): Self-employed persons with income above the minimum wage.

Exclusions: Self-employed persons with income below the minimum wage.

Social assistance: Severely disabled, indigent, unemployed, or self-employed persons with income below the minimum wage.

Source of Funds

Mandatory individual account

Insured person: 2.28% of gross earnings (to be raised gradually to 2.88% of gross earnings by 2008), plus a fixed 1% of gross earnings for disability and survivor insurance and up to a maximum of 0.6% of gross earnings for administrative fees.

The minimum earnings for contribution purposes are equal to the minimum wage.

The maximum earnings for contribution purposes are equal to 20 times the minimum wage.

Self-employed person: None.

Employer: 5.72% of payroll; includes 0.4% of payroll to finance minimum pensions (Social Solidarity Fund). (To be raised gradually to 7.12% of payroll by 2008.)

The minimum earnings for contribution purposes are equal to the minimum wage.

The maximum earnings for contribution purposes are equal to 20 times the minimum wage.

Contributions include administrative fees for the pension fund and management companies (AFPs) and the operating costs of the Superintendent of Pensions, the supervisory organization.

Government: Finances the subsidized mandatory individual account and guarantees the minimum pension.

Contributions include administrative fees for the pension fund and management companies (AFPs) and the operating costs of the Superintendent of Pensions, the supervisory organization.

Social assistance

Insured person: None.

Self-employed person: None.

Employer: None.

Government: Total cost.

Qualifying Conditions

Old-age pension (mandatory individual account): Age 60 with at least 30 years of contributions; age 55 if the individual account balance is sufficient to finance a pension equal to the minimum pension.

Pensioners are not required to cease gainful activity.

Early pension: Aged 57 or older, unemployed, and with at least 300 months of contributions; with less than 300 months, the insured can receive a pension based on the accumulated funds or continue contributing until reaching 300 months.

The pension is not payable abroad.

Old-age pension (subsidized mandatory individual account): Age 65 with at least 25 years of contributions.

The pension is not payable abroad.

Social assistance old-age pension (income-tested): Age 60 and indigent.

Disability pension (mandatory individual account): The insured has a chronic illness or injury (nonwork- or work-related) and has exhausted entitlement to sickness benefits or work injury benefits. A total disability is defined as a loss of at least 2/3 of earning capacity; partial disability, between 1/2 and 2/3 loss of earning capacity.

The insured's degree of disability is assessed by a regional medical committee. The national medical committee may revise, validate, or reject the decision of a regional medical committee.

The pension is not payable abroad.

Social assistance disability pension (income-tested): Payable at any age if severely disabled and indigent.

Survivor pension (mandatory individual account): The deceased was insured or a pensioner at the time of death.

Eligible survivors are a widow(er) or partner and unmarried children younger than age 18 (up to age 21 if a full-time student, no limit if disabled).

The pension is not payable abroad.

Social assistance survivor pension (income-tested): Payable to indigent survivors.

Eligible survivors are a widow(er) or partner and unmarried children younger than age 18 (age 21 if a full-time student, no limit if disabled).

Old-Age Benefits

Old-age pension (mandatory individual account): The pension is based on the value of the accumulated capital plus accrued interest. The accumulated capital can be used to purchase a price-indexed annuity or to make programmed withdrawals. (The value of accrued rights under the old system is combined with the individual account balance.)

Early pension: The minimum old-age pension is paid until age 60. The maximum early pension is equal to the insured's final salary.

The minimum old-age pension is equal to the lowest legal minimum wage.

There is no maximum old-age pension.

Benefit adjustment: Pensions are adjusted according to changes in the minimum public-sector wage.

Old-age pension (subsidized mandatory individual account): The pension is based on the value of the accumulated capital plus accrued interest. The accumulated capital can be used to purchase a price-indexed annuity or to make programmed withdrawals.

The minimum old-age pension (subsidized) is equal to 70% of the private-sector minimum wage.

Benefit adjustment: Pensions are adjusted according to changes in the consumer price index.

Social assistance old-age pension: The pension is equal to 60% of the minimum public-sector wage (plus a Christmas bonus).

Benefit adjustment: Pensions are adjusted according to changes in the consumer price index.

Permanent Disability Benefits

Disability pension (mandatory individual account): For a total disability, the pension is equal to 60% of the insured's indexed average earnings in the 3 years immediately before the onset of disability. The disability pension ceases at the normal pensionable age and the old-age pension is payable. (Disability insurance tops up the accumulated capital in the individual account if the balance is less than the required minimum to finance the permanent disability pension.)

Partial disability: The pension is equal to 30% of the insured's indexed average earnings in the 3 years immediately before the onset of disability.

There is no minimum disability pension.

There is no maximum disability pension.

Benefit adjustment: Pensions are adjusted according to changes in the consumer price index.

Social assistance disability pension: The pension is equal to 60% of the minimum public-sector wage (plus a Christmas bonus).

Benefit adjustment: Pensions are adjusted according to changes in the consumer price index.

Survivor Benefits

Survivor pension (mandatory individual account): The pension is equal to 60% of the deceased's indexed average earnings in the previous 3 years. (Life insurance tops up the accumulated capital in the deceased's individual account if the balance is less than the required minimum to finance the survivor pension.)

A spouse older than age 50 receives the pension for life; a spouse between ages 50 and 55 receives a pension for 6 years only (5 years if younger than age 50).

If there are orphans younger than age 18 (up to age 21 if a full-time student, no limit if disabled), the pension is split between the spouse and the orphans.

There is no minimum survivor pension.

Benefit adjustment: Pensions are adjusted according to changes in the consumer price index.

Social assistance survivor pension: The pension is equal to 60% of the minimum public-sector wage (plus a Christmas bonus).

Benefit adjustment: Pensions are adjusted according to changes in the consumer price index.

Administrative Organization

National Social Security Board (CNSS) (http://www.cnss.gov.do) provides overall governance of the social security system.

Mandatory individual account: Superintendent of Pensions (SIPEN) (http://www.sipen.gov.do) provides general supervision.

Individual pension fund management companies (AFPs) administer the individual accounts.

Authorized insurance companies sell annuity products.

Sickness and Maternity

Regulatory Framework

First law: 1947.

Current laws: 1948 (social insurance), implemented in 1949, with 1966 and 1988 amendments; and 2001 (social security), implemented in 2003.

Type of program: Social insurance system. Cash and universal medical benefits.

Coverage

Cash and medical benefits (nonsubsidized): Employed persons and their spouses or partners, the insured's children up to age 21 if a full-time student (no limit if disabled), and pensioners.

Cash and medical benefits (subsidized): Pensioners receiving subsidized benefits and the self-employed and home workers and their dependents.

Source of Funds

Insured person: 2.7% of gross earnings (2003). (To be raised gradually to 3% of gross earnings by 2008.)

There are no minimum earnings for contribution purposes.

The maximum earnings for contribution purposes are equal to 10 times the minimum wage.

Self-employed person: Part of the cost for the subsidized program.

Employer: 6.3% of payroll (2003). (To be raised gradually to 7% of payroll by 2008.)

There are no minimum earnings for contribution purposes.

The maximum earnings for contribution purposes are equal to 10 times the minimum wage.

Government: Total cost of social assistance and part of the cost for the subsidized program and the pediatric health care program.

Qualifying Conditions

Cash sickness benefits (nonsubsidized): Must have 12 months of contributions or be a pensioner.

Cash maternity benefits (nonsubsidized): Must have 8 months of contributions in the 12 months before childbirth or have been without paid work in the 12 months before childbirth.

Medical benefits

Basic health plan: Universal coverage.

Pediatric health care: Universal coverage.

Sickness and Maternity Benefits

Sickness benefit (nonsubsidized): The benefit is equal to 60% of earnings in the last 6 months (40% if hospitalized) and is payable after a 3-day waiting period, for up to 26 weeks.

Maternity benefit (nonsubsidized): The total benefit is equal to 3 months' insured earnings and is payable for 6 weeks before and 6 weeks after the expected date of childbirth.

Nursing allowance: If the insured's salary is less than three times the minimum national wage, an allowance is paid for up to 12 months after the child's birth.

Workers' Medical Benefits

Benefits under the basic health plan include preventive, inpatient and outpatient, pediatric, and specialist care; medicines; and prosthesis for disabled persons, according to the schedule in law.

Cost sharing: The insured is reimbursed for 70% of the cost of some medicines.

Social assistance beneficiaries receive basic medicines free of charge.

Dependents' Medical Benefits

Benefits under the basic health plan include preventive, inpatient and outpatient, pediatric, and specialist care; medicines; dental treatment for children; and prosthesis for disabled persons, according to the schedule in law.

Pediatric health care: Provided from the 45th day after birth until age 5. Benefits include nutrition, pediatric care, and child development programs.

Administrative Organization

National Health Insurance (http://www.senasa.gov.do) and Health Risk Management Companies administer the basic health plan.

Health Risk Management Companies may be private, public, or mixed entities.

Superintendent of Health and Labor Risks (http://www.sisalril.gov.do) supervises the National Health Insurance and Health Risk Management Companies.

Superintendent of Health and Labor Risks supervises the pediatric health care program.

Social Insurance Institute (IDSS) (http://www.idss.org.do) administers pediatric health care.

Work Injury

Regulatory Framework

First law: 1932.

Current law: 2001 (social security).

Type of program: Social insurance system.

Coverage

All insured workers.

Source of Funds

Insured person: None.

Self-employed person: Not applicable.

Employer: Total cost, met through contributions that vary according to the assessed degree of risk. The average contribution is 1.2% of payroll.

There are no minimum earnings for contribution purposes.

The maximum earnings for contribution purposes are equal to 10 times the minimum average national wage.

Government: None.

Qualifying Conditions

Work injury benefits: There is no minimum qualifying period.

Temporary Disability Benefits

The labor law requires that cash benefits are provided for temporary disability.

Permanent Disability Benefits

Permanent disability pension: Benefits are provided according to four degrees of assessed disability.

- Severe total disability (totally disabled and in need of constant attendance),
- Permanent total disability (unable to perform any occupation),
- Permanent total disability for usual occupation (unable to perform usual occupation), and
- Permanent partial disability for current occupation (the loss of at least 50% of earning capacity).

All benefits are calculated using the base salary. The base salary is equal to the insured's average covered earnings in the 6 months before the onset of injury or occupational disease. For insured workers with less than 6 months of covered earnings, the base salary is 50% of total covered earnings.

For a severe total disability, a monthly pension is paid equal to 100% of the base salary. For an assessed degree of disability of at least 67%, a monthly pension is paid equal to 70% of the base salary. For an assessed degree of disability of more than 50% and up to 67%, a monthly pension is paid equal to 50% of the base salary. For an assessed degree of disability of more than 15% and up to 50%, a lump sum is paid equal to between 5 and 10 times the base salary.

Workers' Medical Benefits

Medical benefits are the same as provided under the basic health plan. Benefits include general, specialist, and surgical care; hospitalization; medicines; and prostheses.

Survivor Benefits

Survivor pension: 50% of the deceased's pension is payable to a widow(er) aged 45 or older or disabled.

The pension ceases on remarriage, and a lump sum equal to 2 years' pension is paid.

A widow(er) younger than age 45 receives a lump sum equal to 2 years' pension.

Orphan's pension: 20% of the deceased's pension is payable to each orphan younger than age 18 (age 21 if a full-time student, no limit if disabled).

Administrative Organization

Superintendent of Health and Labor Risks (http://www.sisalril.gov.do) supervises, monitors, and controls the program.

Family Allowances

Regulatory Framework

Benefits are payable to unemployed single mothers with unmarried children younger than age 18 (age 21 if a full-time student, no limit if disabled) who are without sufficient resources to meet basic needs. (The social assistance benefits are provided under the Old Age, Disability, and Survivors program, above).

Ecuador

Exchange rate: Uses the US dollar (US$).

Old Age, Disability, and Survivors

Regulatory Framework

First law: 1928.

Current laws: 1998 and 2001 (social security).

Type of program: Social insurance system.

Note: The provision under the 2001 law to create a system of individual accounts to complement the social insurance old-age pension program was not implemented.

A government-financed program provides basic social assistance cash benefits to needy persons aged 65 or older and persons aged 18 to 65 assessed as at least 70% disabled.

Coverage

Employees in industry, commerce, and agriculture; government employees; domestic workers; and the self-employed.

Voluntary coverage for the President and Vice-President of the Republic and government ministers.

Exclusions: Congressmen and family labor (including a father, mother, spouse, sons younger than age 18, and dependents).

Special systems for small farmers and armed forces and police personnel.

Source of Funds

Insured person: 9.15% to 17.5% of gross earnings, according to occupation.

The minimum earnings for contribution purposes are equal to the legal minimum wage. The legal minimum wage varies according to the nature of employment or work.

The maximum earnings for contribution purposes are equal to 10 times the minimum wage.

Contributions also finance sickness and maternity benefits, work injury benefits, and unemployment benefits (individual severance account).

Self-employed person: 17.5% to 20.5% of declared earnings.

The minimum declared earnings for contribution purposes are equal to the legal minimum wage. The legal minimum wage varies according to the nature of employment or work.

The maximum declared earnings for contribution purposes are equal to 10 times the minimum wage.

Contributions also finance sickness benefits, maternity benefits, and work injury benefits.

Employer: 9.15% to 20.5% of payroll, according to occupation.

The minimum earnings for contribution purposes are equal to the legal minimum wage. The legal minimum wage varies according to the nature of employment or work.

The maximum earnings for contribution purposes are equal to 10 times the minimum wage.

Contributions also finance sickness and maternity benefits, work injury benefits, and unemployment benefits (individual severance account).

Government: A subsidy for old-age, disability, and survivor pensions; contributes as an employer.

Qualifying Conditions

Old-age pension: Age 55 with at least 360 months of contributions if born before November 30, 1946, or age 65 with at least 180 months of contributions. (To be phased in gradually beginning February 2006, age 60 with at least 360 months of contributions.) The required minimum number of monthly contributions is reduced if aged 66 or older.

Early pension: Aged 45 or older before November 30, 2001, with at least 300 months of contributions or unemployed for 6 months.

Disability pension: Must have 5 years of contributions including the 6 months before the onset of disability and a loss of more than 50% of earning capacity.

Survivor pension: The deceased had 5 years of contributions or was a pensioner at the time of death.

Eligible survivors include a widow(er), a partner who had children with the deceased or who cohabited with the deceased for at least 2 years before death, children younger than age 18 (no limit if disabled), a dependent mother and father, and brothers and sisters younger than age 18 (no limit if disabled).

Survivor settlement: The insured did not meet the qualifying conditions for a pension but had up to 59 contributions.

Funeral grant: The deceased had 6 months of contributions in the last 12 months or was a pensioner. The grant is also payable for a dependent.

Old-Age Benefits

Old-age pension: The monthly pension is equal to 50% of the insured's monthly average earnings with at least 120 months of contributions; 75% of the insured's monthly average earnings with 360 months of contributions; and 100% of the insured's monthly average earnings with 480 months of contributions. With more than 480 months of contributions, the pension is increased for each additional year of coverage.

Average earnings for benefit calculation purposes are based on the 5 best years of earnings.

The minimum pension is US$25; US$12 for domestic workers.

The maximum pension is US$240.

Working old-age pensioners may also receive pension benefits if they rejoin the social security scheme.

Early pension: A reduced pension is paid.

Schedule of payment: Fourteen payments a year.

Benefit adjustment: Pensions are adjusted annually according to scheme reserve funds.

Permanent Disability Benefits

Disability pension: The pension is based on monthly average earnings and the number of years of paid contributions. After 40 years of contributions, the pension is increased for each additional year of coverage.

Average earnings for benefit calculation purposes are based on the 5 best years of earnings.

The minimum pension is US$25; US$12 for domestic workers.

Schedule of payment: Fourteen payments a year.

Benefit adjustment: Pensions are adjusted annually according to scheme reserve funds.

Survivor Benefits

Survivor pension: 40% of the deceased's pension is payable to a widow(er) or partner.

Orphan's pension: Each orphan younger than age 18 (no limit if disabled) receives 20% of the deceased's pension; 40% for a full orphan.

Other dependent survivor's pension: A mother or father receives 20% of the insured's pension; each brother or sister who is younger than age 18, disabled, or a student receives 10% of the insured's pension.

The minimum survivor pension is equal to the legal minimum wage, plus income support for a family group.

The maximum survivor pension is equal to 100% of the deceased's pension for a family group.

Survivor settlement: The total contributions are refunded as a lump sum.

Death grant: Twenty-one times the minimum wage, minus the value of the funeral grant, is paid to the person who pays for the funeral.

Funeral grant: Up to US$450.

Administrative Organization

Under the direction of the Minister of Social Welfare, the Advisory Council (http://www.mbs.gov.ec) provides general supervision.

Social Security Institute administers the program.

Sickness and Maternity

Regulatory Framework

First law: 1935.

Current laws: 1942, 1964, and 2001 (social security).

Type of program: Social insurance system. Cash and medical benefits.

Coverage

Employees in industry, commerce, and agriculture; government employees; domestic workers; and the self-employed.

Voluntary coverage for the President and Vice-President of the Republic, government ministers, and part-time workers.

Exclusions: Congressmen and family labor (including a father, mother, spouse, sons younger than age 18, and dependents).

Medical benefits are available to all insured persons.

Special system for small farmers.

Source of Funds

Insured person: See source of funds under Old Age, Disability, and Survivors, above.

Self-employed person: See source of funds under Old Age, Disability, and Survivors, above.

Employer: See source of funds under Old Age, Disability, and Survivors, above.

Government: See source of funds under Old Age, Disability, and Survivors, above.

Qualifying Conditions

Cash sickness benefits: Must have at least 6 months of contributions before the onset of incapacity.

Cash maternity benefits: Must have at least 360 days of contributions in the year before giving birth or at least 378 days of contributions in the 16 months before giving birth. Prenatal care is provided with at least 6 months of contributions.

Medical benefits: Must have at least 180 days of consecutive contributions in the 6 months before the onset of illness or at least 189 days of contributions in the 8 months before the onset of illness. For the voluntarily insured, 360 days of consecutive contributions in the 12 months before the onset of illness or at least 378 days of contributions in the 16 months before the onset of illness. Benefits are provided for 60 days after the insured ceases to pay contributions.

Sickness and Maternity Benefits

Sickness benefit: For the first 10 weeks, the benefit is equal to 75% of the insured's average earnings in the 3 months before the onset of incapacity. The benefit is payable after a 4-day waiting period for up to 70 days; thereafter, 66% of earnings for up to a maximum of 182 days.

Maternity benefit: The benefit is equal to 75% of the insured's last earnings and is payable 2 weeks before and 10 weeks after the expected date of childbirth. (The employer pays 25% of the insured's last earnings for the same period.)

Workers' Medical Benefits

Medical services are ordinarily provided directly to patients through the medical facilities of the Social Security Institute. Medical care in private clinics is possible under certain conditions. A refund for the cost of medical care provided through medical facilities not belonging to the Social Security Institute is possible in certain cases. Benefits include general and specialist care, home care, surgery, hospitalization, medicines, appliances, rehabilitation, laboratory services, and dental care.

Dependents' Medical Benefits

Full medical care is provided for infants during their first year.

Administrative Organization

Under the direction of the Minister of Social Welfare, the Advisory Council (http://www.mbs.gov.ec) provides general supervision.

Social Security Institute administers the program.

Social Security Institute operates its own clinics, dispensaries, and hospitals.

Work Injury

Regulatory Framework

First law: 1921.

Current laws: 1964 and 2001 (social security).

Type of program: Social insurance system.

Coverage

All insured persons, including public employees, domestic workers, and self-employed workers.

Exclusions: Congressmen and family labor (including a father, mother, spouse, sons younger than age 18, and dependents).

Source of Funds

Insured person: See source of funds under Old Age, Disability, and Survivors, above.

Self-employed person: See source of funds under Old Age, Disability, and Survivors, above.

Employer: See source of funds under Old Age, Disability, and Survivors, above.

Government: See source of funds under Old Age, Disability, and Survivors, above.

Qualifying Conditions

Work injury benefits: There is no minimum qualifying period.

Occupational disease benefits: Must have 6 months of contributions; 12 months for voluntary contributors.

Temporary Disability Benefits

For the first 10 weeks, the benefit is equal to 75% of average earnings in the 10 weeks before the onset of disability; thereafter, 66% of average earnings until the end of the 12th month. If the disability lasts for more than a year, the benefit is increased to 80% of average earnings. Benefits are paid from the day after the onset of disability for a work injury and after a three-day waiting period for an occupational disease.

Permanent Disability Benefits

Permanent disability pension: The pension is equal to 80% of average earnings in the last year or in the previous 5 years if earnings were higher (100% of average earnings in cases of severe disability requiring constant attendance).

Partial disability: A percentage of the full pension is paid according to the assessed degree of disability, based on the schedule in law.

The minimum pension is US$25; US$12 for domestic workers.

Schedule of payments: Fifteen payments a year.

Benefit adjustment: Pensions are adjusted annually according to scheme reserve funds.

Workers' Medical Benefits

Benefits include medical and surgical care, hospitalization, appliances, medicines, and rehabilitation.

Survivor Benefits

Survivor pension: 40% of the deceased's pension is payable to a widow(er) or partner.

Orphan's pension: Each orphan younger than age 18 (no limit if disabled) receives 20% of the deceased's pension; 40% for a full orphan.

Funeral grant: Twenty-four times the minimum wage is paid to the person who pays for the cost of the funeral.

Administrative Organization

Under the direction of the Minister of Social Welfare, the Advisory Council (http://www.mbs.gov.ec) provides general supervision.

Social Security Institute administers the program.

Unemployment

Regulatory Framework

First law: 1951.

Current laws: 1958 and 2001 (social security).

Type of program: Individual severance account and social insurance system.

Note: In 2001, a system of individual severance accounts was introduced. Participation is mandatory for workers younger than age 40 when the program was implemented. The previous social insurance system providing lump-sum benefits is being phased out.

Coverage

Individual severance account: Employees in the private and public sectors.

Social insurance: Employees in the private and public sectors.

Exclusions: Volunteer workers.

Source of Funds

Individual severance account

Insured person: See source of funds under Old Age, Disability, and Survivors, above.

Self-employed person: Not applicable.

Employer: See source of funds under Old Age, Disability, and Survivors, above.

Government: See source of funds under Old Age, Disability, and Survivors, above.

Social insurance

Insured person: 2% of earnings.

Self-employed person: Not applicable.

Employer: 1% of payroll.

Government: None; contributes as an employer.

Qualifying Conditions

Unemployment benefits

Individual severance account: The insured must be involuntarily unemployed with at least 48 monthly contributions.

Social insurance: Must have at least 60 months of contributions. The benefit is payable after 90 days of unemployment or if unemployment is the result of the onset of a permanent disability.

Unemployment Benefits

Individual severance account: A lump sum equal to three times the insured's average wage in the last 12 months is paid. (The total accumulated capital can be drawn down if the insured retires or is assessed as disabled, or by survivors in the event of the insured's death.)

The maximum benefit is equal to the accumulated capital in the individual account, plus interest.

Benefit adjustment: Benefit amounts are fixed annually.

Unemployment benefit (social insurance): A lump sum equal to three times the insured's average wage in the last 12 months is paid.

Survivor benefit (social insurance): A lump sum is paid to a widow, a disabled widower, and children younger than age 21. In the absence of a spouse and children, certain other surviving relatives of an insured person born before November 30, 1961, may be eligible.

Benefit adjustment: Benefit amounts are fixed annually.

Administrative Organization

Individual severance account: Savings managing institutions (EDAPs) manage the accounts.

Banking Superintendent (http://www.superban.gov.ec) supervises the EDAPs.

Social insurance: Under the direction of the Minister of Social Welfare, the Advisory Council (http://www.mbs.gov.ec) provides general supervision.

Social Security Institute administers the program.

Family Allowances

Regulatory Framework

No statutory benefits are provided.

Mothers assessed as needy with at least one child (younger than age 18) and low-income families receive a monthly allowance under the Bono de Desarrollo Humano program.

El Salvador

Exchange rate: Uses the US dollar (US$).

Old Age, Disability, and Survivors

Regulatory Framework

First law: 1953, implemented in 1969.

Current law: 1996 (individual account), implemented in 1998.

Type of program: Mandatory individual account and social insurance system.

Note: The 1996 law established a system of mandatory individual accounts. The social insurance system is closed to new entrants and will be phased out. Those who were younger than age 36 in 1997 transferred to the private insurance system; those who were aged 36 or older but younger than age 55 (men) or age 50 (women) could join voluntarily.

Coverage

Mandatory individual account: All employees in the private, public, and municipal sectors not covered under social insurance.

Voluntary coverage for the self-employed.

Social insurance: All insured persons who were older than age 55 (men) or age 50 (women) in 1998.

Voluntary coverage for those who were aged 36 or older in 1998.

Source of Funds

Mandatory individual account

Insured person: 3.25% of earnings, plus up to a maximum of 1.28% of earnings for disability and survivor insurance and up to a maximum of 1.71% of earnings for administrative fees.

The minimum earnings for contribution purposes are equal to the legal monthly minimum wage. (US$151.20 in the manufacturing for export sector; US$158.40 for all other sectors.)

The maximum earnings for contribution purposes are equal to gross monthly earnings. Gross monthly earnings must not exceed the national public-sector maximum wage.

Self-employed person: A voluntary contribution of 13% of declared income, plus up to a maximum of 1.28% of declared income for disability and survivor insurance and up to a maximum of 1.71% of declared income for administrative fees.

The minimum earnings for contribution purposes are equal to the legal monthly minimum wage. (US$151.20 in the manufacturing for export sector; US$158.40 for all other sectors.)

The maximum earnings for contribution purposes are equal to gross monthly earnings. Gross monthly earnings must not exceed the national public-sector maximum wage.

Employer: 6.75% of earnings.

The minimum earnings for contribution purposes are equal to the legal monthly minimum wage. (US$151.20 in the manufacturing for export sector; US$158.40 for all other sectors.)

The maximum earnings for contribution purposes are equal to gross monthly earnings. Gross monthly earnings must not exceed the national public-sector maximum wage.

Government: Subsidizes the guaranteed minimum pension.

Social insurance

Insured person: 7% of earnings.

Self-employed person: Not applicable.

Employer: 7% of payroll.

Government: The government finances an indexed bond provided to individuals who switched to the mandatory individual account system. The bond represents the value of the insured's contributions to the old social insurance system plus interest.

Qualifying Conditions

Mandatory individual account

Old-age pension: Age 60 (men) or age 55 (women) with 25 years of contributions. Retirement is permitted before the normal retirement age if the pension equals at least 60% of the base salary (average earnings in the last 20 months of contributions) and 160% of the current minimum pension.

Guaranteed minimum pension: Age 60 (men) or age 55 (women) with 25 years of contributions. The pension (based on the value of the accumulated capital plus accrued interest) is less than the minimum pension set by law.

Disability pension: The insured was actively contributing to an individual account before the onset of disability (in the case of a common accident); unemployed persons must have 6 months of contributions in the 12 months before the onset of disability.

The degree of disability is assessed by the Disability Commission.

Guaranteed minimum pension: Must have 10 years of contributions or contributions in 3 of the 5 years before the onset of disability. The pension (based on the value of the accumulated capital plus accrued interest) is less than the minimum pension set by law.

Constant-attendance supplement: Paid if the insured requires the constant attendance of another person.

Survivor pension: The deceased was a pensioner or actively contributing to an individual account before death; unemployed persons must have had 6 months of contributions in the 12 months before the date of death.

Eligible survivors are the deceased's spouse or cohabiting partner, children younger than age 18 (age 24 if a student, no limit if disabled), and dependent parents.

Guaranteed minimum pension: The deceased had 10 years of contributions or contributions in 3 of the 5 years before death. The survivor pension (based on the value of the accumulated capital plus accrued interest) is less than the minimum pension set by law.

Social insurance

Old-age pension: Age 60 (men) or age 55 (women) with at least 25 years of contributions. There is no age requirement if the insured has 30 years of contributions.

Disability pension: Must be younger than age 60 (men) or age 55 (women) and assessed as disabled with at least 36 months of contributions, including 18 months in the 36 months before the onset of disability.

The degree of disability is assessed by the Disability Commission.

Survivor pension: The deceased was a pensioner or had at least 5 years of contributions.

Old-Age Benefits

Mandatory individual account

Old-age pension: The pension is equal to the insured's contributions plus accrued interest. At retirement, the insured may either make periodic withdrawals from the individual account to guarantee income for the duration of the expected life span or buy an annuity from a private insurance company, or use a combination of both. (The value of accrued rights under the social insurance system is combined with the individual account balance.)

Guaranteed minimum pension: US$114 a month.

Social insurance

Old-age pension: The pension is equal to 30% of the base salary for the first 3 years' contributions, plus 1.5% for each additional year.

The base salary is equal to the insured's average earnings in the last 120 months.

The minimum monthly pension is US$114.

The maximum monthly pension is equal to 100% of the base salary.

Permanent Disability Benefits

Mandatory individual account

Disability pension: The pension is equal to 70% of the base salary for a total disability. (Disability insurance tops up the accumulated capital in the individual account if the balance is less than the required minimum to finance the permanent disability pension.)

Partial disability: The pension is equal to 50% of the base salary.

The base salary is equal to the insured's average earnings in the last 120 months.

Guaranteed minimum pension: US$114 a month for a total disability; US$79.80 a month for a partial disability.

The minimum disability pension is replaced by the minimum old-age pension at the normal retirement age.

Social insurance

Disability pension: The pension is equal to 30% of the base salary for the first 3 years' contributions, plus 1.5% for each additional year.

The base salary is equal to the insured's average earnings in the last 120 months.

The minimum monthly pension is US$114.

The minimum disability pension is replaced by the minimum old-age pension at the normal retirement age.

Survivor Benefits

Mandatory individual account

Survivor pension: 50% of the deceased's pension is payable to a spouse (or partner) with children; 60% if there are no eligible children. (Life insurance tops up the accumulated capital in the deceased's individual account if the balance is less than the required minimum to finance the survivor pension.)

Orphan's pension: Each eligible child receives 25% of the deceased's pension.

Parent's pension: Each parent receives 20% of the deceased's pension; 30% if there is only one surviving parent.

In the absence of a surviving spouse (or partner), the pension for surviving children or parents is increased.

Guaranteed minimum pension: US$114 a month.

The minimum survivor pension is a percentage of the minimum old-age pension.

Social insurance

Survivor pension: 50% of the deceased's pension is payable to a widow who was married to the insured for at least 6 months (or who is pregnant or had a child with the deceased) or disabled, a female partner who cohabited with the deceased for the last 3 years (or who is pregnant or had a child with the deceased) or is disabled, and a disabled widower.

Orphan's pension: Each eligible child receives 25% of the deceased's pension; 40% for a full orphan.

Other eligible survivors (in the absence of the above): 30% of the deceased's pension is payable to a mother aged 55 or older; 30% to a father aged 60 or older; 40% if there is only one surviving eligible parent.

The minimum survivor pension is a percentage of the minimum old age pension.

The total survivor pension must not exceed 100% of the deceased's old-age pension.

Administrative Organization

Mandatory individual account: Superintendent of Pensions (http://www.spensiones.gob.sv) provides general supervision.

Individual pension fund management companies (AFPs) administer individual accounts.

Social insurance: Superintendent of Pensions (http://www.spensiones.gob.sv) provides general supervision.

Supervised by a board of 12 directors including the Minister of Labor, representatives of other ministries, the Director of Social Insurance, and representatives of management, labor, and other professional groups, the Social Insurance Institute plans, manages, and administers the program.

Sickness and Maternity

Regulatory Framework

First law: 1949.

Current laws: 1953 and 1993.

Type of program: Social insurance system. Cash and medical benefits.

Coverage

Employed and self-employed persons in industry and commerce and pensioners.

Exclusions: Agricultural, domestic, and casual employees.

Source of Funds

Insured person: 3% of earnings. Pensioners contribute 7.8% of the old-age pension or disability pension and 6% of work injury pensions.

The minimum earnings for contribution purposes are equal to the legal monthly minimum wage. (US$151.20 in the manufacturing for export sector; US$158.40 for all other sectors.)

The maximum earnings for contribution purposes are equal to gross monthly earnings. Gross monthly earnings must not exceed the national public-sector maximum wage.

The above contributions also finance work injury benefits.

Self-employed person: 10.5% of declared income.

The minimum earnings for contribution purposes are equal to the legal monthly minimum wage. (US$151.20 in the manufacturing for export sector; US$158.40 for all other sectors.)

The maximum earnings for contribution purposes are equal to gross monthly earnings. Gross monthly earnings must not exceed the national public-sector maximum wage.

The above contributions also finance work injury benefits.

Employer: 7.5% of payroll.

The minimum earnings for contribution purposes are equal to the legal monthly minimum wage. (US$151.20 in the manufacturing for export sector; US$158.40 for all other sectors.)

The maximum earnings for contribution purposes are equal to gross monthly earnings. Gross monthly earnings must not exceed the national public-sector maximum wage.

The above contributions also finance work injury benefits.

Government: An annual subsidy.

The above subsidy also finances work injury benefits.

Qualifying Conditions

Cash sickness benefits: There is no minimum qualifying period if the insured is in current employment; if unemployed, 8 weeks of contributions in the last 3 months before the onset of incapacity.

Cash maternity benefits: Must have 12 weeks of contributions in the 12 months before the expected date of childbirth.

Medical benefits: There is no minimum qualifying period if the insured is currently employed; if unemployed, 8 weeks of contributions in the last 4 months.

Sickness and Maternity Benefits

Sickness benefit: The benefit is equal to 75% of average monthly earnings and is payable after a 3-day waiting period for up to 52 weeks for the same incapacity.

Maternity benefit: The benefit is equal to 75% of average earnings and is payable for up to 12 weeks; other benefits include a milk allowance for up to 12 weeks (with a medical prescription) and a layette (clothing and other necessities for the newborn).

Workers' Medical Benefits

Benefits include complete medical and maternity care, hospitalization, medicines, auxiliary services for diagnosis and treatment, and dental care (except for cosmetic reasons).

Dependents' Medical Benefits

The insured's wife receives prenatal and postnatal care and in-kind benefits and medical and dental benefits for sickness and accidents. Children up to age 6 receive ambulatory care and preventative dental care.

Administrative Organization

Supervised by a board of 12 directors including the Minister of Labor, representatives of other ministries, the Director of Social Insurance, and representatives of management, labor, and other professional groups, the Social Insurance Institute plans, manages, and administers the program.

Social Insurance Institute operates its own clinics and hospitals and contracts services from the Ministry of Health and the private sector where required.

Work Injury

Regulatory Framework

First law: 1949.

Current laws: 1953 and 1993.

Type of program: Social insurance system.

Coverage

Public- and private-sector employees and self-employed persons in industry and commerce.

Exclusions: Domestic and casual employees and teachers.

Source of Funds

Insured person: See source of funds under Sickness and Maternity, above.

Self-employed person: See source of funds under Sickness and Maternity, above.

Employer: See source of funds under Sickness and Maternity, above.

Government: See source of funds under Sickness and Maternity, above.

Qualifying Conditions

Work injury benefits: There is no minimum qualifying period.

Temporary Disability Benefits

The benefit is equal to 75% of the insured's average monthly earnings in the first 3 of the last 4 months. The benefit is payable from the day after the onset of disability for up to 52 weeks.

Permanent Disability Benefits

Permanent disability pension: With an assessed degree of disability greater than 66%, the pension is equal to 70% of the insured's average monthly earnings in the last year.

The minimum monthly pension is US$114.

Dependent child allowance: A monthly amount for each dependent child younger than age 16 (age 21 if a student) or disabled.

Constant-attendance supplement: Up to 50% of the pension.

Partial disability: If the assessed degree of disability is between 35% and 66%, a percentage of the full pension is paid according to the assessed degree of disability. If the assessed degree of disability is between 20% and 35%, a pension equal to double the amount of the permanent disability pension based on the assessed degree of disability is payable for a limited period of up to 3 years.

Workers' Medical Benefits

Benefits include complete medical care, hospitalization, drugs, auxiliary services for diagnosis and treatment, and dental care.

Survivor Benefits

Survivor pension: 60% of the deceased's pension is payable to a spouse.

Orphan's pension: Each child receives 30% of the deceased's pension.

The maximum survivor pension is equal to 100% of the deceased's pension.

Funeral grant: Equal to twice the deceased's average monthly salary.

Administrative Organization

Supervised by a board of 12 directors including the Minister of Labor, representatives of other ministries, the Director of Social Insurance, and representatives of management, labor, and other professional groups, the Social Insurance Institute plans, manages, and administers the program.

Social Insurance Institute operates its own clinics and hospitals and contracts services from the Ministry of Health and the private sector where required.

Grenada

Exchange rate: US$1.00 equals
2.70 East Caribbean dollars (EC$).

Old Age, Disability, and Survivors

Regulatory Framework

First law: 1969 (provident fund).

Current law: 1983 (social insurance), with 1988 amendments.

Type of program: Social insurance system.

Coverage

All private- and public-sector employees and self-employed persons aged 16 to 59.

There are no special systems for any specified groups of employees.

Source of Funds

Insured person: 4% of monthly gross earnings.

There are no minimum earnings for contribution purposes.

The maximum monthly earnings for contribution purposes are EC$3,000.

The insured's contributions also finance sickness benefits, maternity benefits, and work injury benefits.

Self-employed person: 6.75% of monthly gross earnings.

There are no minimum earnings for contribution purposes.

The maximum monthly earnings for contribution purposes are EC$3,000.

The self-employed person's contributions also finance sickness and maternity benefits.

Employer: 5% of monthly gross wages.

There are no minimum earnings for contribution purposes.

The maximum monthly earnings for contribution purposes are EC$3,000.

The employer's contributions also finance sickness benefits, maternity benefits, and work injury benefits.

Government: None; contributes as an employer.

Qualifying Conditions

Old-age pension: Age 60 with at least 500 weeks of coverage, including at least 150 weeks of paid contributions.

Partial pension: Age 60 with at least 260 weeks of coverage, including at least 150 weeks of paid contributions.

Early pension: There is no early pension.

Deferred pension: There is no deferred pension. (For late application, the insured will receive only 1 year of any retroactive payment due.)

Old-age grant: Age 60 and does not meet the qualifying conditions for the old-age pension. Must have at least 50 weeks of paid or credited contributions.

Old-age benefits are payable abroad.

Disability pension: Younger than age 60 with 150 weeks of paid contributions and an assessed degree of disability of 30% or more.

The degree of disability is assessed by the insured's doctor only once.

Disability grant: Younger than age 60 with an assessed degree of disability of less than 30%. There are no qualifying conditions for contributions.

The degree of disability is assessed by a doctor only once.

Disability benefits are payable abroad.

Survivor pension: The deceased was a pensioner or was eligible for a pension at the time of death.

Survivor grant: The deceased was eligible for an old-age grant or a disability grant at the time of death.

Eligible survivors are the deceased's widow(er) and children.

Survivor benefits are payable abroad.

Funeral grant: The deceased was a pensioner or was eligible for an old-age grant or a disability grant at the time of death. The grant is payable for the funeral of the insured, the insured's spouse, and the insured's children. The funeral grant is payable to the person who meets the cost of the funeral.

Old-Age Benefits

Old-age pension: The pension is equal to 30% of average weekly earnings, plus 1% of earnings for each 50-week period of contributions over 500 weeks.

The minimum weekly pension is EC$40.

The maximum weekly pension is EC$297.70.

Partial pension: The pension is equal to 16% of average weekly earnings, plus 1% of earnings for each 25-week period of contributions over 150 weeks up to 499 weeks.

Average weekly earnings are based on average annual earnings in the best 3 years divided by 52.

Early pension: There is no early pension.

Deferred pension: There is no deferred pension. (For late application, the insured will receive only 1 year of any retroactive payment due.)

Old-age grant: A lump sum equal to five times average weekly insurable earnings is paid for each 50-week period of contributions.

Average weekly insurable earnings are based on the sum of the weekly earnings for the relevant period divided by the number of weeks.

Benefit adjustment: Benefits are reviewed periodically.

Permanent Disability Benefits

Disability pension: The pension is equal to 30% of average weekly earnings, plus 1% of earnings for each 50-week period of contributions over 500 weeks.

Average weekly earnings are based on average annual earnings in the best 3 years divided by 52.

The minimum weekly pension is EC$40.

The maximum weekly pension is equal to 60% of average earnings.

Disability grant: A lump sum equal to five times average weekly insurable earnings is paid for each 50-week period of contributions.

Average weekly insurable earnings are based on the sum of the weekly earnings for the relevant period divided by the number of weeks.

Benefit adjustment: Benefits are reviewed periodically.

Survivor Benefits

Survivor pension: 75% of the deceased's pension is payable to a widow aged 50 or older or disabled or to a dependent disabled widower. A limited pension is payable for a year to a widow who is younger than age 50.

Orphan's pension: 25% of the deceased's pension is paid for each child younger than age 16 (age 18 if a full-time student); 50% for each disabled child or full orphan.

The minimum weekly pension is EC$8.50; EC$17 for a disabled child or full orphan.

The maximum survivor pension is equal to 100% of the deceased's pension.

Survivor grant: A lump sum equal to five times average weekly insurable earnings for each 50-week period of contributions.

Average weekly insurable earnings are based on the sum of the weekly earnings for the relevant period divided by the number of weeks.

Funeral grant: EC$2,000 is paid for the insured's funeral; EC$1,500 for the funeral of the insured's spouse; EC$750 for the funeral of the insured's child.

Benefit adjustment: Benefits are reviewed periodically.

Administrative Organization

Ministry of Health, Social Security, the Environment, and Ecclesiastical Relations provides general supervision.

National Insurance Board (http://www.nisgrenada.org) administers the program.

Sickness and Maternity

Regulatory Framework

First and current law: 1980 (maternity leave) and 1983 (social insurance), with 1988 amendments.

Type of program: Social insurance system. Cash benefits only.

Coverage

All private- and public-sector employees and self-employed persons aged 16 to 59.

There are no special systems for any specified groups of employees.

Source of Funds

Insured person: See source of funds under Old Age, Disability, and Survivors, above.

Self-employed person: See source of funds under Old Age, Disability, and Survivors, above.

Employer: See source of funds under Old Age, Disability, and Survivors, above.

Government: See source of funds under Old Age, Disability, and Survivors, above.

Qualifying Conditions

Cash sickness benefits: Employed on the day before the onset of incapacity with at least 13 weeks of contributions, including 8 of the 13 weeks before the onset of incapacity.

Cash maternity benefits: Must have at least 30 weeks of contributions, including 20 weeks in the 30-week period ending 6 weeks before the expected date of childbirth.

Maternity grant: The grant is payable to the uninsured wife of an insured man.

Maternity leave: Provided by employers to insured employees.

Funeral grant: The deceased was receiving or was entitled to receive sickness or maternity benefits at the time of death. The grant is payable to the person who meets the cost of the funeral.

Sickness and Maternity Benefits

Sickness benefit: The benefit is equal to 65% of average weekly insurable earnings in the 13 weeks before the onset of incapacity. The benefit is payable from the first day of incapacity for up to 26 weeks; for up to 52 weeks with at least 75 weeks of paid or credited contributions in the last 3 years.

Maternity benefit: The benefit is equal to 65% of average weekly insurable earnings in the 30 weeks before the start of the claim. The benefit is payable for a maximum of 12 weeks, beginning 6 weeks before the expected date of childbirth and up to 6 weeks after.

The minimum maternity benefit is EC$450.

Maternity leave: The employer provides an additional 40% of average insurable earnings for 2 months of the 3-month maternity leave period.

Maternity grant: The minimum grant is EC$450.

Funeral grant: EC$2,000.

Benefit adjustment: Benefits are reviewed periodically.

Workers' Medical Benefits

No statutory benefits are provided.

Dependents' Medical Benefits

No statutory benefits are provided.

Administrative Organization

Ministry of Health, Social Security, the Environment, and Ecclesiastical Relations provides general supervision.

National Insurance Board (http://www.nisgrenada.org) administers the program.

Work Injury

Regulatory Framework

First and current laws: 1982 (workmen's compensation), with 1982 amendment; and 1983 (social insurance), with 1998 amendment.

Type of program: Social insurance system.

Coverage

All private- and public-sector employees aged 16 to 59.

Exclusions: The self-employed. (Coverage may be extended to the self-employed before the end of 2006.)

There are no special systems for any specified groups of employees.

Source of Funds

Insured person: None.

Self-employed person: Not applicable.

Employer: 1% of the total 5% of gross monthly wages paid under Old Age, Disability, and Survivors, above.

Government: None; contributes as an employer.

Qualifying Conditions

Work injury benefits: There is no minimum qualifying period.

Temporary Disability Benefits

The benefit is equal to 70% of average weekly insurable earnings in the last 13 weeks. The benefit is payable from the day of the accident or certified onset of the occupational disease until recovery, up to a maximum of 26 weeks.

The degree of disability is assessed by the insured's doctor only once.

Benefit adjustment: Benefits are reviewed periodically.

Permanent Disability Benefits

For total disability (100%), the benefit is equal to 70% of average weekly insurable earnings in the last 13 weeks. For an assessed degree of disability of less than 100%, the benefit is proportionately reduced. The degree of assessed disability must be greater than 1%.

If the assessed degree of disability is less than 30%, a lump sum is paid.

The degree of disability is assessed by the insured's doctor only once.

There is no maximum period for which the benefit is payable.

Constant-attendance allowance: Equal to 50% of the benefit, if 100% disabled.

Benefit adjustment: Benefits are reviewed periodically.

Workers' Medical Benefits

Benefits include medical, surgical, dental, and hospital treatment; skilled nursing services; the cost of medicines; prostheses; overseas treatment; and the cost of transportation.

Survivor Benefits

Survivor pension: 75% of the deceased's pension is payable to a widow(er) for life.

The pension ceases on remarriage.

Orphan's pension: Each child younger than age 16 (age 18 if a full-time student) receives 25% of the deceased's pension; 50% for each disabled child or full orphan.

The minimum weekly pension is EC$8.50; EC$17 for a disabled child or full orphan.

Other dependent's pension: 50% of the deceased's pension is paid if the survivor was totally dependent on the insured; 25% if partially dependent. The pension is payable for a maximum of 52 weeks from the insured's date of death.

The minimum weekly pension is EC$8.50; EC$17 for a disabled child or full orphan.

The maximum total survivor pension is 100% of the deceased's pension.

Funeral grant: EC$2,000 is payable to the person who meets the cost of the funeral.

Benefit adjustment: Benefits are reviewed periodically.

Administrative Organization

Ministry of Housing, Social Security, and Women's Affairs provides general supervision.

National Insurance Board (http://www.nisgrenada.org) administers the program.

Guatemala

Exchange rate: US$1.00 equals 7.59 quetzales.

Old Age, Disability, and Survivors

Regulatory Framework

First law: 1969, implemented on a national level in 1977.

Current law: 2003 (old-age, disability, and survivors).

Type of program: Social insurance system.

Coverage

Employees, including agricultural workers and some public-sector employees.

Voluntary coverage for the self-employed.

Special system for other public-sector employees.

Source of Funds

Insured person: 1.83% of gross earnings.

There are no minimum earnings for contribution purposes.

The maximum monthly earnings for contribution and benefit purposes are 6,000 quetzales.

Self-employed person: Voluntary contributions of 5.5% of declared earnings.

There are no minimum earnings for contribution purposes.

The maximum monthly earnings for contribution and benefit purposes are 6,000 quetzales.

Employer: 3.67% of payroll.

There are no minimum earnings for contribution purposes.

The maximum monthly earnings for contribution and benefit purposes are 6,000 quetzales.

Government: 25% of the cost of benefits paid; also contributes as an employer. The minimum monthly pension is not guaranteed by government.

Qualifying Conditions

Old-age pension: Age 60 with at least 180 months of contributions. If the insured does not fully meet the qualifying conditions, no pension or other cash benefit is paid.

Early pension: There is no early pension.

Deferred pension: There is no deferred pension.

The pension is not payable abroad.

Disability pension: Assessed as disabled with at least 36 months of contributions in the last 6 years and younger than age 45; at least 60 months of contributions in the last 9 years and aged 45 to 54; at least 120 months of contributions in the last 12 years and age 55 (younger in certain cases) or older.

The disability pension is awarded according to two degrees of disability: total disability, involving the loss of 2/3 of earning capacity; and severe disability, involving the complete loss of earning capacity and the need for the constant attendance of another person.

The pension is not payable abroad.

Survivor pension: The deceased had at least 36 months of contributions in the last 6 years or was receiving a pension or qualified for the old-age pension at the time of death.

Old-Age Benefits

Old-age pension: The pension is equal to 50% of the insured's average earnings in the last 60 months, plus an additional 0.5% for each 6-month period of contributions beyond 120 months.

Dependent's supplement: 10% of the insured's pension for a wife or partner or a disabled husband, for each child younger than age 18 or disabled, and for a dependent mother and a dependent disabled father.

The minimum monthly pension, including supplements, is 340 quetzales.

The maximum monthly pension, including supplements, is 4,800 quetzales.

The maximum pension received by a family is 80% of the insured's earnings, up to 6,000 quetzales.

Schedule of payments: Twelve payments a year.

Benefit adjustment: Benefits are adjusted at least every 3 years according to an actuarial assessment.

Permanent Disability Benefits

Disability pension: For a total disability, the pension is equal to 50% of the insured's average earnings in the last 36 months, plus an additional 0.5% for each 6-month period of contributions beyond 120 months. If the insured has worked for less than 36 months, the pension is equal to 50% of average earnings for the total number of months worked.

Dependent's supplement: 10% of the insured's pension for a wife or partner or a disabled husband, for each child younger than age 18 or disabled, and for a dependent mother and a dependent disabled father.

The minimum monthly pension, including supplements, is 340 quetzales.

The maximum monthly pension, including supplements, is 4,800 quetzales.

Constant-attendance supplement: 25% of the insured's pension is paid for a severe disability.

Schedule of payments: Twelve payments a year.

Benefit adjustment: Benefits are adjusted at least every 3 years according to an actuarial assessment.

Survivor Benefits

Survivor pension: The spouse's pension is equal to 50% of the total disability or old-age pension paid or payable to the deceased.

The minimum monthly pension for a spouse is 170 quetzales.

Orphan's pension: Each orphan receives 25% of the deceased's pension; 50% for each full orphan.

The minimum monthly orphan's pension is 85 quetzales; 170 quetzales for a full orphan.

Dependent parent's pension: Each receives 25% of the deceased's pension.

The minimum monthly pension for a dependent parent is 85 quetzales.

Schedule of payments: Twelve payments a year.

The maximum total survivor pension is 100% of the deceased's pension; the sum of the minimum monthly pensions must not exceed 340 quetzales.

Funeral grant: A lump sum of 600 quetzales.

Benefit adjustment: Benefits are adjusted at least every 3 years according to an actuarial assessment.

Administrative Organization

Ministry of Labor and Social Welfare (http://www.mintrabajo.gob.gt) provides general supervision.

Social Security Institute (http://www.igssgt.org) administers the program.

Sickness and Maternity

Regulatory Framework

First law: 1952 (maternity and children).

Current law: 1964 (sickness and maternity), implemented in 1968, with 2003 amendment.

Type of program: Social insurance system. Cash and medical benefits.

Coverage

Employees of firms with three or more workers. Freight or passenger transport enterprises with one or more workers.

Exclusions: The self-employed.

Source of Funds

Insured person: 2% of gross earnings.

There are no maximum earnings for contribution purposes.

Self-employed person: Not applicable.

Employer: 4% of payroll.

There are no maximum earnings for contribution purposes.

Government: 2% of payroll.

There are no maximum earnings for contribution purposes.

Qualifying Conditions

Cash sickness and maternity benefits: Three months of contributions in the 6 months before the onset of incapacity.

Medical benefits: Must be in covered employment.

Sickness and Maternity Benefits

Sickness benefit: The benefit is equal to 2/3 of average earnings (according to the applicable formula). The benefit is payable after a 3-day waiting period for up to 26 weeks; may be extended to 39 weeks. The receipt of benefits for multiple periods of illness must not exceed 52 weeks in a 24-month period.

The maximum monthly benefit is 2,400 quetzales.

Maternity benefit: The benefit is equal to 100% of earnings and is payable for 30 days before and 54 days after the expected date of childbirth. Nursing mothers are also permitted 1 hour a day at work to nurse their child, for up to a maximum of 10 months.

Benefit adjustment: Benefits are adjusted at least every 3 years according to an actuarial assessment.

Workers' Medical Benefits

Benefits include general, specialist, and maternity care; surgery; hospitalization; pharmaceuticals; laboratory services; X-rays; appliances; transportation; rehabilitation; and retraining. Medical services are normally provided directly to patients through the medical facilities of the Social Security Institute.

Free medical benefits for accidents, sickness, and maternity care are provided for pensioners through the old-age, disability, and survivors program in 19 departments.

Dependents' Medical Benefits

The wife or companion of an insured man receives the same maternity care as an insured woman and in 19 departments also receives sickness and accident benefits.

Free medical benefits for accidents, sickness, and maternity care are provided for pensioners through the old-age, disability, and survivors program in 19 departments.

Administrative Organization

Ministry of Labor and Social Welfare (http://www .mintrabajo.gob.gt) provides general supervision.

Social Security Institute (http://www.igssgt.org) administers the program and operates 24 hospitals, 35 clinics, 16 first-aid stations, and other medical services.

Work Injury

Regulatory Framework

First law: 1947.

Current law: 1994, implemented in 1995, with 2003 amendment.

Type of program: Social insurance system.

Note: Work injury benefits are administered as part of the old-age, disability, and survivor program.

Coverage

All insured workers in the country.

Exclusions: The self-employed.

Source of Funds

Insured person: 1% of gross earnings.

There are no minimum and maximum earnings for contribution purposes.

Self-employed person: Not applicable.

Employer: 3% of payroll.

There are no minimum and maximum earnings for contribution purposes.

Government: 1.5% of payroll.

There are no minimum and maximum earnings for contribution purposes.

Qualifying Conditions

Work injury benefits: Must have 3 months of contributions before the onset of the work injury or occupational disease.

Temporary Disability Benefits

The benefit is equal to 2/3 of earnings and is payable after a 1-day waiting period.

The minimum daily benefit is 8 quetzales.

The maximum monthly benefit is 2,400 quetzales.

Benefit adjustment: Benefits are adjusted at least every 3 years according to an actuarial assessment.

Permanent Disability Benefits

A lump sum of between 495 quetzales and 4,950 quetzales is paid according to the assessed degree of disability.

Benefit adjustment: Benefits are adjusted at least every 3 years according to an actuarial assessment.

Workers' Medical Benefits

Benefits include medical treatment, surgery, hospitalization, medicines, appliances, transportation, rehabilitation services, X-rays, laboratory tests, and retraining.

Survivor Benefits

Funeral grant: A lump sum of 412.50 quetzales is paid toward the cost of funeral expenses.

Benefit adjustment: Benefits are adjusted at least every 3 years according to an actuarial assessment.

Administrative Organization

Ministry of Labor and Social Welfare (http:// www.mintrabajo.gob.gt) provides general supervision.

Social Security Institute (http://www.igssgt.org) administers contributions and benefits and provides medical benefits through its 24 hospitals and 35 clinics as well as through private clinics.

Guyana

Exchange rate: US$1.00 equals
203 Guyana dollars (G$).

Old Age, Disability, and Survivors

Regulatory Framework

First law: 1944 (old-age assistance).

Current law: 1969 (social security), with amendments.

Type of program: Social insurance system.

Coverage

All public- and private-sector employees and the self-employed between ages 16 and 59.

Voluntary coverage is possible for previously insured persons until age 60.

Exclusions: Employees earning below G$7.50 a week, casual employees, and family labor.

Source of Funds

Insured person: 5.2% of gross earnings. The voluntarily insured contribute 9.3% of average weekly income in the last 2 years before covered employment ceased.

The maximum weekly earnings for contribution and benefit purposes are G$21,420. The maximum insurable earnings for contribution and benefit purposes are adjusted annually.

Contributions are paid weekly or monthly, depending on the nature of employment.

The insured's contributions also finance cash sickness, maternity, and work injury benefits.

Self-employed person: 11.5% of declared income, up to a maximum.

Contributions are paid weekly or monthly, depending on the nature of employment.

The self-employed person's contributions also finance cash sickness and maternity benefits.

Employer: 7.8% of monthly payroll.

The maximum weekly earnings for contribution and benefit purposes are G$21,420. The maximum insurable earnings for contribution and benefit purposes are adjusted annually.

The employer's contributions also finance cash sickness, maternity, and work injury benefits.

Government: None; contributes as an employer; provides loans to cover any deficits.

Qualifying Conditions

Old-age pension: Age 60 with 750 weeks of paid or credited contributions, including at least 150 weeks of paid contributions; 25 weeks of contributions are credited for each year that the insured was older than age 35 in 1969, up to a maximum credit of 600 weeks.

Retirement is not necessary.

Old-age grant: The insured does not meet the qualifying conditions for a pension but made at least 50 weeks of contributions before age 60.

Old-age benefits are not payable abroad.

Disability pension: Aged 16 to 59 and permanently disabled with a minimum of 250 weekly paid or credited contributions, including at least 150 weeks of paid contributions; 25 weeks of contributions are credited for each year between the onset of disability and age 60.

The assessed degree of disability is reviewed by the National Insurance Medical Board when required.

Disability grant: The insured does not meet the qualifying conditions for a pension but made at least 50 weeks of contributions before the onset of disability.

Disability benefits are not payable abroad.

Survivor pension: The deceased was a pensioner or was eligible for an old-age pension or disability pension at the time of death; or aged 16 to 59 with a minimum of 250 weekly paid or credited contributions, including at least 150 paid contributions.

Eligible survivors are the widow(er) and orphans younger than age 18.

Survivor grant: The deceased would have been eligible for an old-age grant or a disability grant.

Eligible survivors are the widow(er) and orphans younger than age 18.

Survivor benefits are not payable abroad.

Funeral grant: The insured has paid at least 50 weeks of contributions. The grant is payable to help meet the cost of the funeral for the insured or his or her spouse.

Old-Age Benefits

Old-age pension: The pension is equal to 40% of the insured's average weekly covered earnings, plus 1% of average weekly covered earnings for every 50-week period of contributions above 750.

Average weekly covered earnings are based on the insured's best 3 years of the last 5 years before age 60.

The maximum weekly earnings for benefit calculation purposes are G$21,420.

The minimum pension is 50% of the minimum wage.

The public service minimum wage is G$24,192.

The maximum pension is 60% of the insured's average weekly covered earnings.

Old-age grant: The grant is equal to 1/12 of the insured's average annual covered earnings for every 50-week period of paid or credited contributions.

Average weekly covered earnings are based on the insured's best 3 years of the last 5 years before age 60.

Permanent Disability Benefits

Disability pension: The pension is equal to 30% of the insured's average weekly covered earnings, plus 1% of average weekly covered earnings for every 50-week period of contributions above 250.

Average weekly covered earnings are based on the insured's best 3 years of the last 5 years before the onset of disability.

The maximum weekly earnings for benefit calculation purposes are G$21,420.

The minimum pension is 40% of the minimum wage.

The public service minimum wage is G$24,192.

The maximum pension is 60% of the insured's average weekly covered earnings.

Constant-attendance allowance: G$200 a day if dependent on the care and attendance of another person for carrying out daily activities.

Disability grant: The grant is equal to 1/12 of the insured's average annual covered earnings for every 50-week period of paid or credited contributions.

Average weekly covered earnings are based on the insured's best 3 years of the last 5 years before the onset of disability.

Survivor Benefits

Survivor pension: The widow(er)'s pension is equal to 50% of the pension paid or payable to the deceased.

Child's supplement: 16.6% of the deceased's pension is paid for each child, up to a maximum of three children.

Full orphan's pension: Each orphan receives a pension equal to 33.3% of the pension paid or payable to the deceased, up to a maximum of three orphans.

The total maximum survivor pension is equal to 100% of the deceased's pension.

Survivor grant: A lump sum is paid if the deceased did not meet the qualifying conditions for a pension.

Funeral grant: G$12,860 is paid to the person who meets the cost of the funeral.

Administrative Organization

Minister of Finance provides general supervision.

Ministry of Labour, Human Services, and Social Security administers the program.

Sickness and Maternity

Regulatory Framework

First and current law: 1969 (social security).

Type of program: Social insurance system. Cash benefits only.

Coverage

All public- and private-sector employees and the self-employed between ages 16 and 59.

Exclusions: Employees earning below G$7.50 a week, casual employees, and family labor.

Source of Funds

Insured person: See source of funds under Old Age, Disability, and Survivors, above.

Self-employed person: See source of funds under Old Age, Disability, and Survivors, above.

Employer: See source of funds under Old Age, Disability, and Survivors, above.

Government: None; contributes as an employer; provides loans to cover any deficits.

Qualifying Conditions

Cash sickness benefits: The insured must be younger than age 60, be in covered employment in 8 of the 13 weeks before the onset of incapacity, and have 50 weeks of contributions.

Cash maternity benefits: The insured must have 15 weeks of contributions, including 7 in the 26-week period ending 6 weeks before the expected date of childbirth.

Cash maternity grant: Payable to an insured woman who does not meet the qualifying conditions for a maternity benefit but whose insured husband does.

Sickness and Maternity Benefits

Sickness benefit: The benefit is equal to 70% of average weekly covered earnings in the best 8 weeks in the 13 weeks before the onset of incapacity. The benefit is payable from the fourth day of incapacity, for up to a maximum of 26 weeks.

Maternity benefit: The benefit is equal to 70% of average weekly covered earnings in the best 7 weeks in the 26 weeks before the start of the benefit. The benefit is payable for

13 weeks, including the week of childbirth plus 6 weeks before and 6 weeks after; may be extended for up to 13 additional weeks if complications arise.

Maternity grant: A lump sum of G$2,000.

Workers' Medical Benefits

No statutory benefits are provided.

Medical care is available in public hospitals and health centers. Medical care involves cost sharing on an income-tested basis.

Dependents' Medical Benefits

No statutory benefits are provided.

Medical care is available in public hospitals and health centers. Medical care involves cost sharing on an income-tested basis.

Administrative Organization

Minister of Finance provides general supervision.

Ministry of Labour, Human Services, and Social Security administers the program.

Work Injury

Regulatory Framework

First law: 1916.

Current law: 1969 (social security).

Type of program: Social insurance system.

Coverage

All public- and private-sector employees.

Exclusions: Employees earning below G$7.50 a week, casual employees, family labor, and the self-employed.

Source of Funds

Insured person: See source of funds under Old Age, Disability, and Survivors, above.

Self-employed person: Not applicable.

Employer: See source of funds under Old Age, Disability, and Survivors, above; also contributes an additional 1.53% of insurable earnings to finance work injury benefits for workers younger than age 16 or older than age 59.

Government: None; contributes as an employer; provides loans to cover any deficits.

Qualifying Conditions

Work injury benefits: There is no minimum qualifying period.

Temporary Disability Benefits

The benefit is equal to 70% of average weekly covered earnings during the best 8 weeks in the 13 weeks before the onset of disability. The benefit is payable after the first day if the injury lasts for more than 3 days, for up to 26 weeks.

Permanent Disability Benefits

Permanent disability pension: For a total disability (100%), the pension is equal to 70% of average weekly covered earnings in the best 8 weeks in the 13 weeks before the onset of disability.

Constant-attendance allowance: G$200 a day if the insured is dependent on the care and attendance of another person for carrying out daily activities.

Partial disability: If the assessed degree of disability is at least 15%, a reduced pension is paid according to the assessed degree of disability. If the assessed degree of disability is less than 15%, a lump sum is paid equal to 260 times the weekly disability benefit times the assessed degree of disability.

The assessed degree of disability is reviewed by the National Insurance Medical Board when required.

Workers' Medical Benefits

Benefits include hospitalization, general and specialist care, medicines, and transportation.

Survivor Benefits

Survivor pension: The pension is equal to 35% of the deceased's weekly earnings for a widow(er) or parent and 11.6% for each other dependent, up to a maximum of 70% of the deceased's weekly earnings.

Eligible survivors are the deceased's spouse, a dependent parent, and any other dependent person.

The minimum pension for a widow(er) or parent is 50% of the old-age or disability minimum pension; for a child, 16.6% of the old-age or disability minimum pension.

Full orphan's pension: Each orphan younger than age 18 receives a pension equal to 23.3% of the deceased's weekly earnings.

The minimum orphan's pension is 33.3% of the old-age or disability minimum pension.

Death benefit: Up to G$250 to the insured's creditors or estate, in the absence of any dependents.

Administrative Organization

Minister of Finance provides general supervision.

National Insurance Board administers the program.

Haiti

Exchange rate: US$1.00 equals 38.15 gourdes.

Old Age, Disability, and Survivors

Regulatory Framework

First law: 1965 (old-age insurance).

Current law: 1967.

Type of program: Social insurance system.

Coverage

Employees of industrial, commercial, and agricultural firms.

Exclusions: Unpaid family labor, the self-employed, members of religious communities, and foreign diplomats.

Special system for public-sector employees.

Source of Funds

Insured person: 6% of earnings.

Self-employed person: Not applicable.

Employer: 6% of earnings.

Government: Subsidies as needed.

Qualifying Conditions

Old-age pension: Age 55 with at least 20 years of contributions.

Old-age settlement: The insured does not meet the qualifying conditions for a pension.

Disability pension: Total incapacity for work with between 10 and 20 years of contributions. The disability must not be caused by a work injury.

Survivor pension: The insured was a pensioner or was eligible for a pension at the time of death.

Survivor settlement: The insured did not meet the qualifying conditions for a pension at the time of death.

Old-Age Benefits

Old-age pension: The pension is equal to 33% of the insured's average earnings in the last 10 years.

The national monthly minimum wage is 2,100 gourdes.

Average earnings are not adjusted for inflation.

Benefit adjustment: Benefits are not indexed.

Old-age settlement: A refund of contributions without accrued interest.

Permanent Disability Benefits

Disability pension: The pension is equal to 1/60 of the insured's average earnings for each year of coverage in the 10 years before the onset of disability.

The national monthly minimum wage is 2,100 gourdes.

Average earnings are not adjusted for inflation.

Benefit adjustment: Benefits are not indexed.

Survivor Benefits

Survivor pension: The pension is equal to 50% of the pension paid or payable to the deceased. The pension is split among the widow, orphans younger than age 18 (no limit if a student or disabled), and other dependents.

Benefit adjustment: Benefits are not indexed.

Survivor settlement: A refund of contributions without accrued interest.

Administrative Organization

Ministry of Social Affairs provides general supervision.

National Office of Old-Age Insurance of the Social Insurance Institute administers the program.

Social Insurance Institute is managed by a tripartite board and a director general.

Work Injury

Regulatory Framework

First law: 1951.

Current law: 1967.

Type of program: Social insurance system.

Coverage

Public-sector employees and employees of industrial, commercial, and agricultural firms in specified districts.

Exclusions: The self-employed.

Source of Funds

Insured person: None.

Self-employed person: Not applicable.

Employer: 2% of payroll (commerce), 3% of payroll (industry, construction, and agriculture), or 6% of payroll (mining).

Government: None; contributes as an employer.

Qualifying Conditions

Work injury benefits: There is no minimum qualifying period.

Temporary Disability Benefits

The benefit is equal to 66.6% of the insured's earnings and is payable after a 3-day waiting period for the duration of the incapacity. The employer pays benefits during the waiting period. The insured must be younger than age 55.

The national monthly minimum wage is 2,100 gourdes.

Permanent Disability Benefits

Permanent disability pension: For a total disability, the pension is equal to 66.6% of the insured's earnings. The insured must be younger than age 55.

The national monthly minimum wage is 2,100 gourdes.

Partial disability: For an assessed degree of disability of 10% or more, a percentage of the total pension according to the assessed degree of disability is paid. For an assessed degree of disability of less than 10%, a lump sum is paid.

All disability pensions may be paid as a lump sum.

Benefit adjustment: Benefits are not indexed.

Workers' Medical Benefits

Benefits include medical and dental care, surgery, hospitalization, medicines, and appliances. Benefits are provided until full recovery or the stabilization of the disability.

Survivor Benefits

Survivor pension: 50% of the deceased's total disability pension is paid to a widow or a dependent disabled widower.

Orphan's pension: 30% of the deceased's pension is paid for each orphan younger than age 21.

Dependent parent's or grandparent's pension (in the absence of the above): 40% of the deceased's pension is paid.

The maximum total survivor pension is 80% of the deceased's pension.

Funeral grant: The grant is equal to a month of the deceased's earnings.

Benefit adjustment: Benefits are not indexed.

Administrative Organization

Ministry of Social Affairs provides general supervision.

Office of Work Accidents and Sickness and Maternity Insurance of the Social Insurance Institute administers the program.

Social Insurance Institute operates its own dispensaries and hospital in Port-au-Prince.

Social Insurance Institute is managed by a tripartite board and a director general.

Honduras

Exchange rate: US$1.00 equals 18.86 lempiras.

Old Age, Disability, and Survivors

Regulatory Framework

First and current law: 1959 (social security), implemented in 1971, with 2001 amendment.

Type of program: Social insurance system.

Coverage

Employed persons in private- and public-sector enterprises in specified regions.

Coverage is being extended gradually to additional regions.

Exclusions: Domestic workers, temporary workers, and some groups of agricultural workers.

Source of Funds

Insured person: 1% of earnings.

The minimum monthly earnings for contribution purposes are 144 lempiras.

The maximum monthly earnings for contribution purposes are 4,800 lempiras.

Self-employed person: Not applicable.

Employer: 2% of payroll.

The minimum monthly earnings for contribution purposes are 144 lempiras.

The maximum monthly earnings for contribution purposes are 4,800 lempiras.

Government: 0.5% of payroll; also contributes as an employer.

The minimum monthly earnings for contribution purposes are 144 lempiras.

The maximum monthly earnings for contribution purposes are 4,800 lempiras.

Qualifying Conditions

Old-age pension: Age 65 (men) or age 60 (women) with at least 180 months of contributions.

Retirement from covered employment is necessary.

Old-age settlement: Age 65 (men) or age 60 (women) with less than 180 months of contributions.

Disability pension: A loss of 2/3 of earning capacity in the usual occupation with 36 months of contributions in the last 6 years; 8 months of contributions in the last 24 months in the case of a nonoccupational accident. (Men aged 45 or older and women aged 40 or older in 1971 must have contributed for 5 years or 60 months at the time they joined the system.)

Disability settlement: Disabled and does not meet the qualifying conditions for a pension.

Survivor pension: In the case of a death resulting from a common illness, the deceased had 36 months of contributions in the last 6 years; 8 months of contributions in the 24 months before the injury resulting in a nonoccupational accident-related death.

Eligible survivors are a widow(er) or partner aged 65 or older or disabled and orphans younger than age 14 (age 18 if a student, no limit if disabled); in the absence of a widow(er) or partner or orphans, a mother of any age and a father older than age 65 or disabled.

Old-Age Benefits

Old-age pension: The pension is equal to 40% of the insured's basic monthly earnings, plus an additional 1% of earnings for each 12-month period of contributions exceeding 60 months.

Basic monthly earnings for pension calculation purposes are equal to 1/36 or 1/60 of insured earnings in the last 3 or 5 years before the month of entitlement, whatever is greater.

Deferred pension: An additional 3% of basic monthly earnings is paid for each year of contributions after age 65 (men) or age 60 (women).

The minimum pension is equal to 50% of basic monthly earnings.

The maximum pension is equal to 80% of basic monthly earnings.

Old-age settlement: The total contributions are refunded as a lump sum.

Permanent Disability Benefits

Disability pension: The pension is equal to 40% of the insured's basic monthly earnings, plus an additional 1% of earnings for each 12-month period of contributions exceeding 60 months.

Basic monthly earnings for pension calculation purposes are equal to 1/36 or 1/60 of insured earnings in the last 3 or 5 years before the month of entitlement, whatever is greater.

Constant-attendance supplement: If assessed as more than 50% disabled, up to a maximum of 50% of the pension.

The maximum pension is equal to 80% of covered earnings.

Disability settlement: The total contributions are refunded as a lump sum.

Survivor Benefits

Survivor pension: A widow(er) receives 40% of the pension paid or payable to the deceased.

The pension ceases on remarriage.

Remarriage settlement: A widow(er) receives a lump sum equal to 12 months' pension.

Orphan's pension: Each orphan receives 20% of the deceased's pension; 40% for a full orphan.

Dependent parent's pension (in the absence of the above): 20% of the deceased's pension is payable to each eligible parent.

The maximum survivor pension is equal to 100% of the deceased's pension and is split as follows: a widow(er) or partner receives 40%; orphans younger than age 14 receive a total of 60%.

Funeral grant: Equal to 50% of basic monthly earnings. The minimum funeral grant is 250 lempiras if the deceased made at least one contribution in the last 6 months; 100 lempiras if the beneficiary is not a member of the deceased's family.

Administrative Organization

Ministry of Labor and Social Welfare provides general supervision.

Managed by a board of directors and director general, the Social Security Institute (http://www.ihss.hn) administers the program.

Sickness and Maternity

Regulatory Framework

First and current law: 1959 (social security), implemented in 1962, with 2001 amendment.

Type of program: Social insurance system. Cash and medical benefits.

Coverage

Public-sector employees and employees of firms in industry and commerce with one or more workers in specified regions; children of insured persons younger than age 5; disability pensioners; and old-age pensioners.

Unemployed female workers are eligible for medical care while pregnant and during childbirth but are not eligible for cash maternity benefits.

Coverage is being extended gradually to additional regions. The labor code is still in force in regions to which social insurance has not yet been extended.

Exclusions: Agricultural, domestic, family, and temporary workers.

Source of Funds

Insured person: 2.5% of earnings.

The minimum monthly earnings for contribution and benefit purposes are 360 lempiras.

The maximum monthly earnings for contribution and benefit purposes are 4,800 lempiras.

The above contributions also finance work injury benefits.

Self-employed person: Not applicable.

Employer: 5% of payroll.

The minimum monthly earnings for contribution and benefit purposes are 360 lempiras.

The maximum monthly earnings for contribution and benefit purposes are 4,800 lempiras.

The above contributions also finance work injury benefits.

Government: Contributes as an employer, plus 0.5% of total covered earnings. (The contribution on total covered earnings has never been paid.)

The minimum monthly earnings for contribution and benefit purposes are 360 lempiras.

The maximum monthly earnings for contribution and benefit purposes are 4,800 lempiras.

The above contributions also finance work injury benefits.

Qualifying Conditions

Cash sickness benefits: Must have 35 days of contributions in the 3 months before the onset of incapacity.

Cash maternity benefits: Must have 75 days of contributions in the last 10 months.

Medical benefits: Currently in insured employment or unemployed.

Sickness and Maternity Benefits

Sickness benefit: The benefit is equal to 66% of the insured's earnings in the last 3 months and is payable after a 3-day waiting period for up to 26 weeks; may be extended to 52 weeks.

The labor code requires employers to provide sick leave to employees not covered by social insurance.

Maternity benefit: The benefit is equal to 66% of the insured's earnings and is payable for 6 weeks before and 6 weeks after the expected date of childbirth.

The labor code requires employers to provide maternity leave to employees not covered by social insurance.

Workers' Medical Benefits

Medical services are provided directly to patients through the health facilities of the Social Security Institute. Benefits include general and specialist care, surgery, hospitalization, necessary medicines, laboratory services, appliances, dental care, and maternity care including postnatal care for up to 42 days.

The period of duration is dependent on continuing to meet the contribution requirements. If the insured person is unemployed, benefits are limited to 60 days of general care and 6 months of specialized care.

Dependents' Medical Benefits

Benefits include maternity care for the insured's wife, including postnatal care for up to 45 days; pediatric care for the insured's children until age 5 and 30 days or for up to 26 weeks after the insured's death.

Administrative Organization

Ministry of Labor and Social Welfare provides general supervision.

Managed by a board of directors and director general, the Social Security Institute (http://www.ihss.hn) administers the program.

Social Security Institute operates its own hospitals and outpatient clinics and contracts the services of private clinics.

Work Injury

Regulatory Framework

First and current law: 1959 (social security), implemented in 1971, with 2001 amendment.

Type of program: Social insurance system.

Coverage

Public-sector employees and employees of firms in industry and commerce with one or more workers in specified regions.

Coverage is being extended gradually to additional regions. The labor code is still in force in regions to which social insurance has not yet been extended.

Exclusions: Agricultural, domestic, family, and temporary workers.

Source of Funds

Insured person: See source of funds under Sickness and Maternity, above.

Self-employed person: Not applicable.

Employer: See source of funds under Sickness and Maternity, above.

Government: See source of funds under Sickness and Maternity, above.

Qualifying Conditions

Work injury benefits: There is no minimum qualifying period.

Survivor benefits: The deceased worked for a month in insured employment.

Temporary Disability Benefits

The benefit is equal to 66% of the insured's daily wage and is payable after a 3-day waiting period for up to 52 weeks.

The maximum daily wage for benefit calculation purposes is 4,800 lempiras.

Permanent Disability Benefits

Permanent disability pension: The pension is equal to 66% of the insured's basic monthly earnings, plus an additional 1% of earnings for each 12-month period of contributions exceeding 60 months.

Basic monthly earnings for pension calculation purposes are equal to 1/36 or 1/60 of insured earnings in the last 3 or 5 years before the month of entitlement, whichever is greater.

Constant-attendance supplement: Up to a maximum of 50% of the insured's pension.

Partial disability: If the assessed degree of disability is greater than 15%, a percentage of the full pension is paid according to the assessed degree of disability. If the calculated monthly pension is less than 10 lempiras, a lump sum is paid.

Workers' Medical Benefits

Benefits include medical, surgical, and hospital care; medicines; and appliances.

Survivor Benefits

Survivor pension: A widow(er) older than age 65 or disabled receives 40% of the pension paid or payable to the deceased.

Orphan's pension: Each orphan younger than age 14 (age 18 if a student, no limit if disabled) receives 20% of the deceased's pension; 40% for a full orphan.

Dependent parent's pension (in the absence of the above): 20% of the deceased's pension is payable to a mother of any age or a father older than age 65 or disabled.

The maximum survivor pension is 100% of the deceased's pension.

Funeral grant: Equal to 50% of the deceased's basic monthly earnings. The minimum funeral grant is 125 lempiras if the deceased had made at least one contribution in the last 6 months.

Administrative Organization

Ministry of Labor and Social Welfare provides general supervision.

Managed by a board of directors and director general, the Social Security Institute (http://www.ihss.hn) administers the program.

Social Security Institute operates its own outpatient clinics and hospitals.

Jamaica
Exchange rate: US$1.00 equals
61.61 Jamaican dollars (J$).

Old Age, Disability, and Survivors

Regulatory Framework

First law and current law: 1965 (national insurance), with amendments.

Type of program: Social insurance system.

Note: Government-financed social assistance benefits of J$400 a month are provided to low-income and vulnerable persons older than age 60 and to low-income and vulnerable disabled persons.

Coverage

Employed and self-employed persons.

Voluntary coverage is possible, if older than age 18 and younger than the normal retirement age.

Exclusions: Casual workers and unpaid family labor.

Source of Funds

Insured person: Employees contribute 2.5% of gross earnings. Domestic workers, Jamaica Defense Force personnel, and the voluntarily insured contribute a flat-rate J$20 a week.

The maximum earnings for employee contribution purposes are J$9,620 a week or J$500,000 a year. (There are no maximum earnings for contribution purposes for domestic workers or Jamaica Defense Force personnel.)

The insured's contributions also finance cash maternity benefits.

Contributions are paid weekly or monthly, depending on how the employee is paid.

Self-employed person: J$20 a week, plus a maximum of 5% of insurable annual earnings.

The maximum earnings for contribution purposes are J$9,620 a week or J$500,000 a year.

Employer: 2.5% of wages.

The maximum earnings for contribution purposes are J$9,620 a week or J$500,000 a year.

The employer's contributions also finance cash maternity benefits and work injury benefits.

Contributions are paid weekly or monthly, depending on how employees are paid.

Government: None; contributes as an employer.

Qualifying Conditions

Old-age pension: Age 65 (men) or age 60 (women) with 1,443 weeks of paid contributions, including an annual average of 39 weeks of paid or credited contributions.

Partial pension: A reduced pension is paid for annual average contributions of between 13 weeks and 38 weeks.

Early pension: There is no early pension.

Deferred pension: A deferred pension is possible.

Old-age settlement: The insured does not meet the qualifying conditions for a pension. A lump sum is paid if the insured has at least 52 weeks or 1 year of contributions. Substantial retirement is necessary until age 70 (men) or age 65 (women).

Old-age benefits are payable abroad if the insured resides abroad for at least a year and has expressed the need for the benefit to be paid overseas.

Disability pension: Assessed as permanently incapable of work with a minimum of 156 weeks of paid contributions, up to a maximum.

The disability is assessed by an independent medical advisor appointed by the Minister of Labor and Social Security. The independent medical advisor recommends the frequency of any reassessment of the disability.

Disability settlement: The insured does not meet the qualifying conditions for a pension. A lump sum is paid if the insured has at least 52 weeks or 1 year of paid contributions.

The disability is assessed by a doctor appointed by the Minister of Labor and Social Security.

Disability benefits are payable abroad for a limited period if the insured is absent from Jamaica to receive medical treatment.

Survivor pension: The deceased had an annual average of 39 weeks of paid or credited contributions or was a pensioner at the time of death.

Eligible survivors are a widow(er) aged 55 or older or caring for children younger than age 18 and full orphans younger than age 18. If eligible, widows may receive duplicate benefits based on their own earnings. A widow(er) younger than age 55 without children receives a limited pension for 1 year.

Survivor benefits are payable abroad if the survivor resides abroad for at least a year and has expressed the need for the benefit to be paid overseas.

Survivor settlement: The deceased did not meet the qualifying conditions for a pension but had at least 52 weeks of contributions. A surviving spouse must have been married or cohabiting with the deceased for at least 3 years.

Special child's benefit: Payable to a guardian caring for an illegitimate child younger than age 18 who is orphaned and whose deceased mother was eligible for a pension and whose father is dead or his whereabouts are unknown; a lump sum is paid if the deceased mother was not eligible for a pension.

Funeral grant: The deceased or the deceased's spouse was a pensioner or eligible to receive a pension at the time of death.

Old-Age Benefits

Old-age pension: A basic benefit of J$900 a week with an annual average of 39 weeks of paid or credited contributions (reduced to J$675 a week with annual average contributions of between 26 weeks and 38 weeks; J$450 with 13 weeks to 25 weeks), plus an earnings-related benefit of J$0.06 a week for every J$13 of employer–employee contributions paid during the working lifetime.

Spouse's supplement: J$300 a week for a dependent wife aged 55 or older or a disabled husband aged 60 or older.

Early pension: There is no early pension.

Deferred pension: Calculated in the same way as the old-age pension, above.

Old-age settlement: A lump sum of J$8,100.

Permanent Disability Benefits

Disability pension: If assessed as 100% disabled, a basic benefit of between J$100 and J$1,740 a week is paid.

Disability settlement: A lump sum is paid equal to nine times the maximum weekly basic old-age pension (J$8,100).

Survivor Benefits

Survivor pension: A basic benefit of J$900 a week if the deceased had an annual average of 39 weeks of paid or credited contributions (reduced to J$675 a week with annual average contributions of between 26 weeks and 38 weeks; J$450 with 13 weeks to 25 weeks), plus an earnings-related benefit of J$0.03 a week for every J$13 of employer–employee contributions paid during the working lifetime.

Remarriage settlement: The pension ceases if the widow(er) remarries (or cohabits), and a lump sum equal to a year's pension is paid.

Survivor settlement: A lump sum of J$8,100.

Orphan's pension: J$1,575 a week for full orphans younger than age 18.

Orphan's settlement: A lump sum of J$8,100 for full orphans younger than age 18.

Special child's benefit: J$1,575 is paid each week until the child is age 18; a lump sum of J$14,625 is paid if the deceased mother was not eligible for a pension.

Funeral grant: A lump sum of J$30,000 is payable to the person who meets all or part of the cost of the funeral. The funeral grant is normally not payable for a death occurring abroad.

Administrative Organization

Ministry of Labor and Social Security administers the program through its National Insurance Division and local offices.

Public Assistance Division of the Ministry of Labor and Social Security assesses eligibility and administers social assistance benefits as part of the Programme of Advancement Through Health and Education (PATH).

Sickness and Maternity

Regulatory Framework

First and current laws: 1965 (national insurance), with amendments; and 2003 (national health insurance).

Type of program: Social insurance system. Cash maternity benefits and medical benefits.

Coverage

Cash maternity benefits: Resident female employees aged 18 or older.

Exclusions: Self-employed women.

Medical benefits: All residents.

Source of Funds

Insured person: See source of funds under Old Age, Disability, and Survivors, above.

Self-employed person: None for cash maternity benefits.

Employer: See source of funds under Old Age, Disability, and Survivors, above.

Government: See source of funds under Old Age, Disability, and Survivors, above.

Medical benefits are financed mainly from general taxation, with a small portion financed through cost-sharing copayments. The complementary universal National Health Fund is financed by a percentage of the total contributions made to the social insurance program and by earmarked taxes on tobacco and alcohol. The National Insurance Gold program for social insurance pensioners is funded by contributions made to the social insurance program only.

Qualifying Conditions

Cash sickness benefits: No statutory benefits are provided.

Cash maternity benefits: Must have 26 weeks of paid contributions in the 52 weeks before the expected date of childbirth.

Medical benefits: Resident in Jamaica.

Sickness and Maternity Benefits

Sickness benefit: No statutory benefits are provided.

Maternity benefit: The benefits is equal to the national minimum weekly wage and is payable for 8 weeks.

The national minimum weekly wage is J$2,400.

Workers' Medical Benefits

Medical care is provided free or at a nominal cost in public dispensaries and hospitals. The National Health Fund gives universal complementary coverage for prescription drugs for some chronic illnesses.

A complementary health insurance program, National Insurance Gold, offers additional health coverage for social insurance pensioners.

Dependents' Medical Benefits

Medical care is provided free or at a nominal cost in public dispensaries and hospitals. The National Health Fund gives universal complementary coverage for prescription drugs for some chronic illnesses.

A complementary health insurance program, National Insurance Gold, offers additional health coverage for social insurance pensioners.

Administrative Organization

Ministry of Labor and Social Security administers the program through its National Insurance Division and local offices.

Work Injury

Regulatory Framework

First law: 1938 (workmen's compensation).

Current law: 1965 (national insurance), implemented in 1970, with amendments.

Type of program: Social insurance system.

Coverage

Employees aged 18 to 70 (men) or aged 18 to 65 (women).

Exclusions: Domestic workers, unpaid family labor, the self-employed, and Jamaica Defense Force personnel.

Source of Funds

Insured person: None.

Self-employed person: Not applicable.

Employer: See source of funds under Old Age, Disability, and Survivors, above.

Government: None; contributes as an employer.

Qualifying Conditions

Work injury benefits: There is no minimum qualifying period.

Temporary Disability Benefits

The minimum weekly benefit is equal to 75% of the minimum wage and is payable after a 3-day waiting period for up to 52 weeks.

The maximum benefit is J$1,740 a week.

The minimum wage is J$2,000.

Permanent Disability Benefits

Permanent disability pension: If assessed as between 95% and 100% disabled, the pension is equal to 75% of average insurable earnings.

The maximum daily earnings for benefit calculation purposes are J$290.

Partial disability: For an assessed degree of disability of at least 10%, a percentage of the full pension is paid according to the loss of earning capacity.

The disability is assessed by a medical board or medical appeal tribunal.

The minimum benefit is J$100 a week.

The maximum benefit is J$1,740 a week.

Workers' Medical Benefits

Benefits include necessary medical, surgical, and rehabilitative treatment; appliances; hospitalization; and drugs.

Survivor Benefits

Survivor pension: The maximum work injury benefit is payable for the first 52 weeks; thereafter, if the contribution conditions are satisfied, a widow(er) pension is payable.

The minimum survivor pension is J$450 a week.

The maximum survivor pension is J$900 a week.

The pension is payable for 52 weeks after the insured's death to a widow(er) of any age; in the absence of a widow(er), to a child or children or a dependent mother aged 55 or older.

Funeral grant: A lump sum of J$30,000 is payable to the person who meets all or part of the cost of the funeral. The funeral grant is normally not payable for a death occurring abroad.

Administrative Organization

Ministry of Labor and Social Security administers the program through its National Insurance Division and local offices.

Family Allowances

Regulatory Framework

First law: 1941.

Current law: 2001.

Type of program: Social assistance system.

Coverage

Low-income and vulnerable persons.

Source of Funds

Insured person: None.

Self-employed person: None.

Employer: None.

Government: Total cost.

Qualifying Conditions

Family allowances: Children younger than age 18, pregnant women, and nursing mothers. (Social assistance is also provided to persons older than age 60 or disabled, see Old Age, Disability, and Survivors, above.)

Benefits for school-age children are conditional on maintaining an 85% attendance level at school.

Benefits for pregnant women and nursing mothers are conditional on maintaining regular visits to heath centers.

Family Allowance Benefits

Family allowances: Each eligible family member receives J$400 a month.

Eligible persons are also entitled to receive in-kind benefits, including free school lunches, exemption for secondary school tuition fees, and free medical care at public health centers and hospitals.

Administrative Organization

Public Assistance Division of the Ministry of Labor and Social Security assesses eligibility and administers social assistance benefits as part of the Programme of Advancement Through Health and Education (PATH).

Mexico

Exchange rate: US$1.00 equals
10.88 new pesos (NP).

Old Age, Disability, and Survivors

Regulatory Framework

First law: 1943.

Current laws: 1973 (social insurance) and 1995 (social security), implemented in 1997, with 2001 and 2004 amendments.

Type of program: Mandatory individual account and social insurance system.

Note: As of July 1, 1997, all workers must join the mandatory individual account system, and the social insurance system is being phased out. There are no contributors to the social insurance system. At retirement, employees covered by the social insurance system before 1997 can choose to receive benefits from either the social insurance system or the mandatory individual account system.

Coverage

Mandatory individual account: All workers and cooperative members entering the labor force on or after January 1, 1997.

Voluntary coverage for public-sector employees not covered by other laws and the self-employed.

Social insurance: Employees and members of producers', agricultural, and credit union cooperatives who were first covered before 1997.

Special systems for petroleum workers, public-sector employees, and military personnel.

Source of Funds

Insured person: 1.125% of earnings for old-age benefits, plus an average 0.625% of earnings for disability and survivor benefits and an additional amount for administrative fees.

The minimum earnings for contribution purposes are equal to the regional minimum wage.

The maximum earnings for contribution purposes are equal to 25 times the minimum monthly wage in Mexico City (1,631.12 NP).

Self-employed person: 6.275% of declared earnings for old-age benefits; 2.375% for disability and survivor benefits and an additional amount for administrative fees.

Declared earnings for contribution purposes are equal to the minimum monthly wage in Mexico City (1,631.12 NP).

Employer: 5.15% of payroll for old-age benefits, plus an average 1.75% of payroll for disability and survivor benefits. Also finances unemployment benefits.

The minimum earnings for contribution purposes are equal to the regional minimum wage.

The maximum earnings for contribution purposes are equal to 25 times the minimum monthly wage in Mexico City (1,631.12 NP).

Government: An amount equal to 10.14% of the total employer contributions for old-age benefits, plus an average 0.125% of earnings for disability and survivor benefits and a flat-rate amount to finance the guaranteed minimum pension. Also provides an additional contribution on behalf of persons actively contributing to an individual account.

Qualifying Conditions

Mandatory individual account

Old-age pension: Age 65 (men and women) with at least 1,250 weeks of contributions; with less than 1,250 weekly contributions, a lump sum is paid or the insured may continue contributing.

Early pension: Aged 60 to 64 (men and women), retired from covered employment, and with at least 1,250 weekly contributions; with less than 1,250 weekly contributions, a lump sum is paid.

Guaranteed minimum pension: Age 65 (men and women) with at least 1,250 weeks of contributions and the pension (based on the value of the accumulated capital plus accrued interest) is less than the minimum pension.

Disability pension: The insured has at least 150 weeks of contributions with a loss of at least 75% in normal earning capacity; at least 250 weeks of contributions with a loss of between 50% and 70% of normal earning capacity.

Guaranteed minimum pension: The insured is eligible for a disability pension and the pension (based on the value of the accumulated capital plus accrued interest) is less than the minimum monthly pension of 1,631.12 NP.

The Mexican Social Security Institute assesses the loss of normal earning capacity.

Survivor pension: The insured was a pensioner or had at least 150 weeks of contributions at the time of death. The death must not be the result of an occupational injury.

Eligible survivors are a widow(er) or cohabiting partner with children; a widow(er) without children who was married to the deceased for at least 6 months, subject to the deceased being younger than age 55 at the date of marriage; if the deceased was age 55 or older at the date of marriage or if the deceased was a pensioner, the marriage must have lasted at least 12 months. Other survivors are a cohabiting partner without children who lived with the deceased for at least 5 years; children up to age 16 (age 25 if a student); and parents in the absence of other eligible survivors. All eligible survivors must have been dependent on the deceased.

Social insurance

Old-age pension: Age 65 (men and women) with at least 500 weeks of contributions.

Early pension: Aged 60 to 64 (men or women) with at least 500 weeks of contributions.

Retirement from covered employment is necessary.

The pension is suspended if the pensioner leaves Mexico, and the pensioner may request a lump sum equal to 2 years' pension.

Disability pension: Must have a 50% reduction in normal earning capacity with 150 weeks of contributions. The insured may continue to work in a different job.

The Mexican Social Security Institute assesses the level of reduced earning capacity.

Survivor pension: The insured was a pensioner or had at least 150 weeks of contributions at the time of death. The death must not be the result of an occupational injury.

Eligible survivors are a widow(er) or cohabiting partner with children; a widow(er) without children who was married to the deceased for at least 6 months, subject to the deceased being younger than age 55 at the date of marriage; if the deceased was age 55 or older at the date of marriage or if the deceased was a pensioner, the marriage must have lasted at least 12 months. Other survivors are a cohabiting partner without children who lived with the deceased for at least 5 years; children up to age 16 (age 25 if a student); and parents in the absence of other eligible survivors. All eligible survivors must have been dependent on the deceased.

Funeral grant: The deceased had 12 weeks of contributions in the last 9 months or was a pensioner at the time of death.

Old-Age Benefits

Old-age pension

Mandatory individual account: The monthly benefit is based on the value of the accumulated capital plus accrued interest. At retirement, the insured can either purchase an annuity or make programmed withdrawals based on life expectancy.

Early pension: The monthly benefit is based on the value of the accumulated capital plus accrued interest. At retirement, the insured can either purchase an annuity or make pro-grammed withdrawals based on life expectancy.

Guaranteed minimum pension: The guaranteed minimum pension is equal to the minimum monthly wage in Mexico City (1,631.12 NP).

Old-age pensions are payable abroad under bilateral agreement.

Benefit adjustment: Pensions are adjusted annually in February for changes in the price index.

Social insurance: The monthly benefit is a variable percentage (inversely proportional to earnings) of average earnings during the last 250 weeks of contributions, plus 1.25% of earnings for every year of contributions beyond 500 weeks. The pension is increased by 15% if there are no dependents.

Dependent's supplement: 15% of the insured's pension is payable for a wife or partner and 10% is payable for each child younger than age 16 (age 25 if a student, no limit if disabled). In the absence of a wife or partner or children, 10% is payable for each dependent parent.

The minimum pension is equal to 100% of the minimum monthly wage in Mexico City (1,631.12 NP).

The maximum pension is equal to 100% of the insured's average earnings in the last 250 weeks of contributions. The percentage may be increased, depending on total number of weeks of contributions.

Christmas bonus: Equal to a month's pension without supplements.

Early pension: The monthly benefit is equal to 75% of the old-age pension for an insured person who retires at age 60 and increases by 5% for each additional year of age up to age 64. The pension is increased by 15% if there are no dependents.

Old-age pensions are payable abroad under bilateral agreement.

Benefit adjustment: Pensions are adjusted annually in February for changes in the price index.

Permanent Disability Benefits

Disability pension

Mandatory individual account: The monthly benefit is equal to 35% of average adjusted earnings in the last 500 weeks of contributions.

Dependent's supplement: 15% of the insured's pension is payable for a wife or partner and 10% is payable for each child younger than age 16 (age 25 if a student, no limit if disabled). In the absence of a wife or partner or children, 10% is payable for each dependent parent.

Constant-attendance allowance: Up to 20% of the insured's pension.

The minimum pension is equal to 100% of the minimum monthly wage in Mexico City (1,631.12 NP).

The maximum pension is equal to 100% of the insured's average earnings in the last 500 weeks of contributions.

Guaranteed minimum pension: If the insured is eligible for a disability pension and the pension (based on the value of the accumulated capital plus accrued interest) is higher than the minimum pension, the insured may withdraw the sum exceeding the amount needed for the minimum pension.

Christmas bonus: Equal to a month's pension without supplements.

Disability pensions are payable abroad under bilateral agreement.

Benefit adjustment: Pensions are adjusted annually in February for changes in the price index.

Social insurance: The monthly pension is a variable percentage (inversely proportional to earnings) of average earnings during the last 250 weeks of contributions, plus 1.25% of earnings for every year of contributions beyond 500 weeks. The pension is increased by 15% if there are no dependents.

Constant-attendance allowance: Up to 20% of the insured's pension.

Dependent's supplement: 15% of the insured's pension is payable for a wife or partner and 10% is payable for each child younger than age 16 (age 25 if a student, no limit if disabled). In the absence of a wife or partner or children, 10% is payable for each dependent parent.

The minimum pension is equal to 100% of the minimum monthly wage in Mexico City (1,631.12 NP).

The maximum pension is equal to 100% of average earnings in the last 250 weeks of contributions. The percentage may be increased, depending on total number of weeks of contributions.

Christmas bonus: Equal to a month's pension without supplements.

Disability pensions are payable abroad under bilateral agreement.

Benefit adjustment: Pensions are adjusted annually in February for changes in the price index.

Survivor Benefits

Survivor pension (mandatory individual account and social insurance): The monthly pension is equal to 90% of the pension based on the individual account paid or payable to the deceased.

Eligibility ceases if the widow(er) or partner remarries or cohabits with a new partner.

Remarriage settlement: If a widow(er) or a partner remarries, a lump sum equal to 3 years' pension is paid.

Constant-attendance allowance: Up to 20% of the pension may be paid to a widow(er) or a partner.

Orphan's pension (mandatory individual account and social insurance): 20% of the deceased's pension is paid for each orphan younger than age 16 (age 25 if a student, no limit if disabled); 30% for a full orphan. When eligibility ceases, orphans receive a final benefit equal to 3 months of the deceased's pension.

Other eligible survivors (mandatory individual account and social insurance): In the absence of the above, 20% of the deceased's pension is paid for each eligible survivor.

The amount payable may be recalculated if the number of eligible survivors changes.

The maximum pension is equal to 100% of the pension paid or payable to the deceased.

Survivor pensions are payable abroad under bilateral agreement.

Funeral grant: A lump sum equal to twice the insured's monthly salary or pension.

Benefit adjustment: Pensions are adjusted annually in February for changes in the price index.

Administrative Organization

Mandatory individual account: Managed by a general assembly, technical council, oversight commission, and director general, the Mexican Social Security Institute (http://www.imss.gob.mx) administers the program.

National Commission for the Retirement Savings System (CONSAR) (http://www.consar.gob.mx) supervises the pension fund management companies (AFORES).

Social insurance: Managed by a general assembly, technical council, oversight commission, and director general, the Mexican Social Security Institute (http://www.imss.gob.mx) administers the program through regional and local boards.

Sickness and Maternity

Regulatory Framework

First law: 1943.

Current law: 1995 (social insurance), implemented in 1997, with 2001 and 2004 amendments.

Type of program: Social insurance system. Cash and medical benefits.

Coverage

Employees; members of producers', agricultural, and credit union cooperatives; pensioners; and dependents.

Voluntary coverage for self-employed persons, domestic workers, public-sector employees not covered by other laws, family labor, and employers.

Special systems for public-sector employees.

Source of Funds

Insured person

Cash benefits: 0.25% of gross monthly earnings.

Medical benefits: None; 0.88% of earnings exceeding 4,893.36 NP if the insured's earnings are greater than three times the minimum monthly wage in Mexico City (1,631.12 NP). Pensioners contribute 0.375% of gross monthly earnings.

The minimum earnings for contribution purposes are equal to the regional minimum wage.

The maximum earnings for contribution purposes are equal to 25 times the minimum monthly wage in Mexico City (1,631.12 NP).

Voluntary contributors pay a flat rate equal to 22.4% of the minimum monthly wage in Mexico City (1,631.12 NP).

Self-employed person

Cash benefits: 0.7% of declared earnings.

Medical benefits: A flat rate of 18.45% of the minimum monthly wage in Mexico City; plus 2.57% of earnings exceeding 4,893.36 NP if declared earnings are greater than three times the minimum monthly wage in Mexico City (1,631.12 NP). Self-employed pensioners contribute 1.425% of gross earnings.

The minimum earnings for contribution purposes are equal to the regional minimum wage.

The maximum earnings for contribution purposes are equal to 25 times the minimum monthly wage in Mexico City (1,631.12 NP).

Employer

Cash benefits: 0.7% of gross monthly earnings.

Medical benefits: A flat rate equal to 18.45% of the minimum monthly wage in Mexico City per employee; plus 2.57% of earnings exceeding 4,893.36 NP if earnings are greater than three times the minimum monthly wage in Mexico City (1,631.12 NP). Pensioners who are employers contribute 1.05% of gross earnings.

The minimum earnings for contribution purposes are equal to the regional minimum wage.

The maximum earnings for contribution purposes are equal to 25 times the minimum monthly wage in Mexico City (1,631.12 NP).

Government

Cash benefits: 0.05% of gross earnings.

Medical benefits: A flat-rate contribution equal to 18.45% of the minimum monthly wage in Mexico City (1,631.12 NP); 0.75% of gross earnings on behalf of pensioners.

Qualifying Conditions

Cash sickness benefits: Must have 4 weeks of contributions immediately before the onset of the incapacity; for casual workers, at least 6 weeks of contributions in the last 4 months.

Coverage is extended for up to 8 weeks after covered employment ceases if the insured had at least 8 continuous weeks of contributions.

Insured persons older than age 65 (men and women) are eligible, as are all unemployed persons older than age 60 with 750 weeks of contributions.

Cash maternity benefits: Must have at least 30 weeks of contributions in the 12 months before the benefit is payable.

Medical benefits: Currently insured, a pensioner, or an eligible dependent.

Sickness and Maternity Benefits

Sickness benefit: The benefit is equal to 60% of the last daily earnings and is payable after a 3-day waiting period for up to 52 weeks; may be extended in some cases to 78 weeks.

The minimum benefit is equal to 60% of the regional minimum wage.

The maximum earnings for benefit calculation purposes are equal to 25 times the minimum monthly wage in Mexico City (1,631.12 NP).

Maternity benefit: The benefit is equal to 100% of the last daily earnings and is payable for 42 days before and 42 days after the expected date of childbirth. (If incapable of work when maternity benefit ceases, the mother is eligible for a cash sickness benefit.)

The minimum benefit is equal to the regional minimum wage.

The maximum earnings for benefit calculation purposes are equal to 25 times the minimum monthly wage in Mexico City (1,631.12 NP).

Nursing allowance: In-kind assistance is provided for up to 6 months after childbirth. A layette (clothing and other necessities for the newborn) is also provided.

Workers' Medical Benefits

Medical services are normally provided directly to patients (including old-age pensioners covered by the 1997 law) through the health facilities of the Mexican Social Security Institute. Benefits include general and specialist care, surgery, maternity care, hospitalization or care in a convalescent home, medicines, laboratory services, dental care, and appliances. Benefits are payable for 52 weeks; may be extended in some cases to 104 weeks.

Dependents' Medical Benefits

Medical services are normally provided directly to patients through the health facilities of the Mexican Social Security Institute. Benefits include general and specialist care, surgery, maternity care, hospitalization or care in a convalescent home, medicines, laboratory services, dental care, and appliances. Benefits are payable for 52 weeks; may be extended in some cases to 104 weeks. The wife of an insured man also receives postnatal benefits in kind. Medical services are provided for dependent children up to age 16 (age 25 if a student, no limit if disabled).

Administrative Organization

Managed by a general assembly, technical council, oversight commission, and director general, the Mexican Social Security Institute (http://www.imss.gob.mx) administers the program through regional and local boards.

Mexican Social Security Institute (http://www.imss.gob.mx) operates its own hospitals, clinics, pharmacies, and other medical facilities and also contracts for the use of some facilities.

Work Injury

Regulatory Framework

First law: 1943.

Current law: 1995 (social insurance), implemented in 1997, with 2001 and 2004 amendments.

Type of program: Social insurance system.

Coverage

Employees and members of producers', agricultural, and credit union cooperatives.

Voluntary coverage for domestic workers, public-sector employees not covered by other laws, and employers.

Source of Funds

Insured person: None.

Self-employed person: Not applicable.

Employer: Total cost; contributions vary between 0.25% and 15% of payroll according to the total payroll and the assessed degree of risk.

Government: None.

Qualifying Conditions

Work injury benefits: There is no minimum qualifying period. Accidents that occur while commuting to and from work are covered.

Temporary Disability Benefits

Temporary disability benefit: The benefit is equal to 100% of earnings before the onset of disability. The benefit is payable from the first day of disability for a maximum of 52 weeks or until the insured is assessed as permanently disabled.

The minimum benefit is equal to the regional minimum wage.

The maximum earnings for benefit calculation purposes are equal to 25 times the minimum monthly wage in Mexico City (1,631.12 NP).

Occupational disease benefit: The benefit is equal to 100% of average earnings in the last 52 weeks.

Permanent Disability Benefits

Permanent disability pension: If totally disabled (100%), the monthly benefit is equal to 70% of earnings before the onset of disability.

The minimum earnings for benefit calculation purposes are equal to the regional minimum wage.

The maximum earnings for benefit calculation purposes are equal to 25 times the minimum wage in Mexico City (1,631.12 NP).

Partial disability: With an assessed degree of disability greater than 50%, the pension is a percentage of the full pension according to the assessed degree of disability. If the assessed degree of disability is between 26% and 50%, the pension is paid as a percentage of the full pension according to the assessed degree of disability or paid as a lump sum. If the assessed degree of disability is 25% or less, a lump sum is paid equal to 5 years' pension.

Christmas bonus: A supplement equal to 15 days' pension is paid if the assessed degree of disability is greater than 50%.

An initial pension is payable for 2 years; thereafter, payment is dependent on the disability being assessed as permanent.

Pensions are payable abroad under bilateral agreement.

Benefit adjustment: Pensions are adjusted annually in February for changes in the price index.

Workers' Medical Benefits

Benefits include full medical, surgical, and hospital care; medicines; rehabilitation; transport, and appliances.

The duration of benefit is 52 weeks.

Survivor Benefits

Survivor pension: The monthly pension paid to a widow(er) or partner is equal to 40% of the deceased's disability pension.

Eligibility ceases if the widow(er) or partner remarries or cohabits with a new partner.

Remarriage settlement: If a widow(er) or a partner remarries, a lump sum equal to 3 years' pension is paid.

Orphan's pension: 20% of the deceased's pension is paid for each orphan younger than age 16 (age 25 if a student, no limit if disabled); 30% for a full orphan. When eligibility ceases, orphans receive a final benefit equal to 3 months of the deceased's pension.

Other eligible survivors (in the absence of the above): Each eligible survivor receives 20% of the deceased's pension.

The amount payable may be recalculated if the number of eligible survivors changes.

Christmas bonus: A supplement equal to 15 days' pension.

The maximum pension is equal to 100% of the deceased's disability pension.

Survivor pensions are payable abroad under bilateral agreement.

Funeral grant: A lump sum equal to twice the deceased's monthly salary.

Benefit adjustment: Pensions are adjusted annually in February for changes in the price index.

Administrative Organization

Managed by a general assembly, technical council, oversight commission, and a director general, the Mexican Social Security Institute (http://www.imss.gob.mx) administers contributions and benefits through regional and local boards.

Unemployment

Regulatory Framework

Mexican Social Security Institute (http://www.imss.gob.mx) pays an unemployment benefit of between 75% and 95% of the old-age pension for unemployed persons aged 60 to 64 (the benefit is paid under Old Age, Disability, and Survivors, above).

Labor law requires employers to pay dismissed employees a lump sum equal to 3 months' pay plus 20 days' pay for each year of service.

Unemployed persons may withdraw an amount equal to 65 days of earnings in the last 250 weeks of contributions or 10% of the individual account balance, whichever is lower, after 46 consecutive days of unemployment. One withdrawal is permitted every 5 years.

Family Allowances

Regulatory Framework

First law: 1973.

Current law: 1995 (social insurance), implemented in 1997, with 2001 and 2004 amendments.

Type of program: Social insurance system.

Coverage

Family assistance: Persons assessed as needy.

Exclusions: Self-employed persons, domestic workers, public-sector employees not covered by other laws, family labor, and employers.

Child care allowance: Dependent children of covered women, widowers, or divorced working men.

Exclusions: Self-employed persons, domestic workers, public-sector employees not covered by other laws, family labor, and employers.

Marriage grant: Insured men and women.

Social benefits: Residents.

Source of Funds

Insured person: None.

Self-employed person: Not applicable.

Employer: 1% of payroll.

The minimum earnings for contribution purposes are equal to the regional minimum wage.

The maximum earnings for contribution purposes are equal to 25 times the minimum monthly wage in Mexico City (1,631.12 NP).

Government: None.

Qualifying Conditions

Family assistance (means-tested): Assessed as needy.

Child care allowance: The parent is in covered employment; may be extended for up to 4 weeks after leaving covered employment. The grant is payable for a child from the 43rd day after birth up to age 4.

Marriage grant: Paid to an insured man or woman with at least 150 weeks of contributions. Coverage is extended up to 90 days after the last day of contributions.

Social benefits: Must be resident.

Family Allowance Benefits

Family assistance (means-tested): Cash benefits are provided.

Child care allowance: Child day care facilities are provided.

Marriage grant: A lump sum equal to the minimum monthly wage in Mexico City (1,631.12 NP) is financed by the individual account.

Social benefits: Preventive health care services are provided.

Administrative Organization

Managed by a general assembly, technical council, oversight commission, and a director general, the Mexican Social Security Institute (http://www.imss.gob.mx) administers the program.

Nicaragua

Exchange rate: US$1.00 equals 16.33 cordobas.

Old Age, Disability, and Survivors

Regulatory Framework

First law and current law: 1955 (social security), with 2005 amendment.

Type of program: Social insurance system.

Coverage

All persons receiving remuneration for work or services rendered.

Voluntary coverage for the self-employed, workers who were previously covered by the program, clergy, employers, and unpaid family members working for family-owned companies.

Exclusions: Seasonal agricultural workers, armed forces personnel, and domestic workers.

Noncontributory system for miners, indigents, those who have performed services for the country, and war victims.

Source of Funds

Insured person: 4% of gross earnings.

The minimum earnings for contribution purposes are equal to the minimum wage.

The maximum earnings for contribution purposes are 35,525 cordobas.

The insured's contributions also finance family allowances.

Self-employed person: Voluntary contributions of either 10% of declared earnings (old-age, disability, and survivor benefits and dependent supplements) or 18.25% of declared earnings (old-age, disability, and survivor benefits and dependent supplements; sickness and maternity benefits; and family allowances).

The maximum earnings for contribution purposes are 35,525 cordobas.

Employer: 6% of payroll.

The minimum earnings for contribution purposes are equal to the minimum wage.

The maximum earnings for contribution purposes are 35,525 cordobas.

The employer's contributions also finance family allowances.

Government: Subsidizes benefits for voluntarily covered self-employed persons.

The Nicaraguan Institute of Social Security finances any deficit for the provision of war pensions and special pensions (see source of funds under Work Injury, below).

Qualifying Conditions

Old-age pension: Age 60 (age 55 for persons with a certified physical or mental disability) with 750 weeks of contributions. Qualifying conditions are reduced for those who joined the social insurance system after age 45, with contributions required only for half the number of weeks from the date coverage began until the pensionable age.

Age 60 years with 15 years of contributions for the self-employed. Age 55 for miners and teachers with 30 years of service (men) or 15 years of service (women).

A working pensioner may receive a pension and a salary but must pay contributions to the program.

Old-age pensions are not payable abroad.

Disability pension: Payable for the loss of 67% of earning capacity in the usual or a similar occupation (total disability), with 150 weeks of contributions in the last 6 years; for the loss of at least 50% but less than 67% of usual earning capacity (partial disability), with 150 weeks of contributions in the last 6 years.

The disability pension is replaced by the old-age pension at age 60. If the insured is ineligible for the old-age pension, a partial disability pension is increased to the value of the total disability benefit at age 60 on the condition that the beneficiary retire from all gainful employment.

The assessed loss of earning capacity is reviewed every 3 years.

Disability pensions are not payable abroad.

Survivor pension: The deceased had 150 weeks of contributions in the last 6 years.

Survivor pensions are not payable abroad.

Funeral grant: The deceased had 4 weeks of contributions in the 26 weeks before death.

Noncontributory pension: War victims' pensions are paid to persons who have never contributed to the social insurance system but who have performed services for the country; special pensions are paid to other groups, including indigent persons, miners, and public servants.

Old-Age Benefits

Old-age pension: The pension is equal to 40% of the insured's average earnings (45% if average earnings are less than twice the minimum wage) in the last 5, 4, or 3 years (based on a period of contributions of 15, 20, or 25 years, respectively), plus 1.365% (1.59% if average earnings are less than twice the minimum wage) for each additional 50-week period of contributions. An additional 1% of earnings is paid for each year of work after age 60, up to a maximum of 5%.

Dependent's supplement: 15% of the old-age pension is paid for a wife or partner; 10% each for children younger than age 15 (age 21 if student, no limit if disabled); and 10% for uninsured parents older than age 60 or disabled.

The maximum pension is 80% of average earnings if the insured's average earnings are more than twice the minimum wage; 100% if the insured's average earnings are less than twice the minimum wage.

The minimum monthly benefit is 1,032.70 cordobas.

Schedule of payments: Benefits are paid monthly, with an additional payment made each Christmas.

Benefit adjustment: Pensions are adjusted periodically for wage changes, depending on national economic conditions.

Noncontributory pension: War victims' pensions and special pensions are provided.

Permanent Disability Benefits

Disability pension: The pension is equal to 40% of the insured's average earnings (45% if average earnings are less than twice the minimum wage) in the last 5, 4, or 3 years (based on a period of contributions of 15, 20, or 25 years, respectively), plus 1.365% (1.59% if average earnings are less than twice the minimum wage) for each additional 50-week period of contributions.

If the insured has a spouse and children, the total disability pension must not be less than 50% of the insured's average earnings.

Constant-attendance allowance: Equal to 20% of the total disability pension.

Dependent's supplement (total disability): 15% of the pension is paid for a wife or partner; 10% each for children younger than age 15 (age 21 if student, no limit if disabled); and 10% for uninsured parents older than age 60 or disabled.

Partial disability: Equal to 50% of the total disability pension.

The maximum partial disability pension must be higher than 33% but less than 50% of the minimum wage in the insured's occupation.

Schedule of payments: Benefits are paid monthly, with an additional payment made each Christmas.

Benefit adjustment: Pensions are adjusted periodically for wage changes, depending on national economic conditions.

Noncontributory pension: War victims' pensions and special pensions are provided for total and partial disability.

Survivor Benefits

Survivor pension: 50% of the deceased's pension is payable to a widow aged 45 or older or disabled or to a dependent disabled widower. A pension is payable to a widow younger than age 45 for a limited period of 2 years or for as long as she is caring for a child receiving an orphan's pension.

Orphan's pension: Each orphan younger than age 15 (age 21 if a student, no limit if disabled) receives 25% of the deceased's pension; 50% for a full orphan.

The maximum survivor pension payable to a widow(er) with two or more children is equal to 100% of the deceased's pension.

Funeral grant: The cost of the funeral or an amount equal to 50% of the deceased's monthly wage.

Benefit adjustment: Pensions are adjusted periodically for wage changes, depending on national economic conditions.

Noncontributory pension: War victims' pensions and special pensions are provided for spouses, orphans, and dependent parents.

Administrative Organization

Managed by technical and managing councils, the Nicaraguan Institute of Social Security (http://www.inss.org.ni) administers the program.

Sickness and Maternity

Regulatory Framework

First law and current law: 1955 (social security), with 2005 amendment.

Type of program: Social insurance (cash benefits) and universal (medical benefits) system.

Coverage

Cash benefits: All persons receiving remuneration for work or services rendered.

Voluntary coverage for the self-employed, clergy, employers, ranchers, and unpaid family members working for family-owned companies.

Exclusions: Armed forces personnel.

Medical benefits: Insured persons and their dependents (the wife of an insured man receives prenatal and postnatal care; children receive benefits up to age 12) and old-age pensioners.

Source of Funds

Insured person: 6.25% of gross earnings.

The minimum earnings for contribution purposes are equal to the minimum wage.

The maximum earnings for contribution purposes are 35,525 cordobas.

Self-employed person: See source of funds under Old Age, Disability, and Survivors, above.

Employer: 15% of payroll.

The minimum earnings for contribution purposes are equal to the minimum wage.

The maximum earnings for contribution purposes are 35,525 cordobas.

Government: 0.25% of earnings; contributes as an employer.

Qualifying Conditions

Cash sickness benefits: Must have 8 weeks of contributions in the last 22 weeks. Insured persons with 8 weekly contributions in the last 22 weeks who become unemployed are covered for 14 weeks after the end of employment.

No benefits are payable if the insured is caring for a sick family member.

Cash maternity benefits: Must have 16 weeks of contributions in the 39 weeks before the expected date of childbirth. Insured women with 8 weekly contributions in the last 22 weeks who become unemployed are covered for 14 weeks after the end of employment.

Medical benefits: At least 4 weeks of contributions, even if they are not consecutive; receiving a contributory or noncontributory old-age pension.

Sickness and Maternity Benefits

Sickness benefit: The monthly benefit is equal to 60% of the insured's average earnings in the last 8 weeks and is payable after a 3-day waiting period (waived if hospitalized) for up to 52 weeks.

Maternity benefit: The benefit is equal to 60% of the insured's average earnings in the last 8 weeks and is payable according to eight wage classes. The benefit is payable for 4 weeks before and 8 weeks after the expected date of childbirth.

Nursing allowance: Forty-five pounds of milk are provided in the first 6 months of the child's life.

Workers' Medical Benefits

Medical services are provided directly to patients, depending on available resources.

There is no limit to duration.

Dependents' Medical Benefits

Medical services are provided directly to patients, depending on available resources. The wife of an insured man receives prenatal and postnatal care. Benefits are provided for children up to age 12. Old-age pensioners (contributory and noncontributory) receive medical care for 77 illnesses and 7 types of surgical treatment, according to the schedule in law.

Administrative Organization

Managed by technical and managing councils, the Nicaraguan Institute of Social Security (http://www.inss.org.ni) administers the program.

Medical care and cash benefits are delivered through public and private institutions.

Work Injury

Regulatory Framework

First law: 1945 (labor code).

Current law: 2005 (social security).

Type of program: Social insurance system.

Coverage

All persons receiving remuneration for work or services rendered.

Source of Funds

Insured person: None.

Self-employed person: Not applicable.

Employer: 1.5% of payroll (plus 1.5% of payroll for war victims' pensions).

The maximum earnings for contribution purposes are 35,525 cordobas.

Government: None; contributes as an employer.

Qualifying Conditions

Work injury benefits: There is no minimum qualifying period.

Temporary Disability Benefits

The benefit is equal to 60% of earnings in the last 8 weeks of contributions. The benefit is payable from the day after the onset of disability until medical care ceases or the insured is certified as permanently disabled. (The employer pays the benefit for the first day of disability.)

Permanent Disability Benefits

Permanent disability pension: The pension is equal to 60% of the insured's earnings if the insured has a wife and two or more children; 50% if there are no dependents.

Dependent's supplement (total disability): 15% of the pension is paid for a wife or partner; 10% each for children younger than age 15 (age 21 if student, no limit if disabled).

Partial disability: A percentage of the full pension is paid according to the assessed degree of disability.

Noncontributory pension: Special pensions are provided for total and partial disability for prescribed categories of worker.

Workers' Medical Benefits

Medical benefits are provided for work injuries and occupational diseases.

Survivor Benefits

Survivor pension: The minimum pension is equal to 50% of the deceased's earnings used to calculate the permanent disability pension. The pension is payable to a widow or a dependent disabled widower.

Orphan's pension: Each orphan younger than age 15 (age 21 if a student, no limit if disabled) receives 25% of the deceased's pension; 50% for a full orphan.

Other dependent survivors (in the absence of the above): Each survivor receives 25% of the deceased's pension.

The maximum survivor pension is equal to 100% of the deceased's pension.

Funeral grant: 50% of the deceased's average monthly salary.

Administrative Organization

Managed by technical and managing councils, the Nicaraguan Institute of Social Security (http://www.inss.org.ni) administers the program.

Family Allowances

Regulatory Framework

First and current law: 1955 (social security), implemented in 1956, with 2005 amendment.

Type of program: Social insurance system.

Coverage

All persons receiving remuneration for work or services rendered.

Voluntary coverage for the self-employed, workers who were previously covered by the program, clergy, employers, and unpaid family members working for family-owned companies.

Exclusions: Seasonal agricultural workers and armed forces personnel.

Source of Funds

Insured person: See source of funds under Old Age, Disability, and Survivors, above.

Self-employed person: See source of funds under Old Age, Disability, and Survivors, above.

Employer: See source of funds under Old Age, Disability, and Survivors, above.

Government: See source of funds under Old Age, Disability, and Survivors, above.

Qualifying Conditions

Family allowances (earnings-tested): The child must be younger than age 15; age 21 if a student.

Family Allowance Benefits

Family allowances (earnings-tested): Monthly allowances vary according to family earnings and the age of the child.

Administrative Organization

Managed by technical and managing councils, the Nicaraguan Institute of Social Security (http://www.inss.org.ni) administers the program.

Panama

Exchange rate: US$1.00 equals 1 balboa.

Old Age, Disability, and Survivors

Regulatory Framework

First law: 1941.

Current law: 1954 (social insurance), with 1991, 1992, 2000, and 2004 amendments.

Type of program: Social insurance system.

Coverage

Employees in public- and private-sector employment and domestic workers.

Voluntary coverage for the self-employed.

All foreign workers are covered except for those working in Panama for less than 2 months under a foreign employment contract.

Exclusions: Agricultural workers employed for less than 3 months annually and family labor.

Occasional and seasonal workers are to be covered under subsequent regulation.

Public-sector employees are covered under the general system as well as a special system.

Source of Funds

Insured person: 6.75% of gross earnings.

The minimum earnings for contribution purposes are equal to either the monthly minimum pension (175 balboas) paid by the fund or 100 balboas.

There are no maximum earnings for contribution purposes, except for deputies and managerial staff of the Panama Canal who are subject to maximum earnings of 5,000 balboas and 5,326 balboas, respectively.

Self-employed person: A voluntary contribution of 9.5% of declared earnings.

The minimum declared earnings for contribution purposes must be more than 300 balboas.

There are no maximum earnings for contribution purposes.

Employer: 2.75% of payroll.

The minimum earnings for contribution purposes are equal to either the monthly minimum pension (175 balboas) paid by the fund or 100 balboas.

There are no maximum earnings for contribution purposes, except for deputies and managerial staff of the Panama

Canal who are subject to maximum earnings of 5,000 balboas and 5,326 balboas, respectively.

Government: A percentage of contributions (1.04% of payroll for the administration of old-age, disability, and survivor benefits; sickness and maternity benefits; and work injury benefits) and the proceeds of an earmarked tax on alcohol, plus no less than 20.5 million balboas a year.

Qualifying Conditions

Old-age pension: Age 62 (men) or age 57 (women) with 180 months of contributions. Retirement is necessary.

Early pension: There is no early pension.

Deferred pension: A deferred pension is possible. There is no maximum age of deferral.

The pension is payable abroad.

Old-age settlement: At the normal retirement age, the insured does not meet the contribution conditions for a pension.

Disability pension: Payable for a loss of 2/3 of earning capacity. The insured must have at least 36 months of contributions, including 18 months during the last 3 years; a total of 180 months of contributions. The pension is payable for 2 years (may be extended) and the assessed degree of disability may be reviewed at any time at the request of the insured or the fund.

The Medical Qualification Commission assesses the degree of disability.

The disability pension is payable abroad.

The disability pension is not commuted to an old-age pension at the normal retirement age.

Disability grant: The insured does not meet the qualifying conditions for a full pension but has at least 12 months of contributions, including six contributions in the year before the onset of disability.

Survivor pension: The insured met the qualifying conditions for the disability pension or was a pensioner at the time of death.

The survivor pension is payable abroad.

Old-Age Benefits

Old-age pension: The pension is equal to 60% of the insured's average earnings in the best 7 years of earnings, plus 1.25% of earnings for each 12-month period of contributions above 180 months.

Early pension: There is no early pension.

Deferred pension: An additional 2% of earnings is paid for each 12-month period of contributions after the normal retirement age.

Dependent's supplement (at the normal retirement age): Twenty balboas a month is paid for a wife and 10 balboas for each child younger than age 18 (no limit if disabled), up to a maximum of 100 balboas.

The minimum monthly pension is 175 balboas.

The maximum monthly pension with 25 years of coverage and average monthly earnings of 1,500 balboas is 1,500 balboas.

The pension plus supplements must not exceed 100% of the insured's average earnings used for the pension calculation.

Benefit adjustment: Pensions are adjusted on an ad hoc basis depending on economic conditions.

Old-age settlement: A lump sum is paid equal to 1 month's pension for each 6-month period of contributions.

Permanent Disability Benefits

Disability pension: The pension is equal to 60% of the insured's average earnings in the best 7 years of earnings, plus 1.25% of earnings for each 12-month period of contributions above 180 months. If the total contribution period is less than 7 years, the pension is based on 60% of average earnings in the period credited.

Dependent's supplement: Twenty balboas a month is paid for a wife and 10 balboas for each child younger than age 18 (no limit if disabled), up to a maximum of 100 balboas.

The minimum monthly pension is 175 balboas.

Benefit adjustment: Pensions are adjusted on an ad hoc basis depending on economic conditions.

Disability grant: A lump sum is paid equal to 1 month's pension for each 6-month period of contributions.

Survivor Benefits

Survivor pension: 50% of the pension paid or payable to the deceased is paid to a widow aged 57 or older or disabled or caring for a child. A limited pension is paid to other widows for 5 years only. The pension is also payable to a dependent disabled widower.

Orphan's pension: 20% of the deceased's pension is paid for each orphan younger than age 14 (age 18 if a student, no limit if disabled); 50% for a full orphan.

Other dependents (in the absence of the above): The deceased's mother or aged or disabled father receives 30% of the deceased's pension; eligible brothers and sisters receive 20% of the deceased's pension until age 14.

The minimum pension is equal to 87.50 balboas for a widow, 35 balboas for half orphans, 52.50 for parents in the absence of widow and orphans; 35 balboas for brothers and sisters in the absence of widow, orphans, and parents.

The maximum total survivor pension is 100% of the deceased's pension, up to a maximum of 1,500 balboas.

Benefit adjustment: Pensions are adjusted on an ad hoc basis depending on economic conditions.

Funeral grant: A lump sum of 300 balboas.

Administrative Organization

Managed by a board of directors with tripartite representation and a director general with an advisory board for technical advice, the Social Insurance Fund (http://www.css.org.pa) administers the program.

Sickness and Maternity

Regulatory Framework

First law: 1941.

Current law: 1954 (social insurance), with 1983, 1986, and 1999 amendments.

Type of program: Social insurance system. Cash and medical benefits.

Coverage

Employees in public- and private-sector employment and domestic workers.

Voluntary coverage for the self-employed.

Pensioners are covered for medical benefits.

Exclusions: Agricultural workers employed for less than 3 months annually and family labor.

Temporary workers and seasonal workers will be covered by subsequent regulations.

Source of Funds

Insured person: 0.5% of gross earnings; pensioners contribute 6.75% of the pension.

There are no minimum or maximum earnings for contribution purposes.

Self-employed person: A voluntary contribution of 8.5% of declared gross earnings.

There are no minimum or maximum earnings for contribution purposes.

Employer: 8% of payroll.

There are no minimum or maximum earnings for contribution purposes.

Government: A percentage of contributions (1.04% of payroll for the administration of old-age, disability, and survivor benefits; sickness and maternity benefits; and work injury benefits) and the proceeds of an earmarked tax on alcohol.

Qualifying Conditions

Cash sickness benefits: Must have 6 months of contributions in the last 9 months.

Cash maternity benefits: Must have 4 months of contributions in the 8 months before the claim is made and be certified as pregnant.

Medical benefits: Currently insured or a pensioner; if the insured becomes unemployed, coverage continues for 3 months after the end of employment (24 months for insured persons with 180 months of contributions).

Sickness and Maternity Benefits

Sickness benefit: The benefit is equal to 70% of the insured's average earnings in the previous 2 months. The benefit is payable after a 3-day waiting period for up to 52 weeks for any one incapacity; may be extended for up to 26 additional weeks for the same incapacity with a possible further extension of up to a year with the agreement of the Social Insurance Fund.

There are no minimum or maximum benefits.

Maternity benefit: The benefit is equal to 100% of the insured's average earnings in the last 9 months and is payable for up to 6 weeks before and 8 weeks after the expected date of childbirth.

There is no provision of paid parental leave.

Workers' Medical Benefits

Benefits include general and specialist care, surgery, hospitalization, laboratory services, medicines, dental care, and maternity care.

Medical services are normally provided directly through the facilities of the Social Insurance Fund or are provided by the Ministry of Health, with the cost reimbursed. In special cases, including those in which the Fund or Ministry have no facilities, the cost of private care obtained in the country or abroad may be reimbursed in part or in full, with the authorization of the Fund.

There is no limit to duration if the medical service is necessary.

Dependents' Medical Benefits

Benefits include general and specialist care, surgery, hospitalization, laboratory services, medicines, and dental care. Benefits are provided to the insured's wife and children younger than age 18 (age 25 if a student or disabled), a dependent mother, a disabled father, or parents older than age 60.

Administrative Organization

Managed by a board of directors with tripartite representation and a director general with an advisory board for technical advice, the Social Insurance Fund (http://www.css.org.pa) administers the program.

Social Insurance Fund operates its own hospitals and other medical facilities in larger cities.

Ministry of Health (http://www.minsa.gob.pa) is responsible for national health policy.

Work Injury

Regulatory Framework

First law: 1916.

Current law: 1970 (occupational risks).

Type of program: Employer-liability system, involving compulsory insurance with a public carrier.

Coverage

Employees in public- and private-sector employment.

Source of Funds

Insured person: None.

Self-employed person: Not applicable.

Employer: Total cost met through the payment of insurance premiums. The cost of premiums varies with the assessed degree of risk. The average premium is 1.7% of payroll.

Government: None.

Qualifying Conditions

Work injury benefits: There is no minimum qualifying period.

Temporary Disability Benefits

No statutory benefits are provided.

Permanent Disability Benefits

Permanent disability pension: If the insured is 100% disabled, the pension is equal to 60% of his or her earnings.

The minimum monthly pension is 175 balboas.

The maximum monthly pension is 1,000 balboas.

Partial disability: A percentage of the full pension is paid according to the assessed degree of disability. The pension may be increased if the assessed degree of disability is greater than 35%; may be paid as a lump sum if the assessed degree of disability is 35% or less.

The Medical Qualification Commission assesses the degree of disability.

The pension may be replaced by the old-age pension at age 62 (men) or age 57 (women) if the insured meets the qualifying conditions for the old-age pension.

The pension is payable abroad.

Benefit adjustment: Benefits are reviewed every 2 years.

Workers' Medical Benefits

Benefits include general and specialist care, surgery, medicines, hospitalization, and appliances.

Survivor Benefits

Survivor pension: A widow or a disabled widower receives a pension equal to 25% of the deceased's earnings for life; 30% if the survivor is the sole beneficiary or is disabled.

Orphan's pension: The pension for one orphan younger than age 18 is equal to 15% of the deceased's earnings; for two orphans, 25%; for three orphans, 35%; for four or more orphans, 40%. A sole full orphan receives 30% of the deceased's earnings; for two or more full orphans, 15% of the deceased's earnings each.

Other dependents in the absence of other survivors (in order of priority): The deceased's mother receives between 20% and 30% of the deceased's earnings. The pension is payable for 10 years. Brothers or sisters younger than age 18 (no limit if disabled) and other aged or disabled or older relatives, including great grandparents, receive 10% each, up to a maximum of 30%. The pension is payable for 6 years.

The maximum total survivor pension is 75% of the deceased's earnings; otherwise, the pensions are reduced proportionately.

The pension is payable abroad.

Funeral grant: 300 balboas.

Administrative Organization

Managed by a board of directors with tripartite representation and a director general with an advisory board for technical advice, the Social Insurance Fund (http://www.css.org.pa) administers the program.

Social Insurance Fund operates its own hospitals and other medical facilities in larger cities.

Ministry of Health (http://www.minsa.gob.pa) is responsible for national health policy.

Unemployment

Regulatory Framework

No statutory benefits are provided.

Under the 1972 Labor Code, employers are required to provide workers with a severance payment at the end of the labor contract.

Paraguay

Exchange rate: US$1.00 equals 6,220 guarani.

Old Age, Disability, and Survivors

Regulatory Framework

First law: 1943.

Current law: 1992 (unified pension scheme), with 1994, 1995, 2002, and 2003 amendments.

Type of program: Social insurance system.

Coverage

Employed persons, including employees of decentralized state entities and enterprises partially owned by the state.

Exclusions: Public-sector employees, self-employed persons, domestic workers, and apprentices.

Special systems for public-sector employees, railroad employees, bank employees, elected parliamentary representatives, and military and police personnel.

Source of Funds

Insured person: 9% of gross earnings.

The minimum monthly earnings for contribution purposes are equal to the monthly minimum wage (1,089,000 guaranies).

There are no maximum earnings for contribution purposes.

The insured's contributions also finance sickness and maternity benefits and work injury benefits.

Self-employed person: Not applicable.

Employer: 14% of payroll.

The minimum monthly earnings for contribution purposes are equal to the monthly minimum wage (1,089,000 guaranies).

There are no maximum earnings for contribution purposes.

The employer's contributions also finance sickness and maternity benefits and work injury benefits.

Government: 1.5% of gross earnings; contributes as an employer.

The minimum monthly earnings for contribution purposes are equal to the monthly minimum wage (1,089,000 guaranies).

There are no maximum earnings for contribution purposes.

Government contributions also finance sickness and maternity benefits and work injury benefits.

Qualifying Conditions

Old-age pension: Age 60 (men and women) with 25 years of contributions.

A pension may be claimed by an insured person older than age 60. (If the insured was older than age 60 before January 1999, the number of years of required contributions for a new claim is 15.)

Early pension: Age 55 (men and women) with 30 years of contributions.

Disability pension: The loss of 2/3 of earning capacity with 150 weeks of contributions and younger than age 55; between 150 weeks and 250 weeks of contributions if younger than age 60; between 250 weeks and 400 weeks of contributions if younger than age 65.

A medical commission and three doctors assess the degree of disability. The degree of disability is reviewed at least once every 5 years.

Survivor pension: The insured was a pensioner at the time of death or had 750 weeks of contributions.

Eligible survivors include a widow(er) or a partner who lived with the deceased for at least 5 years (2 years if they had children); a child younger than age 18 (no limit if disabled); and dependent parents if there are no other eligible survivors.

Survivor grant: The deceased had less than 750 weeks of contributions.

Funeral grant: Paid to the person who pays for the funeral.

Old-Age Benefits

Old-age pension: The monthly pension is equal to 100% of the insured's average earnings.

Early pension: The monthly pension is equal to 80% of the insured's average earnings, plus 4% of average earnings for every year the insured is older than age 55, up to age 59.

Average earnings are based on earnings in the last 36 months before retirement.

The minimum monthly old-age pension is 300,000 guaranies.

The maximum monthly old-age pension is equal to 300 times the minimum daily wage. (The minimum monthly wage is 1,089,000 guaranies.)

All gainful activity must cease.

Old-age benefits are payable abroad under bilateral or multilateral agreement.

Benefit adjustment: Benefits are adjusted annually according to changes in the cost-of-living index.

Permanent Disability Benefits

Disability pension: The monthly pension is equal to 50% of the insured's average earnings in the last 36 months before the onset of disability, plus 1.5% of average earnings for every 50-week period of contributions beyond 150 weeks, up to a maximum of 100%.

The minimum monthly disability pension is 300,000 guaranies.

The maximum disability pension is 300 times the minimum daily wage. (The minimum monthly wage is 1,089,000 guaranies.)

Disability benefits are payable abroad under bilateral or multilateral agreement.

Benefit adjustment: Benefits are adjusted annually according to changes in the cost-of-living index.

Survivor Benefits

Survivor pension: The monthly pension is equal to 60% of the pension paid or payable to the deceased. The pension is split equally between a widow(er) or partner older than age 40 and children younger than age 18; in the absence of a widow(er) or partner or children, the deceased's parents may receive the benefit.

If the widow(er) or partner remarries or cohabits, the pension ceases and a lump sum is paid equal to twice the annual pension paid or payable to the deceased.

A widow(er) or partner younger than age 40 receives a lump sum equal to three times the annual pension paid or payable to the deceased.

Survivor grant: A lump sum equal to 1 month's minimum wage for each year of contributions.

Survivor benefits are payable abroad under bilateral or multilateral agreement.

Benefit adjustment: Benefits are adjusted annually according to changes in the cost-of-living index.

Funeral grant: A lump sum equal to 75 times the minimum daily wage. (The minimum monthly wage is 1,089,000 guaranies.)

Administrative Organization

Social Insurance Institute (http://www.ips.gov.py) administers the program and is managed by a tripartite council and a director general.

Sickness and Maternity

Regulatory Framework

First law: 1943.

Current laws: 1950 (social security), 1965 (teachers and domestic workers), 1992 (unified pension scheme), 1996 (medical benefits), 1999 (teachers), and 2003 (cohabitants).

Type of program: Social insurance system. Cash and medical benefits.

Coverage

Employed persons, including domestic workers and employees of decentralized state entities and enterprises partially owned by the state, teachers in public and private schools, university professors, and apprentices.

Pensioners are covered for medical benefits.

Exclusions: Public-sector employees and self-employed persons.

Special systems for public-sector employees, railroad employees, bank employees, and military and police personnel.

Source of Funds

Insured person: See source of funds under Old Age, Disability, and Survivors, above. (Pensioners contribute 6% of pensions; teachers in public and private schools and university professors contribute 5.5% of gross earnings; domestic workers contribute 2.5% of gross earnings.)

The minimum earnings for contribution purposes for domestic workers are equal to the minimum wage for domestic workers (400,000 guaranies).

Self-employed person: Not applicable.

Employer: See source of funds under Old Age, Disability, and Survivors, above. (Employers of teachers in public and private schools and university professors contribute 2.5% of payroll; employers of domestic workers contribute 5.5% of payroll.)

The minimum earnings for contribution purposes for employers of domestic workers are equal to the minimum wage for domestic workers (400,000 guaranies).

Government: See source of funds under Old Age, Disability, and Survivors, above.

Qualifying Conditions

Cash sickness and maternity benefits: Must have 6 weeks of contributions in the last 4 months (insured women cannot receive cash maternity benefits and cash sickness benefits at the same time).

Medical benefits: Currently insured.

Sickness and Maternity Benefits

Sickness benefit: The monthly benefit is equal to 50% of the insured's average earnings in the last 4 months before the onset of incapacity. The benefit is payable from the day after the onset of the incapacity, for up to 26 weeks; may be extended to 50 weeks in special cases. The benefit is reduced by half during periods of hospitalization if there are no dependents.

Maternity benefit: The monthly benefit is equal to 50% of the insured's average earnings in the last 4 months immediately before the maternity leave and is payable for 3 weeks before and 6 weeks after the expected date of childbirth.

Benefits in-kind: Milk vouchers are provided for up to 8 months if the mother is unable to nurse the child.

Workers' Medical Benefits

Medical services are provided directly to patients through the facilities of the Social Insurance Institute. Benefits include general and specialist care, hospitalization, laboratory services, medicines, prosthetics, dental care (with 8 weeks of recent contributions), and maternity care. The duration of benefits is 26 weeks for any one illness; may be extended to 52 weeks in special cases.

Dependents' Medical Benefits

Medical services are provided directly to patients through the facilities of the Social Insurance Institute. Benefits include general and specialist care, hospitalization, laboratory services, medicines, prosthetics, dental care (with 8 weeks of recent contributions), and maternity care. The duration of benefits is 26 weeks for any one illness; may be extended to 52 weeks in special cases.

Eligible dependents include the spouse of the insured or pensioner (or a partner who has lived with the insured or pensioner for at least 2 years); an unemployed spouse of an insured woman; the spouse of a female pensioner if he is needy, unemployed, and older than age 60; unmarried children younger than age 18 (no limit if disabled); and the insured's dependent parents older than age 60.

Administrative Organization

Social Insurance Institute (http://www.ips.gov.py) administers the program and is managed by a tripartite council and a director general.

Social Insurance Institute operates its own clinics and hospitals.

Work Injury

Regulatory Framework

First law: 1927.

Current laws: 1950 (social security), implemented in 1952; and 1992 (unified pension scheme).

Type of program: Social insurance system.

Coverage

Employed persons, including domestic workers and employees of decentralized state entities and enterprises partially owned by the state, teachers in public and private schools, and apprentices.

Exclusions: Public-sector employees and self-employed persons.

Special systems for public-sector employees, railroad employees, bank employees, and military and police personnel.

Source of Funds

Insured person: See source of funds under Old Age, Disability, and Survivors, above. (Teachers in public and private schools contribute 5.5% of gross earnings; domestic workers contribute 2.5% of gross earnings.)

The minimum earnings for contribution purposes for domestic workers are equal to the minimum wage for domestic workers (400,000 guaranies).

Self-employed person: Not applicable.

Employer: See source of funds under Old Age, Disability, and Survivors, above. (Employers of teachers in public and private schools contribute 2.5% of payroll; employers of domestic workers contribute 5.5% of payroll.)

The minimum earnings for contribution purposes for domestic workers are equal to the minimum wage for domestic workers (400,000 guaranies).

Government: See source of funds under Old Age, Disability, and Survivors, above.

Qualifying Conditions

Work injury benefits: There is no minimum qualifying period.

Temporary Disability Benefits

The benefit is equal to 75% of the insured's average earnings in the last 4 months or the total contribution period if shorter. The benefit is payable from the day after the onset of disability, for up to 52 weeks.

A medical commission and three doctors assess the degree of disability. The degree of disability is reviewed at least once every 5 years.

Permanent Disability Benefits

Permanent disability pension: The pension varies between 22% and 100% of the insured's average earnings in the last 36 months before the onset of disability, according to the length of the insured's contribution period and the assessed degree of disability.

Total disability supplement: The supplement is equal to 20% of the insured's average earnings in the last 3 years, plus 0.5% for each year of coverage beyond 3 years.

Partial disability: If the assessed degree of disability is more than 30%, the pension is equal to 60% of lost earnings, according to the schedule in law. If the value of the partial disability pension is less than 30% of the total disability pension, a lump sum is paid equal to 5 years' pension.

Partial disability supplement: The total disability supplement is reduced in proportion to the assessed degree of disability.

A medical commission and three doctors assess the degree of disability. The degree of disability is reviewed at least once every 5 years.

Workers' Medical Benefits

Benefits include general and specialist care, hospitalization, medicines, and prosthetics.

Survivor Benefits

Survivor pension: A widow(er) or partner aged 40 or older receives a monthly pension equal to 40% of the pension paid or payable to the deceased.

If the widow(er) or partner remarries or cohabits, the pension ceases and a lump sum is paid equal to twice the annual pension paid or payable to the deceased.

A widow(er) or partner younger than age 40 receives a lump sum equal to three times the annual pension paid or payable to the deceased.

Orphan's pension: Each child younger than age 16 (no limit if disabled) receives 20% of the pension paid or payable to the deceased.

Other eligible survivors (in absence of the above): The pension is payable to the deceased's parents.

The maximum survivor pension is 100% of the pension paid or payable to the deceased.

Survivor supplement: 75% of the deceased's total disability supplement is paid to eligible survivors.

Survivor grant: If the insured had less than 750 weeks of contributions at the time of death, a lump sum equal to 1 month's minimum wage for each year of contributions is paid.

Survivor benefits are payable abroad under bilateral or multilateral agreement.

Benefit adjustment: Benefits are adjusted annually according to changes in the cost-of-living index.

Funeral grant: A lump sum equal to 75 times the minimum daily wage. (The minimum monthly wage is 1,089,000 guaranies.)

Administrative Organization

Social Insurance Institute (http://www.ips.gov.py) administers the program and is managed by a tripartite council and a director general.

Family Allowances

Regulatory Framework

No statutory benefits are provided. (The 1993 labor code requires employers to provide specified maternity benefits and family allowance benefits.)

Peru

Exchange rate: US$1.00 equals
3.25 nuevos soles.

Old Age, Disability, and Survivors

Regulatory Framework

First laws: 1936 (wage earners) and 1962 (salaried employees).

Current laws: 1973 (unified social security), 1991 (mandatory individual account), and 1995 (mandatory individual account).

Type of program: Social insurance and mandatory individual account system.

Note: When public- and private-sector employees enter the workforce, they may choose between the mandatory individual account system (SPP) and the public social insurance system (SNP). SNP members may switch to the SPP but may not switch back.

Coverage

Social insurance (SNP): Wage earners and salaried employees in the private and public sectors, employees of worker-owned and cooperative enterprises, teachers, self-employed drivers, artists, domestic workers, wage earners, and the self-employed in the agricultural sector.

Special systems for fishermen, stevedores, and employees not covered under the SNP.

Voluntary coverage for the self-employed, for those who are economically active but no longer in covered employment (a minimum of 18 months' previous coverage is required), and housewives.

Mandatory individual account (SPP): Employed persons.

Voluntary coverage for the self-employed.

Source of Funds

Social insurance (SNP)

Insured person: 13% of gross earnings.

The minimum earnings for contribution purposes are equal to the legal monthly minimum wage (460 nuevos soles); for domestic workers, 33.3% of the legal monthly minimum wage.

There are no maximum earnings for contribution purposes.

Self-employed person: 13% of declared earnings.

The minimum earnings for contribution purposes are equal to the legal monthly minimum wage (460 nuevos soles).

There are no maximum earnings for contribution purposes.

Employer: None; employers of domestic workers contribute 13% of payroll.

Government: None; the government finances the minimum pension as well as special subsidies needed to finance the program.

Mandatory individual account (SPP)

Insured person: 8% of gross earnings (10% from January 2006) for old-age benefits, plus an average 0.92% of gross earnings for disability and survivor insurance and an average 2.27% of gross earnings for administrative fees.

There are no maximum earnings for contribution purposes for old-age benefits; 6,486.33 nuevos soles for disability and survivor benefits.

Self-employed person: 8% of gross earnings (10% from January 2006) for old-age benefits, plus an average 0.92% of gross earnings for disability and survivor insurance and an average 2.27% of gross earnings for administrative fees.

There are no maximum earnings for contribution purposes for old-age benefits; 6,486.33 nuevos soles for disability and survivor benefits.

Employer: None.

Government: The government finances the guaranteed minimum pension.

Qualifying Conditions

Social insurance (SNP)

Old-age pension: Men born up to December 18, 1932, and women born up to December 18, 1937, with 15 years and 13 years of contributions, respectively. Men and women born after these respective dates with at least 20 years of contributions and aged 65.

Early pension: Age 55 with 30 years of contributions (men) or age 50 with 25 years of contributions (women).

Disability pension: A loss of 2/3 of earning capacity and employed at the onset of disability; with 36 months of contributions, including 18 months in the last 36 months; 12 months of contributions in the last 36 months with a total of 3 to 15 years of contributions; or 15 or more years of contributions.

Survivor pension: The insured was a pensioner or met the qualifying conditions for a pension at the time of death.

Eligible survivors are a widow, a dependent widower older than age 60 (any age if disabled), children younger than age 18 (age 21 if a student, no limit if disabled), and a father older than age 60 and a mother older than age 55 (no limit if disabled).

Funeral grant: The deceased contributed in the 3 months before the date of death; a total of 4 months of contributions in the 6 months before the date of death.

Mandatory individual account (SPP)

Old-age pension: Age 65; a pension is payable at any age if the individual account has accumulated assets that will replace at least 50% of average indexed earnings in the last 10 years.

Guaranteed minimum pension: The insured was born no later than 1945, satisfies the minimum requirements for contributions (20 years), and the pension (based on the value of the accumulated capital plus accrued interest) is less than the minimum pension.

Disability pension: Younger than age 65 and assessed with at least a 50% loss of earning capacity.

The degree of disability is assessed by the pension fund administrator or the Bank Superintendent.

Survivor pension: The deceased was a pensioner or met the qualifying conditions for a pension at the time of death.

Eligible survivors are a widow or partner, children younger than age 18 (age 21 if a student, no limit if disabled), and a dependent father and a mother older than age 65.

Old-Age Benefits

Social insurance (SNP)

Old-age pension: Men and women born after December 31, 1946, receive between 30% and 45% of average earnings in the last 60 months, according to the insured's age on June 14, 2002 (30% if younger than age 31, 35% if aged 31 to 39, 40% if aged 40 to 49, or 45% if older than age 49), plus 2% for each additional year of contributions exceeding 20, up to a maximum of 100%.

Men born after December 18, 1932, and women born after December 18, 1937, but not later than December 31, 1946, receive 50% of the reference salary, plus 4% for each additional year of contributions exceeding 20 years.

The reference salary with between 20 and 25 years of contributions is equal to average earnings in the last 5 years; with between 25 and 30 years, average earnings in the last 4 years; with more than 30 years, average earnings in the last 3 years.

Men born up to December 18, 1932, and women born up to December 18, 1937, receive 50% of the reference salary, plus 2% (men) or 2.5% (women) for each additional year of contributions exceeding 15 and 13 years, respectively.

The reference salary is equal to average earnings in the last 12 months.

Early pension: The pension is reduced by 4% for each year that the pension is taken before the normal pensionable age.

Dependent's supplement: Between 2% and 10% of earnings for a spouse and between 2% and 5% for each child.

The minimum pension is 415 nuevos soles.

The maximum pension is 857.36 nuevos soles.

Constant-attendance supplement: An amount equal to the minimum wage (460 nuevos soles).

Benefit adjustment: Pensions are adjusted according to changes in the cost of living in Lima.

Mandatory individual account (SPP)

Old-age pension: The value of retirement savings varies according to the insured's contributions to an individual account plus accrued earnings, minus administrative fees. (The value of accrued rights under the social insurance system is combined with the individual account balance.)

Retirement savings can be used to make programmed withdrawals from the individual's account or to purchase a personal annuity, a joint survivor life annuity, or a deferred annuity accompanied by temporary programmed withdrawals.

Guaranteed minimum pension: 415 nuevos soles.

Permanent Disability Benefits

Social insurance (SNP)

Disability pension: The pension is equal to 50% of the reference salary, plus 1.5% for each year of contributions exceeding 3 years. For a contribution period of between 1 and 3 years, 1/6 of average earnings for each year of contributions.

The reference salary is equal to average earnings in the last 12 months; for voluntarily insured self-employed persons, the reference salary is average earnings in the last 60 months.

The minimum pension is three times the minimum wage (460 nuevos soles).

The maximum pension is 80% of total earnings.

Dependent's supplement: 2% to 10% of earnings for a spouse and 2% to 5% for each child. The amount is reduced if earnings plus pension income exceed the insured's former average earnings.

Constant-attendance supplement: An amount equal to the minimum wage (460 nuevos soles).

Benefit adjustment: Pensions are adjusted according to changes in the cost of living in Lima.

Mandatory individual account (SPP)

Disability pension: The pension is calculated on the basis of the insured's average monthly salary and is proportional to the assessed degree of disability. (Disability insurance tops up the accumulated capital in the individual account if the balance is less than the required minimum to finance the permanent disability pension.)

Survivor Benefits

Social insurance (SNP)

Survivor pension: 50% of the pension paid or payable to the deceased is payable to a widow or a disabled widower.

The pension ceases if the widow(er) remarries or if a disabled widower is assessed as capable of work.

The minimum pension is equal to three times the minimum wage (460 nuevos soles).

Orphan's pension: 20% of the deceased's pension is payable to the widow for each orphan younger than age 18 (age 21 if a student, no limit if disabled); 40% is payable to each full orphan.

The minimum orphan's pension is 1.5 times the minimum wage (460 nuevos soles).

Other eligible survivors (in the absence of the above): Each dependent parent receives 20% of the deceased's pension.

The maximum survivor pension is 100% of the deceased's pension.

Funeral grant: Up to five times the minimum wage (460 nuevos soles).

Constant-attendance supplement: An amount equal to the minimum wage (460 nuevos soles) if the survivor is disabled.

Benefit adjustment: Pensions are adjusted according to changes in the cost of living in Lima.

Mandatory individual account (SPP)

Survivor pension: The pension for a spouse, orphans, and dependent parents is calculated on the basis of the deceased's average monthly salary, according to the schedule in law. (Life insurance tops up the accumulated capital in the deceased's individual account if the balance is less than the required minimum to finance the survivor pension. Life insurance also covers the cost of funeral grants.)

Administrative Organization

Social insurance (SNP)

Comptroller General of the Republic (http://www.contraloria.gob.pe) provides general supervision.

Office of Social Security Normalization (http://www.sunat.gob.pe) administers the program.

National Superintendent of Tax Administration (http://www.sunat.gob.pe) collects contributions.

Mandatory individual account (SPP)

Superintendent of Banks and Insurance (http://www.sbs.gob.pe) is responsible for licensing and supervising pension fund administrators and insurance companies.

Investment Classification Commission assesses investment risks.

Pension fund administrators (AFPs) administer the scheme.

Sickness and Maternity

Regulatory Framework

First laws: 1936 (wage earners) and 1948 (salaried employees).

Current laws: 1991 (private pensions), 1997 (modernizing health), 1999 (social security health insurance, EsSalud), and 2004 (domestic workers).

Type of program: Social insurance and private insurance system. Cash and medical benefits.

Note: Insured persons and their dependents can opt out of the social security health insurance program (EsSalud) and receive health care from a private health care provider (EPS).

Coverage

EsSalud

Employed persons in the public and private sectors, employees of worker-owned and cooperative enterprises, professional artists, self-employed drivers, domestic workers, pensioners, self-employed persons and other persons who do not meet the requirements for regular affiliation, employed and self-employed persons in agriculture, spouses or partners of insured persons, and children.

Pensioners are covered for the nursing allowance and the funeral grant only.

Exclusions: Employees whose employers provide health services directly.

Special systems for fishermen, stevedores, and employees not covered under the national system.

EPS

All persons opting out of EsSalud and their dependents.

Source of Funds

Insured person: None; pensioners contribute 4% of the pension.

Self-employed person: No information is available.

Employer: 9% of payroll. (Employers providing health services directly to their employees or who use services provided under contract by a private health care provider (EPS) receive a 25% credit toward the cost of contributions.)

The minimum earnings for contribution purposes are equal to the legal monthly minimum wage (460 nuevos soles).

Government: None; contributes as an employer.

Qualifying Conditions

Sickness cash benefits: Must have 3 months' consecutive contributions or 4 months of contributions in the 6 months before the onset of incapacity.

Maternity care and cash benefits: Insured when the child was conceived.

Sickness and Maternity Benefits

Sickness benefit: The monthly benefit is equal to 100% of the insured's average daily earnings in the last 4 months and is payable after a 20-day waiting period for up to 18 months. The employer pays the full salary during the waiting period.

Maternity benefit: The benefit is equal to 100% of earnings, up to a maximum. The benefit is payable for 45 days before and 45 days after the expected date of childbirth; 30 additional days in case of multiple births.

Nursing allowance: Twice the minimum wage (920 nuevos soles) from 8 months to 14 months of age.

Funeral grant: 2,070 nuevos soles.

Workers' Medical Benefits

Benefits include general, specialist, maternity, and dental care; hospitalization; laboratory services; appliances; medicines; rehabilitation; health education; preventative care; and immunization.

Benefits are provided for up to 12 months; may be extended in certain cases.

Employees have the option of receiving medical benefits from EsSalud or from an EPS provider. In order to opt for an EPS provider, 51% of employees must agree to the change.

Medical benefits provided by an EPS provider require a copayment of 2% of monthly income, up to a maximum of 10% of income or 240 nuevos soles, whichever is lower. The insured may purchase additional coverage.

Dependents' Medical Benefits

The insured's spouse or partner receives the same benefits for sickness and maternity as the insured. Children younger than age 18 (no limit if disabled) receive medical care.

Administrative Organization

Comptroller General of the Republic (http://www.contraloria.gob.pe) provides general supervision.

Social Security Health Insurance (EsSalud) (http://www.essalud.gob.pe) administers the program.

Superintendent of Private Health Providers (http://www.seps.gob.pe) authorizes and supervises private health providers.

Private health care providers (EPS) under contract provide complementary and private medical care.

Work Injury

Regulatory Framework

First laws: 1911 (work injury) and 1935 (occupational diseases).

Current law: 1997.

Type of program: Social insurance system. Cash and medical benefits.

Coverage

Employed persons in the public and private sectors, including fishermen, domestic workers, and journalists working for one employer; and employees of worker-owned and cooperative enterprises.

Source of Funds

Insured person: None.

Self-employed person: A lump sum of 10 to 30 nuevos soles.

Employer: 0.63% to 1.84% of payroll, according to the assessed degree of risk and the accident rate.

The maximum earnings for benefit purposes are equal to six times the local minimum wage.

Government: None; contributes as an employer.

Qualifying Conditions

Work injury benefits: There is no minimum qualifying period. Accidents that occur while commuting to and from work are not covered.

Temporary Disability Benefits

The benefit is equal to 100% of wages and is payable after a 20-day waiting period for up to 11 months and 10 days or 340 days. The employer pays the full salary during the waiting period.

The maximum duration of benefit is 18 months in a 36-month period.

The maximum earnings for benefit calculation are equal to six times the local minimum wage.

Permanent Disability Benefits

Permanent disability pension: The pension is equal to 80% of average wages (100% if the insured requires constant attendance) if totally disabled with an assessed degree of disability of more than 65%.

Partial disability: The pension is proportionately reduced for an assessed degree of disability of between 40% and 65%. A lump sum equal to 2 years' pension is paid if the assessed degree of disability is less than 40%.

Workers' Medical Benefits

Benefits include necessary medical, surgical, and hospital care and appliances until full recovery or certification of permanent disability.

Survivor Benefits

Survivor pension: 50% of the deceased's total disability pension is payable to a widow or a disabled widower.

Orphan's pension: Each orphan younger than age 18 (age 23 if a student) receives 25% of the deceased's pension.

Other eligible survivors (in the absence of the above): Each parent receives 25% of the deceased's pension.

The maximum survivor pension is 100% of the deceased's pension.

Funeral grant: 2,070 nuevos soles.

Administrative Organization

Comptroller General of the Republic (http://www.contraloria.gob.pe) provides general supervision.

Office of Social Security Normalization (http://www.sunat.gob.pe) administers the program.

Unemployment

Regulatory Framework

No statutory benefits are provided.

The labor code requires private-sector employers to provide a severance payment to employees at the end of the labor contract.

Saint Kitts and Nevis

Exchange rate: US$1.00 equals
2.70 East Caribbean dollars (EC$).

Old Age, Disability, and Survivors

Regulatory Framework

First law: 1968 (provident fund).

Current laws: 1977 (social security), implemented in 1978, with 1996 and 2002 amendments; and 1998 (social assistance).

Type of program: Social insurance and social assistance system.

Coverage

Social insurance: Employed (including public-sector employees and apprentices) and self-employed persons aged 16 to 62.

Voluntary coverage for those who cease to be compulsorily covered but who have at least 2 years of contributions.

Exclusions: Unpaid family labor.

Special system for civil servants.

Social assistance: Resident elderly or disabled persons.

Source of Funds

Social insurance

Insured person: 5% of weekly or monthly earnings.

The maximum monthly earnings for contribution and benefit purposes are EC$6,500.

The above contributions also finance cash sickness and maternity benefits.

Self-employed person: 10% of monthly earnings, according to earnings categories ranging from EC$200 to EC$1,350 a week.

The above contributions also finance cash sickness and maternity benefits.

Employer: 5% of monthly payroll.

The maximum monthly earnings for contribution and benefit purposes are EC$6,500.

The above contributions also finance cash sickness and maternity benefits.

Government: None; contributes as an employer.

Social assistance

Insured person: None.

Self-employed person: None.

Employer: None.

Government: Total cost.

Qualifying Conditions

Old-age pension (social insurance): Age 62 with at least 500 weeks of paid or credited contributions, including 150 weeks of paid contributions.

Old-age grant (social insurance): Age 62 and does not qualify for an old-age pension.

Old-age benefits are payable abroad under specific conditions.

Old-age social assistance (means-tested): Older than age 62, not in gainful employment, and does not qualify for the old-age pension.

Social assistance benefits are not payable abroad.

Disability pension (social insurance): Younger than age 62 with at least 150 weeks of paid contributions.

The degree of disability is assessed by the Social Security Medical Board at least every 3 years.

Disability benefits are payable abroad under specific conditions.

Disability social assistance (means-tested): Assessed as disabled, between ages 16 and 62, and does not qualify for a disability pension.

The degree of disability is assessed by the Social Security Medical Board at least every 3 years.

Social assistance benefits are not payable abroad.

Survivor pension (social insurance): The deceased had at least 150 weeks of paid contributions.

Eligible survivors are a widow(er) aged 45 or older who was married to the insured for at least 3 years and orphans younger than age 16 (age 18 if a full-time student, no limit if disabled).

Survivor benefits are payable abroad under specific conditions.

Survivor grant (social insurance): The deceased did not qualify for a pension.

Eligible survivors are a widow(er) aged 45 or older who was married to the insured for at least 3 years and orphans younger than age 16 (age 18 if a full-time student, no limit if disabled).

Survivor benefits are payable abroad under specific conditions.

Funeral grant: The deceased had at least 26 weeks of paid contributions.

Old-Age Benefits

Old-age pension (social insurance): The monthly pension is equal to 30% of the insured's average annual wage, plus

2% for each 50-week period of paid or credited contributions exceeding 500, up to a maximum of 750 contributions, and 1% for each 50-week period of contributions exceeding 750. The pension is determined by dividing this sum by 52.

The average annual wage is based on earnings in the 3 years in which the insured made the most contributions in the last 15 contribution years.

The minimum monthly pension is EC$250.

The maximum monthly pension is 60% of wages or EC$3,900, whichever is less.

Old-age grant (social insurance): The grant is equal to six times the average weekly wage for each 50-week period of paid or credited contributions, up to a maximum of 499 contributions.

Insured persons are entitled to a refund of contributions if they have made less than 50.

Old-age social assistance (means-tested): EC$100 is paid every 2 weeks.

Permanent Disability Benefits

Disability pension: The monthly pension is equal to 30% of the insured's average annual wage, plus 2% for each 50-week period of paid or credited contributions exceeding 500, up to a maximum of 750 contributions, and 1% for each 50-week period of contributions exceeding 750. The pension is determined by dividing this sum by 52.

The average annual wage is based on earnings in the 3 years in which the insured made the most contributions in the last 15 contribution years.

The pension is paid after entitlement to 26 weeks of sickness benefit has ended or after the disability has lasted for at least 26 weeks. It is paid for as long as the disability continues.

The minimum monthly pension is EC$250.

The maximum monthly pension is 60% of wages or EC$3,900, whichever is less.

Disability social assistance (means-tested): EC$100 is paid every 2 weeks.

Survivor Benefits

Survivor pension: The pension is equal to 50% of the deceased's pension or 30% of the deceased's average earnings in the 3 years in which he or she made the most contributions, whichever is higher. The pension is payable for life or until remarriage.

A limited pension is payable for a year if the widow(er) is younger than age 45 or was married to the deceased for less than 3 years.

Orphan's pension: Up to 1/6 of the insured's pension is paid if unmarried, younger than age 16 (age 18 if a full-time

student), and previously living with or supported by the deceased. If the orphan is disabled, the pension is equal to 1/3 of the family maximum.

The minimum survivor pension is EC$720 a year.

The family maximum survivor pension is 100% of the deceased's pension.

Survivor grant: The grant is equal to six times the average weekly wage for each 50-week period of paid or credited contributions.

The contributions are refunded if the deceased made less than 50.

Funeral grant: EC$2,500 for the funeral of the insured or his or her spouse. Up to EC$1,600 for a dependent child, with the maximum payable for a child aged 10 or older or aged 16 to 25 and a full-time student. The grant is payable to the person who pays for the funeral.

Administrative Organization

Social insurance: Ministry of Education, Youth, Social and Community Development, and Gender Affairs provides general supervision.

Social Security Board (http://www.socialsecurity.kn) administers the program.

Social assistance: Social Development Assistance Board administers the program.

Sickness and Maternity

Regulatory Framework

First and current law: 1977 (social security), with amendments.

Type of program: Social insurance system. Cash benefits only.

Coverage

Employed and self-employed persons aged 16 to 62.

There are no special systems for any specified groups of employees.

Source of Funds

Insured person: See source of funds under Old Age, Disability, and Survivors, above.

Self-employed person: See source of funds under Old Age, Disability, and Survivors, above.

Employer: See source of funds under Old Age, Disability, and Survivors, above.

Government: None; contributes as an employer.

Qualifying Conditions

Cash sickness benefits: Younger than age 62 and employed the day before the onset of incapacity with 26 weeks of paid contributions, including 8 in the 13 weeks before the onset of incapacity .

Cash maternity benefit: Must have 39 weeks of contributions, including 20 weeks immediately before making the claim.

Maternity grant: Paid to an insured woman or the wife of an insured man, with a minimum of 39 weeks of contributions including 20 weeks of contributions in the 39 weeks before the expected date of childbirth.

Funeral grant: Must have a minimum of 26 weeks of contributions.

Sickness and Maternity Benefits

Sickness benefit: The benefit is equal to 65% of the average weekly wage divided by six (daily rate) and is payable from the first day if the incapacity lasts for 4 or more days. The benefit is payable for up to 26 weeks.

Maternity benefit: The benefit is equal to 65% of the average weekly wage divided by six (daily rate) and is payable for 13 weeks, beginning up to 6 weeks before the expected date of childbirth.

Maternity grant: EC$450 is paid for every childbirth.

Funeral grant: EC$2,500 is payable to the person who pays for the cost of the funeral for the insured, the insured's spouse, or a dependent child.

Workers' Medical Benefits

No statutory benefits are provided.

Medical care is available at public hospitals and health centers.

Dependents' Medical Benefits

No statutory benefits are provided.

Medical care is available at public hospitals and health centers.

Administrative Organization

Ministry of Education, Youth, Social and Community Development, and Gender Affairs provides general supervision.

Social Security Board (http://www.socialsecurity.kn) administers the program.

Work Injury

Regulatory Framework

First law: 1955 (workmen's compensation).

Current law: 1985 (social security), implemented in 1986.

Type of program: Social insurance system.

Coverage

Employed persons regardless of age.

Exclusions: Unpaid family labor and self-employed persons.

There are no special systems for any specified groups of employees.

Source of Funds

Insured person: None.

Self-employed person: Not applicable.

Employer: 1% of payroll.

The maximum monthly earnings for contribution and benefit purposes are EC$6,500.

Government: None; contributes as an employer.

Qualifying Conditions

Work injury benefits: There is no minimum qualifying period.

Temporary Disability Benefits

The benefit is equal to 75% of average weekly covered wages and is payable from the first day if the disability lasts for 4 or more days. The benefit is payable for up to 26 weeks.

Permanent Disability Benefits

If the insured is totally disabled (100%), the pension is equal to 75% of his or her average weekly wages.

The degree of disability is assessed and reviewed periodically by the Social Security Medical Board.

Constant-attendance supplement: If the insured is totally disabled, the supplement should meet the reasonable cost of providing care.

Partial disability: A percentage of the pension is paid according to the assessed degree of disability. A benefit is payable if the assessed degree of disability is 20% or more.

Workers' Medical Benefits

Benefits include the reimbursement of reasonable expenses for medical, surgical, dental, hospital, and nursing care; medicines; appliances; and transportation.

Survivor Benefits

Survivor pension: 50% of the deceased's permanent total disability pension is payable to a widow(er).

Orphan's pension: Each child younger than age 16 receives up to 1/6 of the deceased's permanent total disability pension; 1/3 for a full orphan.

The maximum survivor pension is equal to 100% of the deceased's permanent total disability pension.

Funeral grant: EC$4,000 is payable to the person who pays for the cost of the funeral for the insured, the insured's spouse, or a dependent child.

Administrative Organization

Ministry of Education, Youth, Social and Community Development, and Gender Affairs provides general supervision.

Social Security Board (http://www.socialsecurity.kn) administers the program.

Saint Lucia

Exchange rate: US$1.00 equals
2.70 East Caribbean dollars (EC$).

Old Age, Disability, and Survivors

Regulatory Framework

First law: 1970 (provident fund).

Current laws: 2000 (national insurance corporation), with 2002 amendment; and 2003 (national insurance).

Type of program: Social insurance system.

Note: A government-financed social assistance program provides EC$80 a month to persons of pensionable age, subject to conditions.

Coverage

Employees, self-employed persons, and apprentices aged 16 to 65.

Exclusions: Civil servants were excluded until February 1, 2003.

Special system for civil servants not covered by the National Insurance Corporation.

Source of Funds

Insured person: 5% of gross earnings.

There are no minimum earnings for contribution purposes.

The maximum annual earnings for contribution purposes are EC$60,000.

The insured's contributions also finance sickness and maternity benefits and work injury benefits.

Self-employed person: 5% of declared average monthly earnings.

There are no minimum earnings for contribution purposes.

The maximum annual earnings for contribution purposes are EC$60,000.

The self-employed person's contributions also finance sickness and maternity benefits.

Employer: 5% of payroll.

There are no minimum earnings for contribution purposes.

The maximum annual earnings for contribution purposes are EC$60,000.

The employer's contributions also finance sickness and maternity benefits and work injury benefits.

Government: 5% of payroll for contributing civil servants.

Qualifying Conditions

Old-age pension: Age 62 (January 2006) with at least 13 years of contributions. Retirement from gainful employment is necessary.

Early pension: Age 60 with at least 13 years of contributions. Retirement from gainful employment is necessary.

Deferred pension: The pension may be deferred until age 65.

Old-age grant: Age 62 (January 2006) and does not meet the qualifying conditions for the old-age pension.

All old-age benefits are payable abroad, subject to authorization.

Disability pension: Younger than age 62 (January 2006) with at least 5 years of contributions, including the 36 months before the onset of disability; a total of 13 years of contributions. The insured must have an assessed degree of disability of 30% or more. If the assessed degree of disability is less than 30%, a disability grant is paid.

The degree of disability is assessed by a medical doctor at least every 2 years.

Disability grant: Must be assessed as disabled with less than 5 years of contributions.

All disability benefits are payable abroad, subject to authorization.

Survivor pension: The insured met the qualifying conditions for a pension or was a pensioner at the time of death.

Eligible survivors are a widow(er), children, parents, grandparents, and orphans younger than age 16 (age 18 if a full-time student).

Survivor grant: Paid to the widow(er) of an insured person who did not meet the qualifying conditions for a pension.

Funeral grant: Payable to an insured person for the death of a dependent child or spouse.

All survivor benefits are payable abroad, subject to authorization.

Old-Age Benefits

Old-age pension: The pension is equal to 40% of the insured's average covered earnings, plus 0.1% of average covered earnings for each month of contributions exceeding 156 months.

Average covered earnings are based on the insured's earnings in the best 5 years.

Early pension: The pension is reduced by 0.5% for each month the pension is taken before age 62.

Deferred pension: The pension is calculated in the same way as the old-age pension.

Old-age grant: A lump-sum refund of 50% of contributions, without interest, is paid. (For those covered previously by the provident fund, 100% of contributions, plus accrued interest.)

Permanent Disability Benefits

Disability pension: The pension is paid in proportion to the assessed degree of disability.

The minimum pension for an assessed degree of disability of at least 30% is 65% of the insured's average insurable earnings in the month of the accident.

The maximum pension is equal to 100% of the insured's average insurable earnings in the month of the accident.

Disability grant: A lump sum equal to the value of 60 months' benefit is paid.

Survivor Benefits

Survivor pension: In the absence of any other survivors, 75% of the deceased's old-age pension or disability pension is payable to a widow(er) aged 62 or older (January 2006). If there are other survivors or dependents, the rate of the survivor pension is reduced to 50%.

A limited pension is paid for a year to a widow(er) younger than age 62 (January 2006) who has no dependent children.

Orphan's pension: In the absence of any other survivors, 50% of the deceased's pension (50% of each insured parent's pension if a full orphan) is payable to a dependent child younger than age 16 (age 18 if a full-time student).

If there are other survivors or dependents, the maximum orphan's pension is split among all eligible children.

The maximum survivor pension is equal to 100% of the deceased's pension.

Survivor grant: A lump sum at least equal to the value of the old-age grant or disability grant that would have been payable to the deceased is paid.

Funeral grant: The cost of the funeral, up to a maximum of EC$1,750.

Administrative Organization

Minister of Finance (http://www.stlucia.gov.lc) provides general supervision.

National Insurance Corporation (http://www.stlucianis.org) administers the program.

Sickness and Maternity

Regulatory Framework

First law: 1978 (national insurance).

Current laws: 2000 (national insurance corporation) and 2003 (national insurance).

Type of program: Social insurance system. Cash benefits only.

Coverage

Employees and apprentices aged 16 to 65.

Exclusions: Civil servants were excluded until February 1, 2003.

Special system for civil servants not covered by the National Insurance Corporation.

Source of Funds

Insured person: See source of funds under Old Age, Disability, and Survivors, above.

Self-employed person: See source of funds under Old Age, Disability, and Survivors, above.

Employer: See source of funds under Old Age, Disability, and Survivors, above.

Government: See source of funds under Old Age, Disability, and Survivors, above.

Qualifying Conditions

Cash sickness benefits: Employed on the day before the onset of incapacity, with at least 6 months of contributions including 2 of the 4 months immediately before the onset of incapacity.

Cash maternity benefits: Must have at least 7 months of contributions in the 10 months immediately before the date of the claim.

Maternity grant: Payable to women receiving cash maternity benefits and to women whose husbands have at least 7 months of contributions.

Sickness and Maternity Benefits

Sickness benefit: The benefit is equal to 65% of the insured's average salary in the last 4 months. The benefit is payable after a 3-day waiting period for up to 26 weeks.

Maternity benefit: The benefit is equal to 65% of the insured's average salary in the last 10 months. The benefit is payable for 3 months, beginning 6 weeks before the expected month of childbirth.

Maternity grant: EC$600.

Workers' Medical Benefits

No statutory benefits are provided.

Dependents' Medical Benefits

No statutory benefits are provided.

Administrative Organization

Minister of Finance (http://www.stlucia.gov.lc) provides general supervision.

National Insurance Corporation (http://www.stlucianis.org) administers the program.

Work Injury

Regulatory Framework

First law: 1964 (employer liability).

Current law: 2000 (national insurance corporation).

Type of program: Social insurance system.

Coverage

Employees and apprentices aged 16 to 65.

Exclusions: The self-employed; civil servants were excluded until February 1, 2003.

Special system for civil servants not covered by the National Insurance Corporation.

Source of Funds

Insured person: See source of funds under Old Age, Disability, and Survivors, above.

Self-employed person: Not applicable.

Employer: See source of funds under Old Age, Disability, and Survivors, above.

Government: See source of funds under Old Age, Disability, and Survivors, above.

Qualifying Conditions

Work injury benefits: There is no minimum qualifying period.

Temporary Disability Benefits

The benefit is equal to 65% of wages and is payable from the day of injury until full recovery for up to 52 weeks.

Permanent Disability Benefits

Permanent disability pension: For a total disability (100%), the monthly pension is equal to 65% of covered earnings; for an assessed degree of disability of less than 100%, the pension is a percentage of the full pension according to the assessed degree of disability.

The disability is assessed every 6 months by an appointed medical board.

Disability pensions are payable abroad, subject to authorization.

Workers' Medical Benefits

All medical expenses, including specialist care abroad if necessary, up to a maximum of EC$20,000.

Survivor Benefits

Survivor benefit: A benefit is paid to a spouse, parents, grandparents, and children who were fully or largely dependent on the deceased.

If the spouse, parent, or grandparent is older than the pensionable age, the benefit is paid for life. If the spouse is younger than the pensionable age, a benefit is paid for a year or until the youngest child reaches age 16 (age 18 if a full-time student). If a survivor is disabled, the benefit is paid for the duration of the disability.

Funeral grant: The cost of the funeral, up to a maximum of EC$1,750.

Administrative Organization

Minister of Finance (http://www.stlucia.gov.lc) provides general supervision.

National Insurance Corporation (http://www.stlucianis.org) administers the program.

Saint Vincent and the Grenadines
Exchange rate: US$1.00 equals
2.70 East Caribbean dollars (EC$).

Old Age, Disability, and Survivors

Regulatory Framework

First law: 1970 (provident fund).

Current law: 1986 (social insurance), with amendments.

Type of program: Social insurance system.

Note: The Family Services Division of the Ministry of Social Development administers social assistance cash benefits for needy persons, including needy elderly persons, the disabled, and orphans.

Coverage

Employed persons aged 16 to 59.

Voluntary coverage for self-employed persons aged 16 to 59, previously insured persons with at least 150 paid or credited contributions, and persons living abroad.

Source of Funds

Insured person: 2.5% of gross earnings.

The minimum weekly earnings for contribution purposes are EC$15.

The maximum monthly earnings for contribution purposes are EC$3,770. (EC$4,330 from January 2006.)

The above contributions also finance sickness and maternity benefits, below.

Self-employed person: A voluntary contribution of 5.5% of declared gross earnings, according to eight income categories.

Contributions may be paid weekly or monthly.

Employer: 3.5% of monthly payroll.

The minimum weekly earnings for contribution purposes are EC$15.

The maximum monthly earnings for contribution purposes are EC$3,770. (EC$4,330 from January 2006.)

The above contributions also finance sickness and maternity benefits, below.

Government: None; contributes as an employer.

Qualifying Conditions

Old-age pension: Age 60. The minimum required number of weeks of contributions is being increased annually by 25%, up to 500 weeks of contributions. In 2005, the insured must have at least 350 weeks of contributions.

Old-age grant: Age 60 with at least 50 weeks of contributions.

Old-age benefits are payable abroad.

Disability pension: Younger than age 60 and disabled with at least 150 weeks of contributions. The insured must have an assessed degree of disability of at least 30%.

Disability grant: Younger than age 60 and disabled with at least 50 weeks of contributions.

The degree of disability is assessed by National Insurance Services inspectors. (The last inspection was in 2004.)

Disability benefits are payable abroad.

Survivor pension: The deceased had at least 150 weeks of contributions.

Survivor grant: The deceased did not meet the qualifying conditions for a pension but was eligible for an old-age grant or disability grant.

Survivor benefits are payable abroad.

Funeral grant: The deceased had paid at least 26 weeks of contributions. The grant is payable for the death of the insured, the insured's spouse, and the insured's dependent children younger than age 16 (age 18 if a full-time student, no limit if disabled).

Old-Age Benefits

Old-age pension: The pension is equal to 30% of the insured's average annual earnings with 350 weeks of contributions. The pension is increased by 0.5% of average annual earnings for each additional 25-week period of contributions beyond 350 weeks. (The minimum required number of weeks of contributions is being increased annually by 25%, up to 500 weeks of contributions.)

Average annual earnings are based on the insured's earnings in the best 3 of the last 15 years before the year in which the insured reaches age 60.

The minimum pension is EC$60 a week. The pension is paid every 2 weeks.

The maximum benefit is 60% of average annual earnings.

Benefit adjustment: Benefits are adjusted for inflation every 3 years, subject to an actuarial review.

Old-age grant: The grant is equal to six times average weekly insurable earnings for each 50-week period of contributions.

Average annual earnings are based on the insured's earnings in the best 3 of the last 15 years before the year in which the insured reaches age 60.

Permanent Disability Benefits

Disability pension: The pension is equal to 30% of the insured's average earnings with 350 weeks of contributions. The pension is increased by 0.5% of average annual earnings for each additional 25-week period of contributions beyond 350 weeks. (The minimum required number of weeks of contributions is being increased annually by 25%, up to 500 weeks of contributions.)

Average annual earnings are the sum of the insured's last 50 weeks of insurable earnings or credits before the onset of disability, divided by 50.

The minimum benefit is EC$60 a week. The pension is paid every 2 weeks.

The maximum benefit is 60% of average annual earnings.

Benefit adjustment: Benefits are adjusted for inflation every 3 years, subject to an actuarial review.

Disability grant: The grant is equal to six times average weekly insurable earnings for each 50-week period of contributions.

Average annual earnings are the sum of the insured's last 50 weeks of insurable earnings or credits before the onset of disability, divided by 50.

Survivor Benefits

Survivor pension: The widow(er) pension is equal to 75% of the pension paid or payable to the deceased.

Eligible survivors are a widow(er), or cohabiting partner who lived with the deceased for at least 3 years, aged 50 or older or disabled or caring for a child who is eligible for survivor benefits.

The pension ceases if the surviving spouse remarries or cohabits.

A limited pension is payable for a year to a pregnant widow younger than age 50 with no dependent children; the benefit continues if the child is born and is eligible for benefits.

Orphan's pension: Each dependent child younger than age 16 (age 18 if a full-time student) receives 25% of the pension paid or payable to the deceased; 50% for a full orphan.

Other eligible survivors (in the absence of the above): Dependent parents aged 60 or older may receive up to 50% of the pension paid or payable to the deceased.

The total survivor pension must not exceed 100% of the deceased's old-age pension or disability pension.

Survivor grant: A lump-sum benefit is paid to survivors.

Funeral grant: EC$3,800 is paid to the person who meets all or part of the cost of the insured's funeral. A reduced grant is paid for the funeral of a spouse or child.

Administrative Organization

National Insurance Board (http://www.nissvg.org) administers the program.

Sickness and Maternity

Regulatory Framework

First and current law: 1986 (social insurance), with amendments.

Type of program: Social insurance system. Cash benefits only.

Coverage

Employed persons aged 16 to 59.

Voluntary coverage for self-employed persons aged 16 to 59.

Special systems for certain categories of civil servant.

Source of Funds

Insured person: See source of funds under Old Age, Disability, and Survivors, above.

Self-employed person: See source of funds under Old Age, Disability, and Survivors, above.

Employer: See source of funds under Old Age, Disability, and Survivors, above.

Government: None; contributes as an employer for certain categories of civil servant.

Qualifying Conditions

Cash sickness benefits: Currently employed with at least 26 weeks of contributions, including 8 weeks in the 13 weeks immediately before the onset of the incapacity.

Cash maternity benefits: Must have at least 30 weeks of contributions, including 20 weeks in the 30 weeks immediately before the claim.

Maternity grant: The woman or her spouse must have at least 20 weeks of contributions in the 30 weeks immediately before the birth of a living child.

Sickness and Maternity Benefits

Sickness benefit: The benefit is equal to 65% of the insured's average earnings in the 13 weeks before the onset of the incapacity. The benefit is payable for up to 26 weeks.

Maternity benefit: The benefit is equal to 65% of the insured's average earnings in the last 30 weeks of employment. The benefit is payable for 13 weeks, starting no earlier than 6 weeks before the expected date of childbirth.

Maternity grant: EC$550.

Workers' Medical Benefits

No statutory benefits are provided.

Dependents' Medical Benefits

No statutory benefits are provided.

Administrative Organization

National Insurance Board (http://www.nissvg.org) administers the program.

Work Injury

Regulatory Framework

First law: 1939.

Current law: 1997 (work injury).

Type of program: Social insurance system.

Coverage

Employed persons.

Voluntary coverage is not possible.

Exclusions: Self-employed persons.

There are no special systems for work injury benefits.

Source of Funds

Insured person: None.

Self-employed person: Not applicable.

Employer: 0.5% of payroll.

Employer contributions may be paid weekly or monthly.

Government: None; contributes as an employer.

Qualifying Conditions

Work injury benefits: The insured must be employed. Employees older than age 59 or younger than age 16 are eligible. Benefits are paid for a work injury or an occupational disease only.

Temporary Disability Benefits

The benefit is equal to 70% of average weekly insurable earnings and is payable for up to 26 weeks in the first instance; thereafter, the benefit is payable for an additional 26 weeks and is equal to 70% of average weekly insurable earnings times the assessed degree of disability.

Average weekly insurable earnings are based on the insured's earnings in the 13 weeks before the onset of disability.

The degree of disability is assessed by a medical doctor and reviewed every 26 weeks.

Permanent Disability Benefits

Permanent disability pension: The pension is equal to 70% of average weekly insurable earnings times the assessed degree of disability. The minimum assessed degree of disability must be greater than 30%, and the insured must have exhausted entitlement to the temporary disability benefit.

The degree of disability is assessed by a medical doctor and reviewed every 26 weeks.

Constant-attendance allowance: Equal to 50% of the disability pension for as long as constant attendance is required. The insured must be an outpatient receiving a permanent disability pension (100% disability) and must need the constant attendance of another person.

If the assessed degree of disability is less than 30%, a lump-sum grant is paid equal to 365 times the insured's average weekly insurable earnings times the assessed degree of disability. The insured must have exhausted entitlement to a temporary disability benefit.

Average weekly insurable earnings are based on the insured's earnings in the 13 weeks before the onset of disability.

Workers' Medical Benefits

Benefits include medical, surgical, and hospital treatment; medicines; appliances; and transportation costs.

Survivor Benefits

Survivor pension: 35% of the deceased's average weekly insurable earnings are paid to the widow(er). The insured's death resulted from a work injury or an occupational disease.

The pension ceases on remarriage.

Average weekly insurable earnings are based on the deceased's earnings in the 13 weeks before the onset of disability.

Orphan's pension: Each child younger than age 16 (age 18 if a full-time student) receives 11.7% of average weekly insurable earnings (23% for a full orphan or if disabled).

Average weekly insurable earnings are based on the deceased's earnings in the 13 weeks before the onset of disability or death.

Other dependent's pension: 11.7% of average weekly insurable earnings is paid for a year.

Average weekly insurable earnings are based on the deceased's earnings in the 13 weeks before the onset of disability or death.

Eligible survivors are a widow(er), unmarried children, and any other person who was fully dependent on the insured. Insured workers have the prior option of naming the beneficiary.

Funeral grant: If the insured died as the result of a work injury or an occupational disease, EC$3,800 is payable to the person who paid for the funeral.

Administrative Organization

National Insurance Board (http://www.nissvg.org) administers the program.

Trinidad and Tobago
Exchange rate: US$1.00 equals
6.19 Trinidad and Tobago dollars (TT$).

Old Age, Disability, and Survivors

Regulatory Framework

First and current laws: 1939 (social assistance) and 1971 (social insurance), with amendments.

Type of program: Social insurance and social assistance system.

Coverage

Social insurance: Employed persons aged 16 to 64, including agricultural and domestic workers, apprentices, and public-sector employees.

Voluntary coverage for the old-age pension, survivor pension, and funeral grant for persons younger than age 60 who cease to work in insured employment.

Exclusions: The self-employed, persons who work less than 10 hours a week and earn less than TT$100 per week or TT$433 per month, and persons employed by international organizations who are granted specific exemptions.

There are no special systems for any specified groups of employees.

Social assistance (means-tested): Citizens aged 65 or older with 20 years' residence; aged 40 or older if blind and needy.

Source of Funds

Social insurance

Insured person: 2.8% of gross weekly or monthly earnings, according to 12 wage classes. The voluntarily insured contribute 7.1% of weekly earnings, according to 12 wage classes.

The minimum weekly earnings for contribution purposes are TT$130.

The maximum weekly earnings for contribution purposes are TT$1,010.

Self-employed person: Not applicable.

Employer: 5.6% of weekly or monthly payroll, according to 12 wage classes.

The minimum weekly earnings for contribution purposes are TT$130.

The maximum weekly earnings for contribution purposes are TT$1,010.

Government: None; contributes as an employer.

Social assistance

Insured person: None.

Self-employed person: None.

Employer: None.

Government: Total cost.

Qualifying Conditions

Old-age pension (social insurance): From age 60 with 750 weeks of contributions paid or credited (in 1972, workers were credited with 25 weeks of coverage for each year of age over 35; up to a maximum 600 weeks). An additional amount is paid for each 25-week period of contributions in excess of 750, excluding the age credits.

Retirement is not necessary if aged 65 or older.

Old-age settlement (social insurance): The insured does not meet the qualifying conditions for a pension.

Retirement is not necessary if aged 65 or older.

Old-age benefits are payable abroad under reciprocal agreements with other Caribbean territories and Canada.

Means-tested old-age pension (social assistance): Aged 65 or older with 20 years' residence and monthly income not exceeding TT$1,000.

The social assistance pension is not payable abroad.

Disability pension (social insurance): Assessed as incapable of work with 150 weeks of contributions, including 50 weeks of contributions in the 3 years immediately before the onset of disability; 250 weeks of contributions in the last 7 years immediately before the onset of disability; or 750 weeks of contributions immediately before the onset of disability.

Disability settlement (social insurance): The insured does not meet the qualifying conditions for a pension.

Disability benefits are payable abroad under reciprocal agreements with other Caribbean territories and Canada.

Means-tested disability pension (social assistance): Certified as blind, aged 40 or older, and with monthly income not exceeding TT$1,000.

The social assistance pension is not payable abroad.

Survivor pension (social insurance): The deceased had at least 50 contributions or was a pensioner.

Eligible survivors are a widow(er), children, and dependent parents.

Survivor benefits are payable abroad under reciprocal agreements with other Caribbean territories and Canada.

Funeral grant: The deceased had at least 25 contributions.

Old-Age Benefits

Old-age pension (social insurance): The pension is equal to between 30% and 48% of the insured's average weekly earnings, according to 12 wage classes, plus between 0.56% and 0.71% of average weekly earnings for each 25-week period of contributions exceeding 750 weeks.

Average weekly earnings are based on career average earnings, according to 12 wage classes.

The minimum old-age pension is TT$1,000.

Old-age settlement (social insurance): A lump sum equal to three times the total employer and employee contributions is payable.

The minimum settlement is TT$200.

Means-tested old-age pension (social assistance): TT$1,050 or TT$1,150 a month, depending on income.

Permanent Disability Benefits

Disability pension (social insurance): The pension is equal to between 30% and 48% of the insured's average weekly earnings, according to 12 wage classes, plus between 0.56% and 0.71% of average weekly earnings for each 25-week period of contributions exceeding 750 weeks.

Average weekly earnings are based on career average earnings, according to 12 wage classes.

There is no minimum disability pension.

The disability pension is commuted to an old-age pension at age 60.

Disability settlement (social insurance): A lump sum equal to three times the total employer and employee contributions is payable.

The minimum settlement is TT$200.

Means-tested disability pension (social assistance): TT$1,050 or TT$1,150 a month, depending on income.

Survivor Benefits

Survivor pension (social insurance): A widow(er) receives 60% of the disability pension paid or payable to the deceased.

The pension ceases on remarriage.

Remarriage settlement: A lump sum equal to 52 weeks' benefit is payable.

Orphan's pension (social insurance): Each orphan receives 30% of the deceased's pension (60% if a full orphan) until age 16 (age 19 if a full-time student).

The minimum monthly orphan's pension is TT$320; TT$640 for a full orphan.

Dependent parent's pension (social insurance): 30% of the deceased's pension is paid to one dependent parent or is split equally between two dependent parents.

The maximum survivor pension is 100% of the deceased's pension.

Funeral grant (social insurance): A lump sum of TT$4,000 is payable to the person who pays for the funeral.

Administrative Organization

Ministry of Finance (http://www.finance.gov.tt) provides general supervision of the social insurance program.

National Insurance Board (http://www.nibtt.co.tt), a tripartite body comprising government, labor, and employer representatives, administers the social insurance program.

Office of the Prime Minister (Social Services Delivery), Social Welfare Division, provides general supervision of the social assistance program.

Sickness and Maternity

Regulatory Framework

First and current laws: 1939 (social assistance) and 1971 (social insurance), with amendments.

Type of program: Social insurance and social assistance system. Cash and medical benefits.

Coverage

Employed persons aged 16 to 64, including agricultural and domestic workers, apprentices, and public-sector employees.

Exclusions: The self-employed, persons who work less than 10 hours a week and earn less than TT$100 per week or TT$433 per month, and persons employed by international organizations who are granted specific exemptions.

There are no special systems for any specified groups of employees.

Source of Funds

Insured person: 0.3% of gross weekly or monthly earnings, according to 12 wage classes.

The minimum weekly earnings for contribution purposes are TT$130.

The maximum weekly earnings for contribution purposes are TT$1,010.

Self-employed person: Not applicable.

Employer: 0.6% of weekly or monthly payroll, according to 12 wage classes.

The minimum weekly earnings for contribution purposes are TT$130.

The maximum weekly earnings for contribution purposes are TT$1,010.

Government: None; contributes as an employer.

Qualifying Conditions

Cash sickness benefits: Must have 10 weeks of contributions in the 13 weeks before the onset of incapacity.

Cash maternity benefits: Must have 10 weeks of contributions in the 13 weeks before the last 6 weeks before the expected date of childbirth; receiving sickness benefits in the 13 weeks before the last 6 weeks before the expected date of childbirth.

Maternity grant: Paid if the pregnancy lasts at least 26 weeks.

Sickness and Maternity Benefits

Sickness benefit: The benefit is equal to 60% of average weekly earnings before the onset of incapacity, according to 12 wage classes. The benefit is payable after a 3-day waiting period, for up to 52 weeks.

Average earnings are based on earnings in the 10 best weekly contributions in the 13 weeks before the onset of incapacity.

Maternity benefit: The benefit is equal to 60% of average weekly earnings in the 13 weeks before the last 6 weeks before the expected date of childbirth, according to 12 wage classes. The benefit is payable for a maximum of 13 weeks.

Average earnings are based on earnings in the 10 best weekly contributions in the 13 weeks before the expected date of childbirth.

Maternity grant: A lump sum of TT$2,000.

Workers' Medical Benefits

No statutory social insurance benefits are provided for nonwork-related medical conditions.

Means-tested social assistance medical benefits are provided to persons receiving care in public hospitals and health centers.

Dependents' Medical Benefits

No statutory benefits are provided.

Means-tested social assistance medical benefits are provided to persons receiving care in public hospitals and health centers.

Administrative Organization

Ministry of Finance (http://www.finance.gov.tt) provides general supervision of the social insurance program.

National Insurance Board (http://www.nibtt.co.tt), a tripartite body comprising government, labor, and employer representatives, administers the social insurance program.

Office of the Prime Minister (Social Services Delivery), Social Welfare Division, provides general supervision of the social insurance program and administers means-tested benefits.

Work Injury

Regulatory Framework

First and current law: 1976 (social insurance), with amendments.

Type of program: Social insurance system.

Coverage

Employed persons, including agricultural and domestic workers, apprentices, and public-sector employees.

Exclusions: The self-employed, persons who work less than 10 hours a week and earn less than TT$100 per week or TT$433 per month, and persons employed by international organizations who are granted specific exemptions.

Source of Funds

Insured person: 0.2% of gross weekly or monthly earnings, according to 12 wage classes.

The minimum weekly earnings for contribution purposes are TT$130.

The maximum weekly earnings for contribution purposes are TT$1,010.

Self-employed person: Not applicable.

Employer: 0.4% of weekly or monthly payroll, according to 12 wage classes.

The minimum weekly earnings for contribution purposes are TT$130.

The maximum weekly earnings for contribution purposes are TT$1,010.

Government: None; contributes as an employer.

Qualifying Conditions

Work injury benefits: There is no minimum qualifying period.

Temporary Disability Benefits

The benefit is equal to 66.6% of average weekly earnings, according to 12 wage classes. The benefit is payable for up to 52 weeks. There is no waiting period.

Average weekly earnings are based on career average earnings, according to 12 wage classes.

Benefits are payable abroad under reciprocal agreements with other Caribbean territories and Canada.

Permanent Disability Benefits

Permanent disability pension: With an assessed degree of disability of at least 20%, the pension is calculated as a percentage of the temporary disability benefit, according to the assessed degree of disability.

The benefit is payable after the temporary disability benefit ceases.

The degree of disability is assessed by the insured's doctor.

Partial disability benefit: For an assessed degree of disability of less than 20%, the benefit is calculated as a percentage of average weekly earnings in proportion to half the assessed degree of disability multiplied by the period of disability (up to a maximum of 365 weeks).

The minimum assessed degree of disability when calculating the partial disability benefit is 3%.

The benefit is payable after the temporary disability benefit ceases.

Average weekly earnings are based on career average earnings, according to 12 wage classes.

Benefits are payable abroad under reciprocal agreements with other Caribbean territories and Canada.

Workers' Medical Benefits

Benefits include medical expenses, including doctor and specialist fees and hospital expenses, drugs and dressings, minor and major operations, and transportation costs.

Medical costs are reimbursed, up to a maximum of TT$18,000 per injury.

Survivor Benefits

Survivor pension: A widow(er) receives 40% of the deceased's average weekly earnings.

Average weekly earnings are based on career average earnings, according to 12 wage classes.

The pension ceases on remarriage.

Remarriage settlement: A lump sum equal to 52 weeks' benefit is payable.

Orphan's pension: Each orphan receives 20% of the deceased's average weekly earnings until age 19.

Average weekly earnings are based on career average earnings, according to 12 wage classes.

The minimum monthly orphan's pension is TT$320; TT$640 for a full orphan.

Dependent parent's pension: 20% of the deceased's average weekly earnings are paid to one dependent parent or split equally between two dependent parents.

Average weekly earnings are based on career average earnings, according to 12 wage classes.

Survivor benefits are payable abroad under reciprocal agreements with other Caribbean territories and Canada.

Funeral grant: TT$2,000.

Administrative Organization

Ministry of Finance (http://www.finance.gov.tt) provides general supervision of the social insurance program.

National Insurance Board (http://www.nibtt.co.tt), a tripartite body comprising government, labor, and employer representatives, administers the social insurance program.

Family Allowances

Regulatory Framework

First and current law: 1939 (social assistance).

Type of program: Social assistance system.

Coverage

Individuals and families assessed as needy.

Source of Funds

Insured person: None.

Self-employed person: None.

Employer: None.

Government: Total cost.

Qualifying Conditions

Family allowances (means-tested): Payable to needy individuals and families with little or no means of support.

Burial assistance: Paid to families to help pay for the cost of a funeral.

Clothing grant: Paid to help purchase clothing, including school uniforms and shoes for children. The grant is payable for a maximum of four persons per household.

Dietary grant: Paid to help purchase prescribed foodstuffs for person diagnosed with certain ailments, such as diabetes or heart disease.

Disability assistance: Paid to persons aged 18 to 65 who are certified as disabled by a doctor. The person must have been resident in Trinidad and Tobago for the last 3 years and have annual income less than TT$3,600.

Education grant: Paid to families to help meet the cost of school fees, school transportation, and other essentials. The grant is payable for a maximum of four children per household. Monthly family income must be less than TT$5,000.

Free bus pass: Provided to social assistance beneficiaries and citizens older than age 65.

House rent assistance: Paid to persons unable to pay housing rental payments.

Medical equipment grant: Paid to help purchase necessary medical aids, such as wheelchairs, eyeglasses, and hearing aids.

Home help grant: Paid to help finance short-term care at home.

School textbook grant: Paid to help purchase necessary textbooks and writing material for school. The grant is payable for a maximum of four children per household.

Special child grant: Paid to parents of children up to age 18 with a mental or physical disability. The grant is payable for a maximum of four children per household.

Family Allowance Benefits

Family allowances (means-tested):

Burial assistance: A lump sum of TT$3,450.

Clothing grant: Up to TT$200 per person, for a maximum of four persons per household.

Dietary grant: Up to TT$150 a month.

Disability assistance: A monthly grant of TT$800.

Education grant: Up to TT$140 a month per child, for a maximum of four children per household.

Free bus pass: Entitled persons receive free travel on public transport.

House rent assistance: Up to TT$2,500 is provided in a 3-month period.

Medical equipment grant: Up to TT$5,000.

Home help grant: The selected caregiver receives TT$350 a month, for up to 3 months.

School textbook grant: TT$500 per child, for a maximum of four children per household.

Special child grant: TT$300 a month is payable to parents, for a maximum of four children per household. The grant is reviewed annually by the local office of the National Insurance Board.

Administrative Organization

Office of the Prime Minister (Social Services Delivery) (http://www.socialservices.gov.tt/opmssd), Social Welfare Division, provides general supervision and administers the program.

United States

Exchange rate: US dollar (US$).

Old Age, Disability, and Survivors

Regulatory Framework

First and current law: 1935 (social security), with amendments.

Type of program: Social insurance system.

Coverage

Gainfully occupied persons, including self-employed persons.

Exclusions: Casual agricultural and domestic employees, some categories of self-employed persons (when annual net income is below $400), and some federal employees hired before 1984.

Voluntary coverage for employees of state and local governments (mandatory coverage for employees of state and local governments not covered under a retirement system, effective July 1, 1991) and clergy. Voluntary coverage applies in the United States, Puerto Rico, Northern Mariana Islands, Virgin Islands, Guam, and American Samoa, and to citizens and residents employed abroad by U.S. employers.

Special systems for railroad employees, federal employees, and many employees of state and local governments.

Source of Funds

Insured person: 6.2% of earnings.

The maximum annual earnings for contribution and benefit purposes are $90,000. (The maximum earnings for contribution and benefit purposes are automatically adjusted to wage levels.)

Self-employed person: 12.4% of earnings.

The maximum annual earnings for contribution and benefit purposes are $90,000. (The maximum earnings for contribution and benefit purposes are automatically adjusted to wage levels.)

Employer: 6.2% of payroll.

The maximum annual earnings for contribution and benefit purposes are $90,000. (The maximum earnings for contribution and benefit purposes are automatically adjusted to wage levels.)

Government: Total cost of the means-tested old-age benefit.

Qualifying Conditions

Old-age pension: Effective for workers retiring at age 65 in 2005, the full retirement age required for a nonreduced pension has been raised from age 65 to age 65 and 6 months. (The full retirement age will increase gradually to age 67 by 2027.) The insured must have 40 quarters of coverage.

Early pension: A reduced pension is payable from age 62.

Deferred pension: The pension may be deferred up to age 70.

Pensions are payable abroad to noncitizens under reciprocal agreement. However, noncitizens' dependents who were first eligible after 1984 generally must meet a residency test.

Old-age supplemental income benefit (means-tested): Aged 65 or older with low income and limited resources. The means test is based on earned and unearned income, including benefits.

Disability pension: Incapable of substantial gainful activity as the result of a physical or mental impairment that is expected to last at least a year or result in death. The insured must have a quarter of coverage for each year since age 21 up to the year of the onset of disability, up to a maximum of 40 quarters of coverage. The insured must also have 20 quarters of coverage in the 10-year period before the onset of disability.

The qualifying conditions for young and blind persons are more liberal.

Pensions are payable abroad to noncitizens under reciprocal agreement. However, noncitizens' dependents who were first eligible after 1984 generally must meet a residency test.

Disability supplemental income benefit (means-tested): Payable to disabled and blind persons younger than age 65 with low income and limited resources. The means test is based on earned and unearned income, including benefits. Certain impairment-related work expenses are deductible from income.

Survivor pension: The deceased was a pensioner or had a quarter of coverage for each year since age 21 up to the year before the year of death, up to a maximum of 40 quarters of coverage.

For orphans or a nonaged widow(er) with an eligible dependent orphan, the deceased had 6 quarters of coverage in the 13 quarters ending with the quarter in which the death occurred.

Eligible survivors are a widow(er) (or a surviving divorced spouse, if the marriage lasted at least 10 years), orphans younger than age 18 or aged 18 to 19 and attending elementary or secondary school full time (no limit if disabled before age 22), and dependent parents aged 62 or older and at least 50% dependent on the deceased.

Pensions are payable abroad to noncitizens under reciprocal agreement. However, noncitizens' survivors who were first eligible after 1984 generally must meet a residency test.

Old-Age Benefits

Old-age pension: The pension is based on the insured's average covered earnings since 1950 (or age 21, if later) and indexed for past wage inflation, up to age 62 (or death, if earlier) excluding the 5 years with the lowest earnings. (Earnings in years outside this period may be substituted, if higher.)

Early pension: The pension is payable from age 62 but is reduced for each month of receipt before the full retirement age.

There is no minimum pension for insured persons reaching age 62 after 1981.

The maximum monthly pension for workers retiring in 2005 at the full retirement age is $1,939.

Deferred pension: An increment is provided for each month the insured defers retirement after the full retirement age, up to age 70. The increment amount depends on the year the insured person reached age 62. In 2005, the annual increment is 8% for those aged 62.

Benefit adjustment: Benefits are adjusted automatically for changes in the cost of living.

Dependent's allowance: 50% of the insured's primary insurance amount is paid to a wife or a husband (or an unmarried divorced spouse, if the marriage lasted at least 10 years) at the full retirement age (reduced from age 62 up to the full retirement age) or to a wife or a husband at any age caring for a child younger than age 16 or disabled; to each child (or dependent grandchild) younger than age 18 or aged 18 to 19 and attending elementary or secondary school full time (no age limit if disabled before age 22).

The primary insurance amount is derived from the insured's covered lifetime earnings and is the basis for determining benefit amounts for the insured and the insured's family members.

The maximum family pension ranges from 150% to 188% of the insured's primary insurance amount.

The maximum monthly family pension for an insured person retiring in 2005 at the full retirement age is $3,393.

Old-age supplemental income benefit (means-tested): The maximum monthly benefit is $579 for an individual; $869 for a couple.

Benefit adjustment: Benefits are adjusted automatically for changes in the cost of living.

Permanent Disability Benefits

Disability pension: The pension is based on the insured's average covered earnings since 1950 (or age 21, if later) and indexed for past wage inflation, up to the onset of disability, excluding up to 5 years with the lowest earnings.

There is no minimum pension for insured persons who became disabled after 1981.

The maximum monthly pension for insured persons who become disabled at age 50 in 2005 is $2,036. The maximum pension for insured persons disabled at any other age is computed on the basis of that age.

Dependent's allowance: 50% of the insured's pension is paid to a wife or a husband (or an unmarried divorced spouse aged 62 or older, if the marriage lasted at least 10 years) at the full retirement age (reduced from age 62 up to the full retirement age) or to a wife or a husband at any age caring for a child younger than age 16 or disabled; to each child (or dependent grandchild) younger than age 18 or aged 18 to 19 and attending elementary or secondary school full time (no age limit if disabled before age 22).

The maximum family benefit ranges from 100% to 150% of the insured's primary insurance amount.

The maximum monthly family pension for an insured person who becomes disabled in 2005 is $3,054.

Benefit adjustment: Benefits are adjusted automatically for changes in the cost of living.

Disability supplemental income benefit (means-tested): The maximum monthly benefit is $579 for an individual; $869 for a couple.

Benefit adjustment: Benefits are adjusted automatically for changes in the cost of living.

Survivor Benefits

Survivor pension: The pension is equal to 100% of the deceased's primary insurance amount at the full retirement age (reduced if at least aged 60 and up to the full retirement age); a reduced pension is paid if the deceased was disabled at age 50 to 59 or received the early retirement benefits.

The pension is payable to a widow(er) (or a surviving divorced spouse, if the marriage lasted at least 10 years); 75% of the insured's primary insurance amount for a widow(er) or surviving divorced spouse at any age caring for a child younger than age 16 or disabled.

The primary insurance amount is derived from the deceased's covered lifetime earnings and is the basis for determining benefit amounts for survivors.

The pension is not payable before age 50 if the survivor is disabled.

The pension ceases if the survivor remarries before age 60.

Death benefit: A lump sum of $255 is also payable to a surviving spouse.

Orphan's pension: 75% of the deceased's pension for each child.

Dependent parent's pension: The pension is equal to 82.5% of the deceased's pension at age 62; 150% for two eligible parents.

The maximum family pension ranges from 150% to 188% of the deceased's primary insurance amount.

The maximum monthly family pension, if the insured died at age 40 in 2005, is $3,602.

Administrative Organization

Social Security Administration (http://www.socialsecurity.gov), an independent agency within the executive branch, administers the program through regional program centers, district offices, and branch offices.

Treasury Department (http://www.treasury.gov) supervises the collection of Social Security taxes through the Internal Revenue Service and supervises the payment of benefits and the management of funds.

Administered by the Social Security Administration, the Supplemental Security Income (SSI) program provides means-tested benefits.

Sickness and Maternity

Regulatory Framework

First and current laws: 1965 (health insurance for older persons) and 1972 (health insurance for the disabled). Medical benefits only.

Type of program: Social insurance system.

Note: Beginning in 2006, subsidized access to prescription drug insurance coverage under the health insurance program for older persons and disabled persons (Medicare) will be provided on a voluntary basis with premium and cost-sharing subsidies for low-income persons.

Coverage

Cash sickness and maternity benefits: There is no national program. Cash benefits may be provided at the state level. (Cash benefits for workers in industry and commerce are available in five states (Rhode Island, California, New Jersey, New York, and Hawaii) and Puerto Rico; agricultural workers are covered to varying degrees in three states (California, Hawaii, and New Jersey) and Puerto Rico. Contribution rates and benefits vary by jurisdiction.)

Special federal system for railroad employees.

Medical benefits

Hospitalization: Persons eligible for a pension and aged 65 or older and certain others who qualify at age 65; persons who have been a disability pensioner for more than 2 years; and persons with end-stage renal disease.

Other medical services: Persons eligible for a pension and aged 65 or older and certain others who qualify at age 65; persons who have been a disability pensioner for more than 2 years; persons with end-stage renal disease; and all other persons aged 65 or older, through voluntary coverage.

Separate federal and state systems for the medically indigent.

Source of Funds

Insured person

Cash benefits: There is no national program.

Hospitalization: 1.45% of earnings is paid by all workers covered for old-age, disability, and survivor benefits, plus some federal, state, and local employees.

There are no maximum earnings for contribution purposes for hospitalization.

Other medical services: Pensioners contribute $78.20 a month.

Self-employed person

Cash benefits: There is no national program.

Hospitalization: 2.9% of declared earnings.

There are no maximum earnings for contribution purposes for hospitalization.

Other medical services: None.

Employer

Cash benefits: There is no national program.

Hospitalization: 1.45% of payroll.

There are no maximum earnings for contribution purposes for hospitalization.

Other medical services: None.

Government

Cash benefits: There is no national program.

Hospitalization: Total cost of hospitalization benefits for certain noninsured elderly persons.

Other medical services: The balance of the cost for voluntary insurance.

Qualifying Conditions

Cash sickness and maternity benefits: There is no national program. Cash benefits may be provided at the state level.

Medical benefits

Hospitalization: Pensioners aged 65 or older, disabled persons who have been entitled to disability benefits for at least 2 years, or persons with end-stage renal disease.

Other medical services: Meets the requirement for hospitalization benefits, election of coverage, and payment of required premiums.

Sickness and Maternity Benefits

Sickness benefit: There is no national program. Cash benefits may be provided at the state level.

Maternity benefit: There is no national program. Cash benefits may be provided at the state level.

Workers' Medical Benefits

Hospitalization: Inpatient care is provided for stays of up to 90 days; the beneficiary is responsible for the first-day deductible of $912 (amount adjusted each year) and, for the 60th to the 90th day, $228 per day. For inpatient care longer than 90 days, coverage is available for up to 60 lifetime reserve days (may be used only once); the beneficiary is responsible for $456 per day. Posthospital skilled nursing facility care for an additional 100 days (the patient pays $115 for the 21st to the 100th day), laboratory and X-ray services for inpatients, and posthospital home health services.

Other medical services: Payment for 80% of medically necessary charges above $110 a year for physician's services, outpatient diagnostic and physical therapy, laboratory services, appliances, and transportation.

Persons eligible for both hospitalization and other medical services under the regular Medicare program, except for those with end-stage renal disease, can as an alternative elect to participate in one of several types of Medicare Advantage plans if one is available in their jurisdiction.

Federal and state assistance programs: Medical services are provided to medically indigent persons of any age.

Dependents' Medical Benefits

Benefits are only for persons aged 65 or older who satisfy other qualifying requirements or who have end-stage renal disease.

Hospitalization: Inpatient care is provided for stays of up to 90 days; the beneficiary is responsible for the first-day deductible of $912 (amount adjusted each year) and, for the 60th to the 90th day, $228 per day. For inpatient care longer than 90 days, coverage is available for up to 60 lifetime reserve days (may be used only once); the beneficiary is responsible for $456 per day. Posthospital skilled nursing facility care for an additional 100 days (the patient pays $115 for the 21st to the 100th day), laboratory and X-ray services for inpatients, and posthospital home health services.

Other medical services: Payment for 80% of medically necessary charges above $110 a year for physician's

services, outpatient diagnostic and physical therapy, laboratory services, appliances, and transportation.

Persons eligible for both hospitalization and other medical services under the regular Medicare program, except for those with end-stage renal disease, can as an alternative elect to participate in one of several types of Medicare Advantage plans if one is available in their jurisdiction.

Federal and state assistance programs: Medical services are provided to medically indigent persons of any age.

Administrative Organization

Medical benefits: Department of Health and Human Services provides general supervision. Centers for Medicare and Medical Services (http://www.cms.hhs.gov) provide the national administration of the program in cooperation with the Public Health Service, Social Security Administration, and state health departments.

Private carriers and public agencies, serving under contract as intermediary administrative agents, determine and make payments to providers of services or to patients.

Medical services are furnished by providers paid for directly by carriers, or through refunds to patients by carriers of part of the medical expenses.

Includes nonprofit Blue Cross and Blue Shield plans, commercial insurance companies, and group-practice prepayment plans.

Work Injury

Regulatory Framework

First laws: 1908 (federal employees) and 1911 (nine state laws).

Current laws: All states, Puerto Rico, District of Columbia, Guam, and Virgin Islands; federal employees, longshoremen, and harbor workers. Most laws were enacted before 1920.

Type of program: Compulsory (elective for employers in one state) insurance through a public or private carrier (according to the state) or self-insurance.

Coverage

Employees in industry and commerce generally and most public-sector employees.

Exclusions: Common exemptions from coverage are domestic service workers, agricultural employees, small employers, and casual labor. However, 39 programs have some coverage for agricultural workers, and 25 programs have some coverage for domestic workers.

Special federal program for miners (pneumoconiosis).

Source of Funds

Insured person: Nominal contributions in a few states.

Self-employed person: Not applicable.

Employer: Total cost in most states and most of the cost in others, met through either insurance premiums varying with the assessed degree of risk or self-insurance. (The average cost in 2002 was 1.58% of payroll.) Total cost of pneumoconiosis benefits for insured persons who entered the workforce after 1973.

Government: None; contributes as an employer. Total cost of pneumoconiosis benefits for insured persons who entered the workforce before 1974.

Qualifying Conditions

Work injury benefits: There is no minimum qualifying period, except for exposure to occupational disease.

Temporary Disability Benefits

In most states, the benefit is equal to 66.6% of earnings. The benefit is payable after a waiting period of 3 to 7 days (first day in Virgin Islands). Benefits are paid retroactively if the disability lasts a specified period, ranging from 4 days to 6 weeks.

Dependent's supplement: About 1/5 of all states provide supplements for dependents, in some instances as a lump sum.

The maximum weekly benefit varies by state.

Benefit adjustment: About 4/5 of all states increase benefits automatically according to increases in state wages.

Permanent Disability Benefits

Permanent disability pension: In most states, the pension is equal to 66.6% of earnings for a total disability. The pension is limited to between 312 days and 500 weeks in nine jurisdictions.

Partial disability: A reduced pension is paid according to the assessed loss of earning capacity, or at the full rate for fewer weeks in the case of scheduled injuries.

Pneumoconiosis pension: The basic monthly pension is $549. The maximum monthly family pension is $1,098 (2004).

Constant-attendance supplement: Provided in some states. The supplement is payable for life or for the duration of the disability in 4/5 of all states. Some states provide limited supplements for a duration of 104 to 500 weeks.

Dependent's supplement: Provided in some states, the supplement is payable for life or for the duration of the disability in 4/5 of all states. Some states provide limited supplements for a duration of 104 to 500 weeks.

Workers' Medical Benefits

Medical care is provided for as long as is required in all states.

Survivor Benefits

Survivor pension: The pension is equal to between 35% and 70% of the deceased's earnings for a widow(er); 60% to 80% for a widow(er) with dependent children.

Other eligible survivors (under some work injury laws) include dependent parents, brothers, and sisters.

Survivor pension (pneumoconiosis): The basic monthly pension is $549. The family maximum monthly is $1,098 (2004).

Other eligible survivors include dependent parents, brothers, and sisters.

Funeral grant: A lump sum is paid. The amount varies by state.

Administrative Organization

Work injury: State workers' compensation agencies administer the program in about 1/2 of all states, state Departments of Labor administer the program in about 3/8 of all states, and courts administer the program in three states.

Employers must insure with the state fund in six states; may insure with the state fund or a private carrier in 14 states and with a private carrier in the remainder.

Self-insurance by employers is also permitted under all but three state laws.

Pneumoconiosis: Department of Labor, Office of Workers' Compensation Programs, administers the program and pays benefits.

Unemployment

Regulatory Framework

Federal law: 1935.

State laws: All states, Puerto Rico, Virgin Islands, and District of Columbia have separate laws creating their own programs. State laws were first enacted between 1932 and 1937.

Type of program: Social insurance system.

Coverage

Employees of firms in industry and commerce and employees of nonprofit organizations with four or more employees during 20 weeks in a year or that pay wages of $1,500 or more in any calendar quarter in a year. Almost all state and local government workers, domestics, and more than 3/4 of farm workers are covered. Federal civilian and military employers are also covered.

Exclusions: Some agricultural employees, employees of religious organizations, casual employees, family labor, and self-employed persons.

Special federal system for railroad employees.

Source of Funds

Insured person: None, except in Alaska, New Jersey, and Pennsylvania.

Self-employed person: Not applicable.

Employer

Federal tax: 0.8% of taxable payroll. (The full amount is 6.2%. However, there is a 5.4% credit if states meet all federal requirements; includes a temporary surcharge of 0.2% on the first $7,000 earned by each worker in covered employment annually.)

State programs: The standard rate is 5.4%. Actual rates vary from zero to 10% or more, according to the individual employer's experience with laying off workers. The first $7,000 to $32,000 earned by each worker in covered employment is subject to this tax annually.

Government: Federal tax revenue is used for the administration of state unemployment compensation programs, loans to states to pay for unemployment benefits, or to finance the extended benefits program. State tax revenue is used for unemployment benefits.

Qualifying Conditions

Unemployment benefit: Most states require minimum earnings in the base period equal to a specified multiple of the weekly benefit amount or high-quarter wages, or a specified total amount of wages. A few states require a specified number of weeks of employment (for example, from 15 to 20 weeks). One state requires a certain number of hours of work. To be eligible, an unemployed worker must be registered with the employment service, be capable of and available for work, and must actively seek work. An unemployed worker will be disqualified for voluntarily leaving a job without good cause, being discharged from employment for misconduct, or refusing an offer of suitable work. Unemployed workers may be disqualified if they are participating in a labor dispute. The length of the disqualification period varies among states and depends on the reason for disqualification.

Unemployment Benefits

Unemployment benefit: The benefit is equal to about 50% of the insured's earnings (usually capped at around 50% of the state's average weekly wage), according to diverse state formulas. The benefit is payable after a 1-week waiting period in most states, for up to a maximum of 26 weeks in most states.

Dependent's supplement: About 1/4 of states provide from $1 to $120 a week for each child and sometimes for other dependents.

Federal law provides for up to 13 additional weeks of benefits in states with high levels of unemployment.

Unemployment assistance: Assistance is available in some states to workers who are ineligible for unemployment benefits because of insufficient periods of covered employment, to unemployed persons who have exhausted benefit rights under the federal and state assistance programs, and to unemployed persons participating in training programs.

Administrative Organization

Department of Labor (http://www.ows.doleta.gov/unemploy) administers the program nationally through its Employment Training Administration and Office of Workforce Security.

State workforce agencies are responsible for the administration of individual state programs. More than half of agencies are within a department of the state government; the remainder are independent boards or commissions.

Family Allowances

Regulatory Framework

A federal and state system of aid (cash payments, social services, and job training) provides temporary assistance to needy families, and a system of liberalized refundable federal tax credits operates for low-income families with eligible children and for some single persons.

Uruguay

Exchange rate: US$1.00 equals
24.15 new pesos (NP).

Old Age, Disability, and Survivors

Regulatory Framework

First laws: Various laws from 1829 to 1954.

Current law: 1995 (social insurance and individual accounts), implemented in 1996.

Type of program: Social insurance, individual account, and social assistance system.

Note: The mixed social insurance and individual account system is mandatory for employed and self-employed persons born after April 1, 1956, with monthly earnings greater than 12,951 NP; the individual account is voluntary for those with monthly income of 12,951 NP or less.

Coverage

Social insurance: Employed and self-employed persons, including rural and domestic workers.

Special systems for bank employees, notaries, university graduates, armed forces personnel, and police force personnel.

Social insurance and individual account: Employed and self-employed persons, including rural and domestic workers, with monthly earnings greater than 12,951 NP.

Voluntary coverage for employed and self-employed persons with monthly earnings of 12,951 NP or less.

Special systems for bank employees, notaries, university graduates, armed forces personnel, and police force personnel.

Social assistance: Needy elderly or disabled persons.

Source of Funds

Insured person: Contributions depend on the insured's level of monthly earnings and whether the insured has an individual account:

- 15% of gross monthly earnings to social insurance, with earnings up to 12,951 NP. (If the insured opted for the individual account, 7.5% of gross monthly earnings to social insurance and 7.5% of gross monthly earnings to the individual account.)

- 15% of gross monthly earnings (up to a ceiling of 12,951 NP) to social insurance and 15% of monthly earnings for earnings above 12,951 NP to the individual account, with monthly earnings from 12,951 NP up to a ceiling of 19,427 NP. (If the insured opted for the indi-

vidual account, 7.5% of monthly earnings (up to a ceiling of 12,951 NP) plus 15% of monthly earnings for earnings above 12,951 NP (up to a ceiling of 19,427 NP) to social insurance and 7.5% (up to a ceiling of 12,951 NP) to the individual account.)

- 15% of monthly earnings (up to a ceiling of 12,951 NP) to social insurance and 15% of monthly earnings for earnings above 12,951 NP (up to a ceiling of 38,854 NP) to the individual account, with earnings of 19,427 NP or more.

The insured's contribution includes an average 0.98% of earnings for disability and survivor insurance and an average 1.88% of earnings for administrative fees.

The minimum monthly earnings for contribution purposes are 1,397 NP.

Earnings for contribution purposes are adjusted according to the civil servants' average wage index.

Self-employed person: 15% of declared earnings, including an average 0.98% of declared earnings for disability and survivor insurance and an average 1.88% of declared earnings for administrative fees.

The minimum monthly declared earnings for contribution purposes are 2,829.42 NP.

Street vendors with annual earnings up to 400,000 NP contribute 27.625% of 1,397 NP for old-age, disability, and survivor benefits (plus an additional amount if covered for sickness benefits).

Employer: 12.5% of payroll for social insurance only.

The minimum monthly earnings for contribution purposes are 1,397 NP.

The maximum monthly earnings for contribution purposes are 38,854 NP.

Government: Earmarked proceeds of various taxes help finance pension deficits; pays the total cost of noncontributory benefits; contributes as an employer.

Qualifying Conditions

Old-age pension

Old-age pension (social insurance): Age 60 (men and women) with at least 35 years of coverage. Additional years of service are credited for hazardous occupations.

Deferred pension: With at least 35 years of coverage, the pension is increased for each year of deferral.

Old-age pension (individual account): Age 60 (men and women) with at least 35 years of coverage; age 65 with no coverage requirement.

Advanced-age pension (social insurance and individual account): Age 70 (men and women) with 15 years of service. Retirement from the current place of employment is necessary.

Noncontributory means-tested pension (social assistance): Age 70 (men and women), assessed as needy, and with at least 15 years of residency.

Disability pension

Permanent disability pension (social insurance and individual account): Must be incapable of any work and have an assessed degree of disability of at least 66%. If the disability is the result of an accident, there are no other qualifying conditions. Must have at least 2 years of recognized service, including the 6 months before the onset of disability; at least 6 months of recognized service before the onset of disability if younger than age 26. Coverage is extended for up to 2 years after employment ceases if the insured has at least 10 years of coverage.

Partial disability benefit (social insurance and individual account): Must be incapable of work in the usual job and have an assessed degree of disability of 50% to 66%. If the disability is the result of an accident, there are no other qualifying conditions. Must have at least 2 years of recognized service, including the 6 months before the onset of disability; at least 6 months of recognized service before the onset of disability if younger than age 26. The benefit is payable on a temporary basis and is subject to a reassessment of the incapacity to work.

District medical commissions of the Social Security Bank assess the degree of incapacity to work.

Noncontributory means-tested pension (social assistance): Assessed as totally and permanently disabled, needy, and with at least 15 years of residency.

Survivor pension

Survivor pension (social insurance and individual account): The deceased was working; a pensioner; a beneficiary of partial disability benefit, sickness benefit, maternity benefit, or work injury benefit; unemployed and receiving unemployment benefits; or death occurred in the 12-month period after unemployment benefit ceased. Coverage is extended for up to 12 months after employment ceases; no limit with at least 10 years of coverage.

Eligible survivors include a widow(er), a divorced spouse, orphans up to age 21 (no limit if disabled), and dependent disabled parents. A widow(er) or a divorced spouse younger than age 30 receives benefits for 2 years; from age 30 to age 39, for 5 years; or without limit if older than age 39. A widow(er) must have average monthly earnings in the 12 months before the insured's death of no more than 38,854 NP; 22,341.33 NP for a divorced spouse.

Funeral grant: The grant is payable to eligible survivors or to the person who paid for the funeral. (If the funeral costs are paid by a pension scheme, only necessary additional funeral costs are paid.)

Old-Age Benefits

Old-age pension

Old-age pension (social insurance): The monthly benefit is 50% of average indexed earnings in the last 10 or 20 years, whichever is higher, with at least 35 years of coverage. The pension is increased by 0.5% for each year of work exceeding 35 years, up to a maximum of 2.5%, and by 2% for each year of work after age 60 if the contribution condition was not met.

Deferred pension: The pension is increased by 3% for each year after age 60, up to a maximum of 30%.

The maximum earnings for benefit calculation purposes are 12,951 NP.

The minimum monthly pension is 1,452.20 NP.

The maximum monthly pension is 10,684.98 NP.

The pension is payable abroad under bilateral or multilateral agreement only.

Benefit adjustment: Pensions are adjusted according to the civil servants' average wage index.

Advanced-age pension (social insurance): The monthly benefit is 50% of average indexed earnings in the last 10 or 20 years, whichever is higher, plus 1% for each year of work exceeding 15 years, up to a maximum of 14%.

The pension is payable abroad under bilateral or multilateral agreement only.

Benefit adjustment: Pensions are adjusted according to the civil servants' average wage index.

Old-age pension (individual account): The value of the pension is dependent on the insured's contributions plus accrued interest, minus administrative fees. At retirement, the insured uses the accumulated capital to purchase an annuity from an insurance company.

The pension is payable abroad under bilateral or multilateral agreement only.

Advanced-age pension (individual account): The value of the pension is dependent on the insured's contributions plus accrued interest, minus administrative fees. At retirement, the insured uses the accumulated capital to purchase an annuity from an insurance company.

The pension is payable abroad under bilateral or multilateral agreement only.

Noncontributory means-tested pension (social assistance): 2,498.73 NP a month.

Benefit adjustment: Pensions are adjusted according to the civil servants' average wage index.

Permanent Disability Benefits

Disability pension

Permanent disability pension (social insurance): The monthly pension is equal to 65% of average indexed earnings in the 10 or 20 years before the onset of disability, whichever is higher, or the total number of years worked if less than 10 years.

Special allowances: A lump sum of 1,036 NP is paid for transportation costs, and a lump sum of 1,921 NP is paid for rehabilitation costs.

Partial disability benefit (social insurance): The monthly benefit is equal to 65% of average indexed earnings in the 10 or 20 years before the onset of disability, whichever is higher, or the total number of years worked if less than 10 years. The benefit is payable for up to 3 years.

The maximum earnings for benefit calculation purposes are 12,951 NP.

The minimum monthly benefit is 2,425.64 NP.

The maximum monthly benefit is 10,684.98 NP.

Benefits are payable abroad under bilateral or multilateral agreement only.

Benefit adjustment: Benefits are adjusted according to the civil servants' average wage index.

Permanent disability pension (individual account): The monthly pension is equal to 45% of average indexed earnings in the 10 years before the onset of disability. (Disability insurance tops up the accumulated capital in the individual account if the balance is less than the required minimum to finance the permanent disability pension.)

Partial disability benefit (individual account): The monthly pension is equal to 45% of average indexed earnings in the 10 years before the onset of disability. The benefit is payable for up to 3 years.

Noncontributory means-tested pension (social assistance): 2,498.73 NP a month.

Benefit adjustment: Pensions are adjusted according to the civil servants' average wage index.

Survivor Benefits

Survivor pension

Survivor pension (social insurance and individual account): A monthly pension equal to between 66% and 75% of the pension paid or payable to the deceased is paid, depending on the number of survivors. (Life insurance tops up the accumulated capital in the deceased's individual account if the balance is less than the required minimum to finance the survivor pension.)

Widow(er)s and divorced spouses share 100% of the pension if there are no other eligible survivors. Widow(er)s and divorced spouses share 70% of the total pension if they have children; 60% if there are no children but other eligible survivors. The remainder is split equally among other eligible survivors. In the absence of a widow(er) or a divorced spouse, 100% of the pension is split equally among other eligible survivors.

Eligibility ceases if the widow(er) or divorced spouse remarries.

For members of an individual account scheme, the accumulated capital in the individual account, equal to the insured's contributions plus accrued interest, minus administrative fees, is transferred to an insurance company, which pays the pension.

Survivor pensions are payable abroad under bilateral or multilateral agreement only.

Benefit adjustment: Pensions are adjusted according to the civil servants' average wage index.

Funeral grant: The cost of the funeral up to 6,015.27 NP. (Additional costs related to the funeral are covered up to 2,978.84 NP.)

Administrative Organization

Ministry of Labor and Social Security (http://www.mtss.gub.uy) provides general supervision.

Social Security Bank (http://www.bps.gub.uy) supervises and administers the social insurance program.

Pension fund management companies (AFAPs) manage the individual accounts.

Central Bank of Uruguay (http://www.bcu.gub.uy) oversees pension fund management companies and insurance companies.

Sickness and Maternity

Regulatory Framework

First laws: 1958 (maternity benefits) and 1960 (sickness benefits for construction workers).

Current laws: 1975 (sickness), 1980 (maternity), 1981 (maternity), 1995 (pensioners), 1999 (maternity), and 2001 (child adoption).

Type of program: Social insurance system.

Coverage

Sickness benefits: Employed persons in the private sector, self-employed persons, persons receiving unemployment benefits, and employers with one employee.

Voluntary coverage for rural workers and their spouses; and pensioners.

Special systems for bank employees and civil servants.

Maternity benefits: Benefits are provided under Family Allowances, below.

Source of Funds

Insured person: 3% of gross earnings; 3% of gross earnings for voluntary coverage.

The minimum earnings for contribution purposes are 1,746.25 NP.

Self-employed person: 8% of declared earnings.

Employer: 5% of payroll, plus an additional amount for medical benefits. Employers with one employee contribute 8% of declared earnings.

Government: Earmarked proceeds of various taxes help finance maternity benefits and any deficits for sickness benefits.

Qualifying Conditions

Cash sickness benefits: Must have 3 months of contributions or 75 days of contributions in the last 12 months.

Cash maternity benefits: See Family Allowances, below.

Sickness and Maternity Benefits

Sickness benefit: The benefit is equal to 70% of earnings and is payable after a 3-day waiting period (no waiting period in case of hospitalization) for up to a year; may be extended for an additional year.

The maximum monthly benefit is 4,191 NP; 978 NP for the self-employed.

Maternity benefit: See Family Allowances, below.

Workers' Medical Benefits

Medical services are available through mutual health institutions. Medical services include medical assistance, surgery, and pharmaceutical products.

Grants for eyeglasses, contact lenses, prostheses, orthopedic appliances, wheelchairs, and psychiatric hospitalization are provided by health institutions.

Prenatal and postnatal medical care is provided for insured women under Family Allowances, below.

Copayments for benefits range from 43 NP to 189 NP.

Dependents' Medical Benefits

Medical services are available through mutual health institutions. Medical services include medical assistance, surgery, and pharmaceutical products.

Grants for eyeglasses, contact lenses, prostheses, orthopedic appliances, wheelchairs, and psychiatric hospitalization are provided by health institutions.

Prenatal and postnatal medical care are provided for insured women under Family Allowances, below.

Maternity care for the wife of an insured man and pediatric care for the insured's children up to age 6 (may be extended to age 14) are provided under Family Allowances, below.

Administrative Organization

Social Security Bank (http://www.bps.gub.uy) supervises and administers the social insurance program.

Collective medical assistance or mutual health institutions contracted by the Social Security Bank provide medical benefits.

Work Injury

Regulatory Framework

First law: 1914.

Current law: 1989 (work injury), with 1990 amendment.

Type of program: Compulsory insurance with a public carrier.

Coverage

Private-sector employees, including agricultural workers; certain public-sector workers; apprentices; and persons working with horses.

Exclusions: Self-employed persons, sportsmen, and actors.

Source of Funds

Insured person: None.

Self-employed person: Not applicable.

Employer: Total cost, met through contributions varying with the assessed degree of risk. For agricultural workers, assessments are made according to the land area the employer has under cultivation.

Government: None.

Qualifying Conditions

Work injury benefits: There is no minimum qualifying period. Accidents that occur while commuting to and from work are not covered.

Temporary Disability Benefits

For a work injury, the benefit is equal to 66% of earnings before the onset of disability; for workers in irregular employment, 66% of total adjusted earnings in the last 6 months divided by 150. The daily benefit is payable after a 4-day waiting period until the insured is assessed as no longer disabled. The benefit for the waiting period is paid retroactively.

For an occupational disease, the benefit is equal to 100% of earnings before the disease was diagnosed. There is no waiting period.

An additional benefit equal to 3.607% of earnings is payable under sickness benefits.

The State Insurance Bank assesses the degree of loss of earnings.

Benefit adjustment: Benefits are adjusted according to the civil servants' average wage index.

Permanent Disability Benefits

Permanent disability pension: For an assessed degree of disability of 20% or more, the monthly pension is equal to the monthly loss of earnings; 115% of earnings before the onset of disability if the insured needs the constant attendance of another person.

For an assessed degree of disability of 10% to 20%, a lump sum is paid equal to 36 times the monthly loss of earnings; for an assessed degree of disability less than 10%, a benefit is paid only if the assessed disability is the result of repeated accidents.

The State Insurance Bank assesses the degree of loss of earnings.

Benefit adjustment: Benefits are adjusted according to the civil servants' average wage index.

Workers' Medical Benefits

Medical services are available through the State Insurance Bank. Benefits include medical, surgical, and dental care; hospitalization; medicines; and appliances.

There is no limit to duration.

Survivor Benefits

Survivor pension: A monthly benefit equal to 50% of the deceased's earnings is payable to a widow(er) or partner with dependents; 66% without dependents. The widow(er) must have been married to the deceased for a year; a partner must have cohabited with the deceased for a year.

Orphan's pension: Between 20% and 100% of the deceased's earnings for dependent orphans younger than age 18 (no limit if disabled), subject to the number of orphans and other eligible survivors.

If the deceased worked for at least 150 days in the last 6 months, the earnings for pension calculation purposes are based on 24 times average half-monthly earnings in the 6 months before the accident; half-monthly earnings if the insured worked less than 15 days.

Benefit adjustment: Benefits are adjusted according to the civil servants' average wage index.

Administrative Organization

State Insurance Bank (http://www.bse.com.uy) administers the program.

Unemployment

Regulatory Framework

First law: 1934.

Current laws: 1981 (industry and commerce) and 2001 (rural workers).

Type of program: Social assistance system.

Coverage

Private-sector employees.

Exclusions: Domestic workers, bank employees, pensioners, and self-employed persons.

Source of Funds

Insured person: None.

Self-employed person: Not applicable.

Employer: None.

Government: Earmarked proceeds of various taxes help finance benefits.

Qualifying Conditions

Unemployment benefits: Workers who are paid monthly must have 6 months (150 days if paid daily) of work in the 12-month period before unemployment; workers who are paid at irregular intervals must have earned 8,382 NP in the 12-month period.

Rural workers who are paid monthly must have 12 months (250 days if paid daily) of work in the 24-month period before unemployment; rural workers who are paid at irregular intervals must have earned 16,764 NP in the 12-month period.

Unemployment must not be the result of dismissal for disciplinary reasons.

Partial unemployment benefit: A benefit is paid to workers who are paid daily or at irregular intervals if working time is reduced by 25% or more.

Dependent's supplement: Payable if the unemployed person is married, has children younger than age 21 (any age if disabled), or has disabled dependents.

There is a 12-month waiting period before a new claim for unemployment benefits can be made.

Unemployment Benefits

Workers who are paid monthly or at irregular intervals receive a benefit equal to 50% of average earnings in the 6 months before unemployment.

Workers who are paid daily receive a monthly benefit equal to 12 days of earnings before unemployment.

Partial unemployment benefit: The monthly benefit is equal to 12 days of earnings before partial unemployment, minus the value of current monthly earnings.

Dependent's supplement: Equal to 20% of the benefit.

The minimum unemployment benefit is 698.50 NP.

The maximum unemployment benefit is 11,176 NP.

Administrative Organization

Ministry of Labor and Social Security (http://www.mtss.gub.uy) provides general supervision.

Social Security Bank (http://www.bps.gub.uy) supervises and administers the unemployment insurance program.

Family Allowances

Regulatory Framework

First law: 1943.

Current laws: 1980 (family allowances), implemented in 1981, with 1999 amendment; 1995 (social security); 2002 (multiple pregnancy); and 2004 (low-income families).

Type of program: Social assistance system.

Coverage

Private-sector employees, domestic workers, unemployment benefit recipients, newspaper vendors, small rural products vendors, and pensioners.

Exclusions: Self-employed persons.

Special system for civil servants.

Source of Funds

Insured person: None.

Self-employed person: Not applicable.

Employer: None.

Government: Earmarked proceeds of various taxes help finance benefits.

Qualifying Conditions

Family allowances: The child must be younger than age 14 (age 18 if a student, no limit if disabled). The benefit is paid from the day the pregnancy is confirmed.

Pensioners with benefits of 4,191 NP or more and employees with earnings of 13,970 NP or more do not receive family allowances. (For employees with earnings of 13,970 NP or more and with three or more dependents, the earnings limit is increased to 1,397 NP for each additional dependent.)

Cash maternity benefit: Payable for the birth of a child.

Multiple birth allowance: Payable to a pregnant woman expecting more than one child. The benefit is paid from the day the pregnancy is confirmed.

Special paid leave: Paid to a salaried worker who adopts a child.

Low-income family allowance: Payable to eligible children in households with monthly earnings of 4,191 NP or less.

Family Allowance Benefits

Family allowances: The allowance is 223.52 NP (447.04 NP for a disabled child) for covered persons with income up to 8,382 NP; 111.76 NP (223.52 NP for a disabled child) with income between 8,382 NP and 13,970 NP.

For a family with children resulting from a multiple pregnancy, the allowance is paid at three times the standard rate until the children reach age 5, at twice the standard rate until the children reach age 12, and at the standard rate until the children reach age 18. The benefit is paid every 2 months.

Cash maternity benefit: The benefit is equal to 100% of average earnings in the last 6 months and is payable for the period 6 weeks before until 6 weeks after the expected date of childbirth. The benefit is paid on the expected date of childbirth.

Multiple birth allowance: The allowance is paid at three times the family allowance standard rate until the children reach age 5, at twice the standard rate until the children reach age 12, and at the standard rate until the children reach age 18. The benefit is paid every 2 months.

The maximum allowance is 20,955 NP.

Special paid leave: Private-sector workers receive benefits equal to 6 weeks' cash maternity benefit.

Low-income family allowance: 223.52 NP (447.04 NP for a disabled child) is payable every 2 weeks.

In-kind benefits include pediatric care for children up to age 6, dental care for children up to age 9, and specialist medical care and transportation for children up to age 14. Medical examinations and medicines for children are free.

Administrative Organization

Social Security Bank (http://www.bps.gub.uy) supervises and administers the program.

Collective medical assistance or mutual health institutions contracted by the Social Security Bank provide medical benefits.

Venezuela

Exchange rate: US$1.00 equals 2,150 bolivares.

Old Age, Disability, and Survivors

Regulatory Framework

First law: 1940.

Current laws: 1966, 1991, and 2002.

Type of program: Social insurance system.

Note: The 1990 labor code established supplementary pension funds financed by employer contributions only.

Coverage

Employees in the private and public sectors and members of cooperatives.

Voluntary coverage for persons who were previously covered, subject to conditions.

Special system for armed forces personnel.

Source of Funds

Insured person: The average contribution is 1.93% of earnings.

The maximum monthly earnings for contribution and benefit purposes are equal to five times the minimum urban wage.

The above contributions also finance the marriage grant (see Family Allowances, below).

Self-employed person: Not applicable.

Employer: The average contribution is 4.82% of payroll.

The maximum monthly earnings for contribution and benefit purposes are equal to five times the minimum urban wage.

The above contributions also finance the marriage grant (see Family Allowances, below).

Government: At least 1.5% of total taxable earnings to cover the cost of administration; contributes as an employer.

Qualifying Conditions

Old-age pension: Age 60 (men) or age 55 (women) with 750 weeks of contributions. The pensionable age is lower for those in unhealthy and arduous occupations.

Retirement is not necessary.

The pension is payable abroad.

Old-age grant: The insured does not meet the qualifying conditions for the pension but has at least 100 weeks of contributions in the last 4 years.

Disability pension: Payable for the permanent or prolonged loss of over 2/3 of working capacity with 250 weeks of contributions (reduced by 20 contributions for each year the insured is younger than age 35), including 100 weeks in the last 3 years before the onset of disability. There is no qualifying period for a disability caused by an accident.

Partial disability pension: The loss of between 25% and 66.6% of working capacity.

Disability grant: For an assessed degree of disability of between 5% and 25%.

Survivor pension: The insured met the qualifying conditions for a pension or was a pensioner at the time of death. There is no qualifying period if the death is caused by an accident.

Eligible survivors are a widow older than age 45 or with children; a partner older than age 45 or with children and who cohabited with the deceased for at least 2 years; a widower older than age 60 or disabled; and children younger than age 14 (age 18 if a student, no limit if disabled). A widow or partner younger than age 45 receives a lump sum payment.

Survivor grant: The insured did not meet the qualifying period for a pension but had at least 100 weeks of contributions during the last 4 years.

Eligible survivors are a widow older than age 45 or with children; a partner older than age 45 or with children and who cohabited with the deceased for at least 2 years; a widower older than age 60 or disabled; and children younger than age 14 (age 18 if a student, no limit if disabled).

Old-Age Benefits

Old-age pension: The pension is equal to 296,524.80 bolivares a month, plus 30% of average earnings in the last 5 years or the average of the best 5 years in the last 10 years (whichever is higher), plus 1% of earnings for each 50-week period of contributions exceeding 750 weeks.

The minimum pension is equal to 40% of earnings.

Deferred pension: An additional 5% of the pension is paid for each year the pension is deferred after the pensionable age.

Benefit adjustment: Pensions are adjusted periodically for changes in prices and wages.

Old-age grant: The grant is equal to 10% of the insured's total covered earning.

Benefit adjustment: Benefits are adjusted periodically for changes in prices and wages.

Permanent Disability Benefits

Disability pension: The pension is equal to 296,524.80 bolivares a month, plus 30% of average earnings (payable after 6 months of disability), plus 1% of earnings for each 50-week period of contributions exceeding 750 weeks.

The minimum pension is equal to 40% of the insured's earnings.

Constant-attendance supplement: Up to 50% of the pension.

Partial disability: For an assessed degree of disability of between 25% and 66.6%, a percentage of the full pension according to the assessed degree of disability (if the disability is the result of a nonoccupational accident).

Benefit adjustment: Pensions are adjusted periodically for changes in prices and wages.

Disability grant: The grant is equal to 36 months' disability pension.

Benefit adjustment: Benefits are adjusted periodically for changes in prices and wages.

Survivor Benefits

Survivor pension: An eligible widow(er) or partner receives 40% of the pension paid or payable to the deceased. Other widows or partners receive a lump sum equal to 2 years' survivor pension.

Orphan's pension: Each orphan younger than age 14 (age 18 if a student, no limit if disabled) receives 20% of the deceased's pension; the first full orphan receives 40% of the pension and other full orphans, 20%.

The maximum survivor pension is 100% of the deceased's pension.

Other eligible survivors (in the absence of the above): Brothers, sisters, and parents may receive an amount equal to 10% of the deceased's total covered earnings.

Benefit adjustment: Pensions are adjusted periodically for changes in prices and wages.

Survivor grant: 10% of the deceased's total covered earnings is payable.

Funeral grant: The grant must not be more than five times the deceased's monthly salary.

Benefit adjustment: Benefits are adjusted periodically for changes in prices and wages.

Administrative Organization

Ministry of Labor (http://www.mintra.gov.ve) provides general supervision.

Managed by a tripartite board and director general, the Social Insurance Institute (http://www.ivss.gov.ve) administers the program.

Sickness and Maternity

Regulatory Framework

First law: 1940.

Current laws: 1966, 1991, and 2002.

Type of program: Social insurance system. Cash and medical benefits.

Coverage

Employees in the private and public sectors.

Source of Funds

Insured person: The average contribution is 1.79% of earnings.

The above contributions also finance work injury benefits.

Self-employed person: No information is available.

Employer: The average contribution is 3.46% of payroll.

The above contributions also finance work injury benefits.

Government: See source of funds under Old Age, Disability, and Survivors, above.

Qualifying Conditions

Cash sickness and maternity benefits: Currently insured.

Medical benefits: Currently insured.

Sickness and Maternity Benefits

Sickness benefit: The benefit is equal to 66.6% of earnings and is payable after a 3-day waiting period for up to 52 weeks; may be extended under certain conditions. The benefit is reduced by 50% when the insured is hospitalized.

Maternity benefit: The benefit is equal to 66.6% of earnings in the last month before maternity leave and is payable for up to 6 months.

Workers' Medical Benefits

Free medical services are normally provided directly to patients by the medical facilities of the Social Security Institute for up to a maximum of 52 weeks; may be extended for another 52 weeks for convalescent care. Benefits include general and specialist care, hospitalization, laboratory services, medicines, dental care, maternity care, appliances, and transportation.

Dependents' Medical Benefits

Free medical services are normally provided directly to patients by the medical facilities of the Social Security Institute. Benefits include general and specialist care, hospitalization, laboratory services, medicines, dental care, maternity care, appliances, and transportation. The maximum duration of medical benefits for dependents of pensioners is 26 weeks; survivors of pensioners are entitled to medical service benefits for up to 52 weeks.

Administrative Organization

Ministry of Labor (http://www.mintra.gov.ve) provides general supervision.

Managed by a tripartite board and director general, the Social Insurance Institute (http://www.ivss.gov.ve) administers the program.

Social Insurance Institute operates its own clinics and hospitals and contracts for other facilities.

Work Injury

Regulatory Framework

First law: 1923.

Current laws: 1966, 1991, and 2002.

Type of program: Social insurance system.

Coverage

Employees in the private and public sectors and members of cooperatives.

Source of Funds

Insured person: See source of funds under Sickness and Maternity, above.

Self-employed person: Not applicable.

Employer: See source of funds under Sickness and Maternity, above.

Government: See source of funds under Old Age, Disability, and Survivors, above.

Qualifying Conditions

Work injury benefits: There is no minimum qualifying period.

Temporary Disability Benefits

The benefit is equal to 66.6% of the insured's earnings. The benefit is payable after a 3-day waiting period for up to 52 weeks; may be extended for an additional 52 weeks if recovery is likely.

Permanent Disability Benefits

Permanent disability pension: The pension is equal to 66.6% of the insured's earnings, if totally disabled.

Constant-attendance supplement: Up to 50% of the pension.

Partial disability: For an assessed degree of disability of between 25% and 66.6%, a percentage of the full pension according to the assessed degree of disability. For an assessed degree of disability of between 6% and 24%, a lump sum equal to 3 years' pension is paid.

Workers' Medical Benefits

Benefits include free general and specialist care, hospitalization, medicines, laboratory services, appliances, and rehabilitation services.

Survivor Benefits

Survivor pension: An eligible widow(er) or partner receives 40% of the pension paid or payable to the deceased. Other widows or partners receive a lump sum equal to 2 years' survivor pension.

Eligible survivors are a widow older than age 45 or with children; a partner older than age 45 or with children and who cohabited with the deceased for at least 2 years; a widower older than age 60 or disabled; and children younger than age 14 (age 18 if a student, no limit if disabled).

Orphan's pension: Each orphan younger than age 14 (age 18 if a student, no limit if disabled) receives 20% of the deceased's pension; the first full orphan receives 40% of the pension and other full orphans, 20%.

Other eligible survivors (in the absence of the above): Brothers, sisters, and parents who were dependent on the deceased may receive an amount equal to 10% of the deceased's total covered earnings.

Survivor settlement: 10% of the deceased's total covered earnings is paid if the deceased did not meet the qualifying period for a pension but had at least 100 weeks of contributions in the last 4 years.

Funeral grant: 5,000 bolivares.

Administrative Organization

Ministry of Labor (http://www.mintra.gov.ve) provides general supervision.

Managed by a tripartite board and director general, the Social Insurance Institute (http://www.ivss.gov.ve) administers contributions and benefits.

Social Insurance Institute provides medical benefits through its own clinics and hospitals.

Unemployment

Regulatory Framework

First law: 1940.

Current laws: 1966, 1991, and 2002.

Type of program: Social insurance system.

Coverage

Employees in the private and public sectors and members of cooperatives.

Source of Funds

Insured: 0.5% of earnings.

The maximum monthly earnings for contribution and benefit purposes are equal to five times the minimum urban wage.

The above contributions also help finance health insurance for the unemployed.

Self-employed person: Not applicable.

Employer: 1.7% of payroll.

The maximum monthly earnings for contribution and benefit purposes are equal to five times the minimum urban wage.

The above contributions also help finance health insurance for the unemployed.

Government: None.

Qualifying Conditions

Unemployment benefits: Must have 52 weeks of contributions in the 18 months before unemployment began. The insured must be available for training or suitable employment.

Unemployment Benefits

The benefit is equal to 60% of the insured's average weekly wage in the last 50 weeks. The benefit is paid for up to 18 weeks; may be extended to 26 weeks.

Unemployed persons are entitled to a transportation grant of 200 bolivares, employment training, and guidance services.

Workers' Medical Benefits

Unemployed insured persons and family members are covered for health insurance for 26 weeks.

Administrative Organization

Ministry of Labor (http://www.mintra.gov.ve) provides general supervision.

Employment services administer training and guidance.

Social Insurance Institute (http://www.ivss.gov.ve) administers the program.

Family Allowances

Regulatory Framework

Marriage grant: A lump sum of 7,000 bolivares is paid with 100 weekly contributions made in the 3 years before marriage. (The grant is provided under Old Age, Disability, and Survivors, above.)

www.socialsecurity.gov/policy

Social Security Administration
Office of Policy
Office of Research, Evaluation, and Statistics
500 E Street, SW, 8th Floor
Washington, DC 20254

SSA Publication No. 13-11804
March 2006

ISBN 0-16-075962-5

90000

9 780160 759628